KU-767-063

# TOTAL QUALITY
# MANAGEMENT
# AND THE SCHOOL

# TOTAL QUALITY MANAGEMENT AND THE SCHOOL

Stephen Murgatroyd and
Colin Morgan

LEARNING
RESOURCES
CENTRE

Open University Press
Buckingham · Philadelphia

371·2

AR

174110

Open University Press
Celtic Court
22 Ballmoor
Buckingham
MK18 1XW

and

1900 Frost Road, Suite 101
Bristol, PA 19007, USA

First Published 1992
Reprinted 1993 (twice), 1994

Copyright © Murgatroyd and Associates/Colin Morgan Associates 1993

All rights reserved. No part of this publication may be
reproduced, stored in a retrieval system or transmitted in
any form or by any means, without written permission from the
publisher.

A catalogue record for this book is available from the British Library

*Library of Congress Cataloging-in-Publication Data*
Murgatroyd, Stephen J.
    Total quality management and the school / Stephen Murgatroyd and
Colin Morgan.
        p.   cm.
    Includes bibliographical references and index.
    ISBN 0–335–15723–8 — ISBN 0–335–15722–X (pbk.)
    1. School management and organization—United States.   2. Total
quality management—United States.   I. Morgan, Colin.   II. Title.
LB2805.M815   1992
371.2′00973—dc20                                                    92–17386
                                                                         CIP

Typeset by Graphicraft Typesetters Ltd, Hong Kong
Printed and bound in Great Britain by
Biddles Ltd, Guildford and King's Lynn

# Dedications

## from Stephen Murgatroyd

This text is dedicated to the teachers, school administrators and educational managers with whom I have worked since 1975. More especially, it is dedicated to Noreen O'Haire of the Alberta Teachers Association, who has helped to make many of these ideas alive in the minds of so many.

## from Colin Morgan

This text is similarly dedicated to the school and college Heads, teachers and students with whom I have worked in Wales and England in recent years; in particular in the following Local Education Authorities: Clwyd, Dyfed, Gwent, Mid-Glamorgan, Gloucester and Warwick.

# Contents

# Preface

There are new concerns emerging in the developed world about the nature of educational services at the primary and secondary levels. Part of the reason for this focus can be called 'return on investment' – government and industry are not happy with the performance of the systems of education, especially in terms of the increasing calls for more and more expenditure. The other driving factor is the growing recognition of the importance of educational investment and performance to the competitive strategy of nations in a world, where information technology and global economy set the context.

In the context of these concerns, government, communities and industry are responding with a variety of initiatives. In Britain, the Government in the late 1980s and early 1990s has sought to change the control strategies for the system by devolving governance of schools to the local level (local management of schools), opening boundaries between schools so as to permit extended parental choice of schools (open enrolment – in theory at least, because government-set building limits restrict the openness of enrolment in many places), creating a core national curriculum and establishing a Citizens Charter which embodies and codifies parental and pupil rights. In Canada at the same time, the Government is seeking to impose standards through value-for-money audits and through the development of performance indicators for schools. In the USA the Government has announced similar developments to those envisaged in Canada.

All of these developments focus on questions about the quality of performance. In completing the statement 'schools need to ...', most governments respond in terms of improving the quality of educational performance within existing resources. Some have called this 'back to the basics ...', but it is more appropriately to be regarded as meeting minimum performance standards in areas of competence seen to be essential in the interests of the economy. In fact, economic needs within the global economy are dictating a higher level of minimum educational standard for the many rather than the minority.

In both the service and manufacturing sectors of the economies of the developed world, the sentence 'the priority of our business ...' is completed with 'is to increase profitability through a focus on quality'. Joel Barker, a futurist, has suggested that there is an epidemic of 'quality' worldwide which, if you don't catch it, may mean you are not in business in ten years' time. Whether the focus is on service quality, product quality or total quality, the world of business is deeply concerned with the quality of its activities to the extent that quality issues dominate the thinking and concerns of top-team members in all major employers in the world. The focus on quality for the customer has led to the development of a body of theory, tools and applications that has become known in management as TQM – total quality management. There are journals devoted to this new branch of management, and training courses in TQM, or Total Quality Customer Service, take place almost every day of the month across the world. This concern with 'Quality' in the sense of performance/ achievement/service has widened from manufacturing industry, where it began, into service provisions and the public sector. Most recently, in some parts of the world it has started to influence education.

This book is about the application of TQM to schools. The claim of this book is that it seeks to provide a comprehensive framework from within which school-based administrators and managers can make a sustainable difference to the quality and performance of the schools for which they are responsible. The book builds on developments taking place elsewhere in the fields of TQM, on experience in applying these ideas to school systems and on the research on school effectiveness. Four ideas are central to the thinking behind this book.

The first is that a school involves a chain of relationships between 'customers' and 'suppliers' – the school is in fact an organization that manages a chain of customers (Schonberger 1989). Teachers are the suppliers of services to pupils and parents; secretaries are suppliers of services to teachers; school administrators are suppliers of services to teachers; teachers supply services to each other. There are internal customers (those who work for the school) and external customers (those who demand services from the school). There are also external suppliers of services to the school. All of these are customer–supplier relationships bounded by the organization we call school.

Many people do not like the wholesale importation of the language of business – 'customers' and 'suppliers' – into the practice of schooling. They claim that the ideological presuppositions such language implies are inappropriate to a public service such as education, and may in fact be harmful. In our view, this argument is weak in two respects. First, the language of business does indeed carry assumptions about the relationships between customers and suppliers – assumptions that are appropriate to the work of a public service for which the customers are paying and are being asked to pay more for (both in terms of taxation and user fees) over time. Second, the use of such language challenges a view of public service and the nature of accountability in a way that is in keeping with the nature of devolved governance and resourcing for schools. Schools are a key part of the service economy and need to be seen as such.

The second key idea is that all of the relationships between customers and suppliers (whether internal or external) are mediated by processes. Whether a teacher is providing learning opportunities to a student, or a secretary is providing typing services or the administrator is creating a timetable for the school year, they are all engaged in managing processes. Quality comes through process improvements intended to make a sustainable difference to the outcomes of these processes.

Third, the people best able to make process improvements are those nearest to the customer for that process. This may look like an obvious statement, but it carries radical implications for the control, management and design of schools as organizations. It implies turning the management pyramid upside-down. At the heart of the organization are its customers – parents and students. Without these there would not be a school. The next most significant process managers in the school are the rank and file of teachers – they are closest to the customers and their performance of the key processes of teaching, learning facilitation, curriculum development and implementation, reflective evaluation, formative and summative evaluation and record keeping are central to the task of schooling. They are, in turn, supported in their work by teacher aides, school librarians and secretaries, who are in turn supported by the school-based administrative or management team. This is the customer-driven hierarchy within the school. After the parents and students, the most significant leaders and managers in the school are teachers. They alone are responsible for the processes in classrooms that enable learning and are consequently the real leaders of performance.

This idea is radical to many school-based managers, who see themselves as appointed to 'lead' the organization. In their organizational charts all are accountable to them and all report to them. There are some very critical roles to be played for those with such leadership roles in the school, as we shall see. The key point to make here is that leadership for vision, quality and performance, and leadership for control, are two very different action-sets.

To secure sustainable quality performance improvements for a school requires visionary leadership, which supports and enhances the work of those closest to the customer.

If, in the tenets of TQM, performance is driven by customer perceptions of quality, it must be recognized that customers will have different definitions of what constitutes quality. It may well be that many customers of schooling have a similar common core definition of quality, but the totalities of their definitions of 'quality' will differ. Schools must therefore determine their own strategy for quality. The final of our four central ideas informing this text is that the strategy a school operates from involves choices. Schools are not all identical – they pursue different objectives, embody different values and work in different ways. While many think that the national curriculum in Britain, or the increased use of performance indicators in North America, may be creating a more uniform system of schooling, the reality is that the changes that are taking place are increasing the range of strategic choices that schools can make. Later we will introduce a model for such choice – the generic strategy model – and indicate the options from which the school can chose. The key point is that the response of the marketplace to the strategy the school adopts is central in determining the success of the school. Schools therefore need to know what identity they want in the 'marketplace' of the community.

This book represents the first major articulation of the application of TQM to schools. Earlier work (Murgatroyd 1989, 1991) outlined some elements of the thinking behind this text – thinking that has been refined, modified and developed in the light of those implementations of TQM that have begun in schools in both North America and Europe. It seeks to provide ideas, resources and insights relevant to the running of schools in several countries. Doing this is always problematic; for example, there are differences of language usage between Britain and North America regarding the terminology of schooling – pupils (instead of students) is the term more generally used in Britain, while 'semester' is unheard of. There are also differences of usage in respect of the way terms in management and administration are used; indeed, in the educational worlds of North America and Britain the terms administration and management have the opposite connotations. We have found no simple solution to this and have decided to use what comes most naturally in the situation and with a bias towards the usages that are becoming generic across occupations, leaving it to the reader to make the necessary adjustments and translations.

It is very early days for TQM in schools, so there are not yet many 'proven' applications available, although there are some TQM pioneers now working in Britain, Canada and the USA. These early adopters will be developing and customizing TQM processes and will show results in the near future. This book therefore provides a framework, not a prescription. It provides what might be referred to as a basis for the development of market-driven effective quality schooling. More specifically, the book does not seek to offer a comprehensive overview of all developments in TQM and their applications to schooling; nor does it seek to offer a step-by-step analysis of how TQM applies in different ways in different school jurisdictions. Our intention is to provide insights, understandings, frameworks and tools from which the reader can develop their own strategies for making our schools totally dedicated to high performance, quality and the satisfaction of parent and pupil expectations.

# CHAPTER 1

# Making sense of schooling in the 1990s: Tools for taking the long view

There are many developments in the field of schooling. Some of these developments – school-based budgeting, local management of schools, new curriculum developments, integration of special needs children into the 'normal' classroom and extended use of new technology in teaching and learning – are understandable in their own right as developments that spring from special interests and concerns that have been expressed over a number of years.

Other developments, such as increasing market-driven competitiveness between urban schools, growth of alternative schooling arrangements (private schools, home schooling), the increasing use of distance education and open learning systems to provide alternative routes through the curriculum in (North America) or the establishment of a national curriculum, attainment targets and devolution of control to the school level in Britain are part of a newer and wider approach about who defines the 'product' of public education systems. Many policymakers are struggling to keep pace with these changes that are taking place in the management of education. Others are struggling against the changes, while not fully understanding the dynamics of these changes.

The underlying dynamic is that schooling is shifting from a public service driven by professionals towards a market-driven service, fuelled by purchasers and customers. In Britain, this market economy for schooling is in its infancy. In the USA and Canada the development is in its birth stages. But the development is clear and discernible in the developed world.

In this chapter we outline a basis for understanding the dynamics of the changes that are taking place in the provision of schooling. We use *industry analysis*, developed by Michael Porter and refined for use in the context of schooling, as a framework for scrutinizing these developments. Later chapters will elaborate this analysis in terms of competitiveness, strategic development and service management. Our aim is to illuminate a simple method for reviewing the developments that are taking place and that could have an impact on your school or the cluster of schools in your region. From the analysis, you will be able to develop a framework that will be valuable when making strategic choices.

Many people dislike the use of business language, industry analysis and reference to the market as a basis for seeking to understand the practice of schooling. The argument is that the very use of this language embodies a set of values and assumptions that are counter to those that education seeks to promote. Some assert that 'education is nothing to do with economy', that it is 'about the whole person and not about specific skills or crude performance as understood in the industrial world.'

Some go further, suggesting that the deliberate linkage of capitalism and schooling is representative of a form of social repression that should be avoided in the development of social justice, social well-being and social policy (Bowles and Gintis 1976). These arguments are ideologically grounded and need to be understood as representing a set of ideological propositions about the nature of schooling, the role of the state in the management of social policy and the relationship between people and capital.

We are not concerned here with such matters; this book is not intended to discuss the ideology of schooling, but to sensitize and help those now leading primary and secondary schools understand and respond to new contexts that governments have legislated. In general, across the world, such legislation has introduced elements of the marketplace so that schools now operate in what might perhaps be better termed a modified marketplace.

Industry analysis is an analytical tool for understanding the system dynamics of the marketplace and therefore has relevance to the new situation facing publicly funded schooling in several countries. By 'industry analysis' we mean the range of approaches initiated by Michael Porter at the Harvard Business School from work on competitive strategy, and by now extended by other writers (Day 1990). However, we are not saying that total quality management (TQM) and industry analysis are only relevant to educationalists because they now operate in a context with elements of a marketplace. We see the thinking and tools of TQM as relevant to the enhancing of schools' performance in the eyes of their 'customers', even if there were no market factors operating, that is, even if the 'opting out' and 'open enrolment' of Britain were to disappear overnight. We are saying, then, that industry analysis can help us even where there is no intention of advocating a full market model of schooling. It is a tool that permits the development of a variety of models of public and private services, not necessarily models that lead to privatization; the analytical frame could lead to propositions that minimized the role of the private sector or led to new ways of thinking about the structural impediments to effective private sector educational strategies.

## The growing problem of investment resource for public educational systems in the western world

Four factors are creating a major challenge to public educational provision; indeed some are calling their effects a crisis. They are:

1 Costs and demands for educational provision by the public purse are outstripping the available revenue.
2 In some countries taxpayers are baulking at paying.
3 Parents and government have been redefining the range of what they expect schools to do for children by adding to the 'entitlement curriculum' personal, health, and social education content.
4 Government and influential groups in society increasingly expect schools to play their part in national economic competitiveness.

In analysing the basic features of public sector education in Britain, Europe, Canada and the USA the problems are the same. They may manifest themselves in different ways in different countries, but the structural features of these problems are identical.

The fundamental problem is that available revenues for educational investment and expenditure are declining relative to both demand and cost. At the same time, taxpayers are becoming increasingly unwilling to pay additional sums in education-related taxation. In particular, the double-income-no-kids (sometimes referred to as 'dinks') and retired persons with pensions and fixed incomes (sometimes referred to as 'woofs' – well-off older folks or worse-off older folks, depending upon the pension arrangements) whose children are long out of school, appear reluctant to invest more in education. Finally, parents with children in school have successive new demands for education: schools are responding to these parental demands by increasing their work in the fields of health and social education, social work and community development. In fact, by mid-1991 only one-tenth of all households in the UK conformed to the popular image of the nuclear family (a man, a woman and two children) – the most common form of household in Britain was a couple with no children, and the number of retired people was the highest recorded. Only 10.8 per cent of households were a couple and two children; couples without children made up 29.2 per cent and one-person households 26.9 per cent – 60 per cent of all households are one or two persons without children. All these

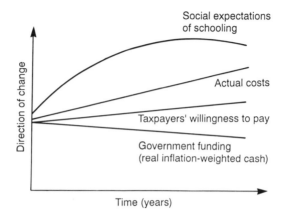

*Fig. 1.1*   The elements of the education 'crisis'.

aspects considered, then, there is something of a crisis developing in public sector education provisions. In terms of this analysis, if education was looked at as an industry then it could be seen to be heading into deep trouble unless responses are made.

The trends can be shown on a single graph. The horizontal axis shows time (in years) and the vertical shows expectations/supply. The message of this simple graph is clear: without change, the expectations and costs of education in the public sector will be both unreasonable (in terms of expectations) and unaffordable (in terms of expenditure) – the education industry is in crisis (Fig. 1.1).

At the level of the individual school the implications of the four factors discussed above, and illustrated for the most part in the graph, are two-fold: (i) schools will have to match their performances more closely to the expectations of their customers; and (ii) school management will have to manage the relationship between income and expenditure in terms of the curriculum programmes delivered. To do this requires a thorough understanding of the strategy a school is pursuing and the dynamics of that strategy. This in turn requires a thorough understanding of the context for strategy: the nature of the educational 'industry' and the dynamics of change in that industry. This is what industry analysis seeks to enable.

## The dynamics of the public education 'industry'

Industry analysis requires the analyst to work systematically at understanding seven key features of the industry they are studying. These seven key features are:

1 Changes in the behaviour of consumer stakeholders (buyers).
2 Changes in the behaviour of provider stakeholders (suppliers).
3 Changes in the use of new technology, which have an effect on operating practices.
4 New providers into the 'business' of schooling.
5 Changes in the competitive strategies of schools.
6 Changes in the requirements of governments that have a direct impact on the way the schools operate.
7 Understanding the key demographic features that will affect the nature of schooling.

We have used the term 'stakeholder' in the list above, and we shall make frequent use of this term in the following discussions. 'Stakeholder' refers to those who have a vested interest in education, its processes and its outcomes.

Each area of the public provision of schooling will be examined in detail in terms of the seven key features suggested by industry analysis. In doing this we shall, in effect, be examining the position of the school in its environment as though it was any other industry in the marketplace and exactly on a par with a manufacturing or commercial enterprise. This approach will be novel to many and some will object that it is irrelevant to the public service context. We see the relevance of this 'industry analysis' approach, however, precisely because governments in many countries have been re-organizing the parameters of both the system and control of publicly provided schooling. They have introduced, by way of greater consumer choice and control, elements of the marketplace. Schools are now in a marketplace, even if it is not a full blown one, hence the relevance, we believe, of the industry analysis approach we are using here (Fig. 1.2).

In reading this analysis, the task is to connect the exemplars we provide to the reality of the situation in your particular school: adjust, add, modify the exemplars under each heading to better understand your environment, your dynamics and your options. As a result of this work you will be able to better understand the pressures that affect your decisions and your strategic choices. Chapter 2 will help you make use of the analysis, which is best done with your senior management team. Engage them in brainstorming or use de Bono's Six Thinking Hats Process (de Bono 1987) and encourage them to highlight the key underlying issues your school has to address through the choice of a sustainable strategy for success. Rather than see all of the pressures and changes that you face as equivalent, categorize them, understand their interrelationship and, wherever possible, collect information about just how the change you identify could affect your school.

This is a practical task, not simply an academic exercise. Only by understanding these environmental forces can you select a sustainable and durable strategy for your school.

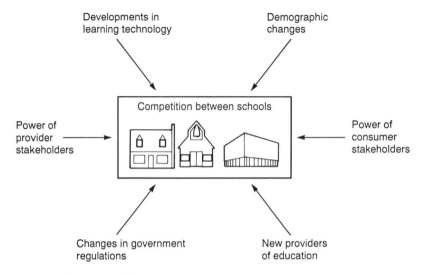

*Fig. 1.2*   Elements of the 'market' in schooling.

**Changes in the behaviour of consumer stakeholders**

Schooling has a variety of 'customers' or stakeholders. They include parents, community leaders, young people, employers, postsecondary educational institutions, community groups and some others. The question to be asked under this heading is simple: 'What are the current developments in the attitudes and behaviour of these groups that have a direct effect on both the current operations of schools and what is likely to happen in the future?' The first part of the question focuses on short-term development, while the second looks at strategic questions.

Some of the changes that are widely reported in this area of the education industry include:

*Parents*

1 Increased demands from parents for primary education to be more directly concerned with health care and social well-being issues.
2 Increased demands from parents for guarantees about literacy, numeracy and social skills.
3 Increasing concern that education equips their children for employment.
4 Increased desire for involvement on the part of parents in the decision-making associated with both the operation of schools and the development of the curriculum.
5 Increased attention required in education, following protests of parents, on both special needs and gifted children.

6 Increased sense of uncertainty about the value of education in the light of unemployment, access issues in relation to postsecondary education (especially in Canada and Britain) and the increased use of 'user fees' in education.

7 An increased demand that schooling should be more tied to jobs or career development so that student learning is seen to be linked to future wage-earning.

8 A desire to have 'rights' protected – in Britain, the Citizens Charter seeks to do this.

## Pupils

1 Increased drop-out rates from school systems over time.

2 Declines in pupil performance on some tests, showing that the system has performance weaknesses (especially in the USA).

3 Increasing use of the 'community' services of the school – health, sports, counselling, guidance, clubs and societies – by students.

4 Concerns over range of choice and subject options – more flexibility sought.

5 Concern to link school with career more firmly.

## Employers

1 Growing concern about the quality of educational services in terms of literacy, numeracy and social skills.

2 Increasing involvement in strategy and resourcing questions in education through industry partnering, joint venturing, curriculum development projects (e.g. junior achievers).

3 Increase in the attempts of employers to secure policy change by Government through lobby pressure.

4 Increase in industry expenditure of training, especially in relation to postschool literacy, numeracy and social skills – this is seen as industry responding to the failure of schooling.

5 Recognition that training investment is a key element in any competitive strategy.

## Postsecondary institutions

1 Changes in entrance requirements (becoming more difficult) as demand for places outstrips supply (Canada and Britain).

2 Concern over the academic base of the school curriculum – continued attempts to influence curriculum of schools in terms of university entrance.

3 Concern over the lack of integration of technological skills (especially information technologies) in the curriculum of the secondary (high) school.
4 Growing interest in the preparation of young people for life-long learning.

*Community groups*

1 Concern among taxpayers who do not have children in school with value for money (also called, by some, return on investment).
2 Advocacy groups increasingly seeing schools as a vehicle for promotion of social issues (e.g. AIDS; environmental concerns; minority language rights within statutory education, e.g. Welsh/French language issues in Wales and Canada).
3 'Politically correct' monitoring of curriculum by some.
4 Religious/ethical/moral monitoring of curriculum by others.
5 Greater demands for access to physical facilities and capital equipment (especially information technology) from community groups.

At the base of these concerns across all stakeholder groups are questions about performance, relevance and rights. Indeed, in making strategic choices there is a need to reconcile four critical stakeholder concerns:

1 *Effectiveness* – the ability of a school to be effective in delivering educational services as measured by some articulated performance standard.
2 *Efficiency* – the ability of the school to meet expectations in a demonstrated cost-effective way. Stakeholders cling to a concept of 'value for money', which has, in our view, both accountancy and perception elements to it. They want the demonstration that an objective is being achieved without waste and in what looks to be a cost-effective manner. They also want evidence to show to what extent their expectations are being achieved.
3 *Individual rights* – the extent to which the work of the school recognizes and respects the rights and concerns of individuals.
4 *Equality of opportunity (equity)* – while curriculum programmes may differ from one school to another, all should have equal rights of access to programmes according to ability – access should be independent of gender, race, class or sexual orientation.

## The importance of school leaders and stakeholders agreeing a strategy

In looking at these concerns, the task is to develop a cohesive and coherent strategy for the school, which has ownership among all of the stakeholders. Chapter 2 will help you focus on strategic choices. However, the starting point here is whether the school has worked out exactly who its stakeholders are? While there will be differences from school to school, in our view, all would probably list in common: parents, governors, school board members, certain local employers and community leaders. How many, though, would list the pupils and teachers as separate stakeholder groups?

The questions to ask about the consumer stakeholder groups that are important in determining the strategy choices are:

1 What are the core values of the stakeholders (i.e. attitudes and beliefs about education) and how are these values reflected in their expectations?
2 What behavioural expectations do stakeholders have for the school – if they were to outline the characteristics of a successful school leaver, what would each stakeholder group say?
3 What social image is expected of the school by each stakeholder group?
4 What criteria are being used by each stakeholder group in evaluating the non-academic performance of the school?
5 How do the stakeholder groups seek to evaluate the teachers in the school – what are the characteristics of effective teachers from their point of view.
6 What are the stakeholders willing to offer the school in terms of support (time, money, commitment) and under what conditions?

By asking these (and other questions important in your local context), how can you design a school that not only meets but exceeds these expectations? Designing a school for these stakeholders is central to the ideas of this book.

## New entrants into the provision of schooling

As schooling becomes more and more influenced by the factors we have discussed above, so that there is a significant degree of real open enrolment and free flow of pupils to the schools their parents choose, other providers will come into the 'business' of schooling and will provide competing curriculum programmes to those that have previously been offered exclusively by publicly provided schools.

Some of these 'new entrants' are already to be found in some systems in the developed world, others are yet to appear. Some of the current developments, which are evidenced in both North America and Europe, include:

1 The growth of private schooling, especially in terms of specialist schools in the area of gifted children, children with special learning needs, science and languages.

2 'Immersion' schools in French and other languages. These may be publicly or privately funded.
3 The growth of private sector involvement in the provision of learning through curriculum resources, partnering and sponsoring and through the growth of industry–education curriculum development projects.
4 The entrance of telecommunications companies into schooling through the development of information technology and distance learning provisions.
5 Significant expansion of home-schooling (parent-guided learning), increasingly supported by information technology.
6 The increasing role of government agencies in the curriculum (e.g. the Training Agency in Britain – TECs – and the multicultural commissions in Canada).

Underlying these developments is the belief held by many in government, and also by those who are influentially placed outside government, that the interests in education go beyond the education professionals and now embrace some other providers with more commercial or 'property' interests in learning. Not all of the interests are philanthropic – distance learning and the telecommunications and computer investments in classrooms of the future are intended to produce income for their companies in terms of the sales of hardware and software. In their terms, educational activity is a 'market area', with significant potential for the future.

Some possible future trends, which have already been discussed or are now beginning to occur, include:

1 Post-16 specialist schools funded jointly by industry and private capital to boost students' chances of achieving the required entry standards for postsecondary institutions.
2 Industry-funded training and education at the post-16 level for apprenticeship and skill development.
3 Private distance learning systems for primary and secondary school systems to support both home learning (using information technology, audiovisual systems and print) and in-school learning.
4 Growth of private tutoring and special skills units managed by educational 'consultants' to bolster publicly funded provision on an individualized/customized basis.

Most of these developments can be seen in terms of 'added value' resources to the basic provisions of a publicly funded education service. Because most would rely on user fees rather than public grants in aid of their work, these developments would give emphasis to a market-driven aspect to the provision of educational services and present stakeholders with genuine alternative (and not necessarily very expensive) choices.

New providers can have certain advantages over existing providers. These advantages include:

1 Being able to focus attention on particular aspects of educational services, rather than having to provide a broad-based service.
2 Being able to recruit staff for the purposes of the new organization, rather than having to gain conversions from old ways of working to new ones.
3 Having fewer points of control.
4 Being able to recoup the full costs of the services they provide from their users, thus making explicit the customer–supplier relationship.

At the level of the school, there is a need to be aware of and in touch with these developments and to examine systematically what can be learned from them.

### Developments in the use of new technology

The development of efficient computing technology, information technology (IT) and expert systems permits a significant rethinking in the nature of learning as a process. Without doubt, the wide availability in the home of computers, video and audio systems remains one of the hitherto unexploited territories for learning enhancement.

The countries of Europe and North America vary widely in their investments in learning technology, in their utilization of information technology for administrative and management activity and in their investments in teacher education for technology use. Britain is notably sluggish in its resourcing of schools and in training its teachers in information technology and has only recently begun to use information technology for management information and control in its schools. Although some staff training is taking place, this aspect – and the much wider use of computers and information technology to support the individual school's curriculum strategy, financial budgeting and cost control, policy review and evaluation systems – is expected to expand rapidly now that the majority of schools have full delegated local management control of their budgets. The fullest implementation of the TQM approaches deriving from industry analysis depend on exploitation of these new technologies. Some schools are aware of this and are aiming at a situation where all their senior managers are networked to the school's databases and skilled in the applications of project control for their own areas of responsibility, school-wide research and evaluation systems, updating the community database, etc.

Examples of key developments taking place, or possible in the future, in the use of technology to enhance learning performance and to aid strategy and management in educational institutions are:

1 Some schools are entirely computerized, with students learning through a combination of traditional teaching and self-paced study using computer managed learning (CML) systems and computer aided learning (CAL) systems.
2 Some curriculum areas have developed major resources for the use of teachers for CML, video-based or text-based self-paced learning.
3 Major publishing houses are developing CML versions of their school texts, thus making possible updates, new editions, special editions or customization.
4 CD ROM computer technology is making the nature of library support for student learning and curriculum development a very different process – vast resources are available to students without leaving home.
5 Videodisc technology can make a range of scientific work (especially laboratory work) readily available in interactive mode. While currently expensive, price is a function of volumes of sales.

Some schools are more advanced than others in their use of computer systems and information technologies. Some are integrating computers systematically across the curriculum, and individualizing instruction as a deliberate strategy to differentiate them from other schools in the area. Others are regarding new technology as an adjunct to their people-focused strategies for learning. The point to note here is that the use of technology is a way in which one school can be differentiated from another at the level of strategy. Indeed, the place of technology in the process of learning is increasingly a centrepiece question for parents when they are making a choice between schools.

For the school-based management team, the issue here is simple: what role will technology have in our future and how are we to ensure that the technology in which we invest carries the outcomes we desire?

This last point is important. While the cost of technology is coming down, it is still the case that a significant investment in technology would be a large cost to a school. In addition, the implications such an investment has for staff training, ongoing capital and recurrent expenditure, and for managing the operation, can be as significant as the initial costs of equipment. Keeping up with developments in technology is also demanding.

In the service economy in general, investment in technology has not been accompanied by any substantial growth in productivity (Roach 1991): there is no automatic relationship between technology investment and efficiency or effectiveness. This implies that technology use has to be a very clear and specific part of a strategy for performance improvement, rather than an adjunct. That is, technology of itself is not necessarily a strategy for improvement – it is what technology is intended to do that counts. As Paul (1991) says 'technology is the answer – now what is the question?'. If technology is to be used as a key element in the design of a school's strategy, then the outcome expectations have to be very clearly specified, along with the steps that will be taken to ensure that technology will make a sustainable difference to the work of the school.

In looking at this area of our analysis, the following questions need to be asked by the school-based management team:

1 What is our current use of technology (audio, video, CAL, CML, IT and expert systems)?
2 How effective is our use of this technology in terms of: (i) enhancing learning through improved performance; (ii) changing the nature of teaching and learning so as to ensure that our pedagogy makes full use of the opportunities of this technology; and (iii) reducing our operating costs as a school?
3 What could we use technology for and how would this make a sustainable difference to our performance as a school?
4 What technology do we need to meet the expectations of our consumer stakeholders ?
5 What training would be required among staff to ensure effective use of technology and where would this training come from?
6 How critical is this technology to our strategy?
7 What would it cost?
8 How could we get others (parents, industry, governments) to meet the costs of this investment?

## Changes in the behaviour, values and expectations of providers

Just as there are stakeholders in the outcomes of education, there are also stakeholders in the inputs into education. These stakeholders include governments (national and local), teacher education centres and teacher unions: all seek to influence the process of education, and hence the outcomes. Because we have created a separate analysis category focusing on government (this is not usually done in industry analysis), we will highlight here changes in the environment of schooling that come from other sources, notably teachers, teacher education providers, industry, developers of intellectual property and teacher unions.

Some of the discernible developments among these stakeholders include:

### Teachers

1 Stress and burn-out appear to be increasing – certainly as issues of concern to teachers.
2 The period of time spent in the teaching profession is getting shorter, with fewer staying a full 40–45 years in the profession.

3 While degree programmes are becoming more narrowly focused, the teacher is increasingly expected to have both specialist and generalist skills.
4 Extensive concern within the profession that too many changes are being introduced too rapidly and with too little emphasis on teacher education and training.
5 Some highly innovative curriculum work is being initiated and completed in the areas of information technology and global education.

### Teacher education providers

1 Significant moves to review and radically change the preparation of teachers as the assumed connection between current training curricula and later effectiveness in the classroom, together with the ability to adapt to a fast changing world, are now questioned.
2 Increasing use of mentors/proctorships (professional teachers trained in teacher guidance/evaluation) to assist training or assess professional competence.
3 Growth of Masters/PhD requirements for administrative positions.
4 Shortages of teachers in key areas (maths, science, certain languages, etc.).
5 Uncertainty as to whether supply of teachers will be adequate for demand in the mid- to late 1990s.

### Industry

1 Sponsorship of schools increasing – donations of hardware, resources, money, people, time and company skills increasing.
2 Partnering between a particular business and a particular school or group of schools is increasing.
3 Attempts to influence school policies and practices are increasing and, in some places, are formalized through school–business councils.

### Developers of intellectual property

1 Changes in copyright laws, which make it more difficult and more expensive for schools to make copies of materials.
2 Rapidly changing knowledge-base reflected in more frequent new editions of textbooks, computer software and other learning resources.
3 Less competition between providers of books, video and audio resources due to mergers, therefore less competitive pricing and fewer alternative sources for learning resources.
4 Stronger ties between publishers and curriculum as the scope of the curriculum is increasingly specified by governments rather than teachers.

5 The national curriculum in Britain and the cross-Provincial/State curriculum alignment in North America create 'knowledge' trading blocs that are distinct between continents at this time but are likely to become global with time – this may make such curriculum bodies as the International Baccalaureate more attractive for schools with globally mobile parent populations.

### Teacher unions

1 Changes in the focus of bargaining, with more balance between pensions, working conditions and pay than previously.
2 More intense local bargaining (especially in Britain) than previously.
3 Local differentials between pay and other conditions are likely to become increasingly important in determining who teaches where and for how long.
4 Job protection focus will intensify as budget pressures become more severe.

The way in which an individual school responds to all these aspects of change in their environment will have a crucial bearing on the strategy they pursue. As schools are service organizations, which depend upon knowledge workers (Handy 1989), the way in which such workers are recruited, trained and sustained will have a crucial bearing on the success of the strategy of the school. The questions the school management team should ask are:

1 What expectations do teachers have about their work environment in this school, and how well are we doing in meeting these expectations?
2 What mechanisms do we have for the continual improvement of the work environment for our teachers, and how well are these mechanisms working?
3 When we recruit new teachers to work in this school, what kind of expectations do we convey to them about the strategy of the school? What kind of orientation do we give them to the nature of this school, its commitment, communication and cultural expectations and its expectations in terms of sensitivity to our consumer stakeholders?
4 What are we willing to pay our teachers?
5 What is the performance management system for the task of meeting the expectations of our stakeholders?
6 How are we managing the process of innovation in this school?
7 Who do we involve in the activity of curriculum development and implementation in this school – which stakeholders?
8 How can we maximize the available learning opportunities for the adults who work in this school?

9  How can we involve our industry/business stakeholders in the learning and innovation tasks of the school in a way that teachers feel to be supportive and valuable as opposed to threatening and disruptive?
10  How can the teacher unions help this school to be outstanding in achieving its goals and sustaining these achievements over time? How can we involve and engage the union(s) in this task?
11  How can this school have an influence on the preparation of its teachers for its work ?

You will notice that these are big and demanding questions – they go to the heart of the work of this book. You may want to return to this list having completed your reading of this text. The important thing is that your answers to these questions will prove central to your success in building strong commitment, effective communication and a powerful performance culture for success in your school. Taken together with the questions about consumer stakeholders, this is the heart of a strategy for market-driven quality schooling. Of course, finding the answers to these questions requires some systematic survey research to yield data that is representative and reliable rather than the hit and miss of anecdotal or fragmented information, which is always so readily available. To achieve the systematic collection of data will need someone in the senior management team who has had training in these skills. What we are talking about here is the school equivalent of the market research officer.

### Changes in the requirements of governments

There are significant changes taking place in all major developed countries in the ways of financing and control of public education provision. In some countries – most notably Britain – these changes are dramatic. In others, such as Canada, these changes are in their infancy. But certain key trends are discernible.

Key among them is the dual realization that:

1  Investment in education is a significant key to the competitive advantage of nations, especially those with limited or a rapidly declining natural resource base (Porter 1990).
2  Current investments in educational systems are not producing the returns that the planners expected at the time investments were made.

Education is now becoming an election issue for both of these reasons, although the public issues revolve more around the second concern than the first. It is expressed in terms of the number of young people who leave school without literacy skills (largely unchanged as a percentage of the cohort across almost a century of public schooling), the number of drop-outs from schooling (and especially in terms of those who do not continue in full time education after the statutory leaving age), growing concerns about the level of capability of teachers and concern about the growth of funding demands from the education sector.

Other aspects of the decisions of governments, which have an impact on the short- and medium-term for the education industry are:

1 Specification of a national curriculum in terms of outcomes – already legislated in Britain and a key issue in Canada and the USA debate about education.
2 Accountability and performance central to the agenda of governments – performance indicators increasingly used as a basis for shaping policy and for funding decisions.
3 Increasing the local management of schools through changes in both the structure of control and the rights of parents.
4 Introduction of open enrolment policies – providing parents with the freedom of choice for their children's schooling (largely an urban choice).
5 School-based financing based on formulae.
6 Proposed privatization (in Britain) of certain functions (e.g. school inspection and evaluation).
7 Focus on individual rights and entitlements protected in law (Canada, Britain and the USA).
8 Recognition that market forces have a part to play in determining the success or otherwise of schools and the public funding they receive (Britain and the USA).
9 Increased partnership between government and business in response to educational development issues (Britain and the USA).
10 Prescription by governments of standard curricula with determined core skills (Britain and the USA).
11 Encouragement of private and non-profit ventures in education and the decline of state monopoly of educational services (linked to privatization developments).

These developments, while having a major impact on how schooling is funded, organized, evaluated and accounted for, are relatively easy to understand. They refer to the concern of government to ensure: (i) value for money; (ii) international competitiveness through the skills of people; and (iii) an increase in the extent to which local people feel in control of local schooling – building on the belief that those nearest the customer are best able to meet the needs of the customer.

Some of the developments speak again to the model of public policy issues outlined earlier. Governments are seeking to reconcile competing public policy issues by the decisions they are making. For example, in Britain individual rights and effectiveness issues are being addressed through a combination of a Citizens Charter, which guarantees rights in law, and a specification of a National Curriculum, with standards set and audited by government-approved agencies. Efficiency is being encouraged in North America by the growth of new technology-based learning systems and an increase in private sector involvement in education. Equity issues are being addressed through distance learning (equity of curriculum choice between rural and urban schools), integration of special needs children into 'normal' classrooms and special projects to encourage girls to enter science, mathematics and technical and vocational subject choice career paths.

In looking at the nature of the changes outlined, you need to be very clear to differentiate between assumptions about what the changes mean and the reality of the changes. For example, it is often assumed that a National Curriculum will increase uniformity of the curriculum; however, what is being specified are the outcomes desired from a teaching–learning process. In reality, schools still have significant degrees of freedom in the delivery of the prescribed curricula and the methods by which the objectives are to be met.

One other thing needs to be made clear here. Most governments in the developed world are running significant public sector deficits. While the reasons for this differ between countries, the reality is that public policy is being undermined by indebtedness. Only four ways to resolve this problem have been tried in modern times: (i) cutting public programmes and privatization; (ii) increasing taxation; (iii) blending expenditure reduction and taxation policies to produce the desired results; and (iv) stimulating the economy by public spending and printing money in the hope that activity levels will rise in such a way as to both pay off the debt and the cost of the new programmes. History shows (Johnson 1989) that this last strategy actually increases indebtedness. With some exceptions, governments in the developed world are pursuing the third of these strategies – adjusting taxation, reducing public spending and moving to an increasingly free-market economy for many 'public' services. It follows, then, that significant new investments for education are unlikely to come from government sources. It is more likely that any new activity is likely to follow from the reallocation of resources from other activities no longer deemed essential. This has been the reality of most postsecondary developments in education for some time.

Some respond to this financial situation by opposing the underlying strategy of governments: they see themselves as victims of the strategy. Others accept the strategy and try to work with it: they see themselves as having opportunities within the strategy. How you chose to see this reality will be a critical factor in shaping the strategy for your school. As Henry Ford said, 'if you think you can or you think you can't, you're probably right.'

Given the comments and the changes outlined here, what questions should your school-based management team ask itself? In the following questions, the word 'government' is used frequently. You should interpret this to mean either the governors/trustees of your school, your local education authority or school board; your State/Provincial or national government; or a combination of all of these:

1  What three changes taking place in the requirements of government are critical to us? How can we manage these three changes exceptionally well?
2  For government to see this school as outperforming the expectations it has of us, what would outperformance look like in terms of the achievements of our students, the quality of our staff and the use of our resources?
3  What would it take for us to meet and then exceed the expectations of government?
4  Who in government knows about the work of this school? How do they know this and what can we do to ensure that what they know is accurate, up-to-date and valued?
5  How can we ensure that we maintain such contact with government that we can anticipate and plan for change rather than always be reactive and 'victims' of change?
6  What are our expectations of government (after all, they are suppliers of services to us) and how can we ensure that they are fully aware of our expectations and needs?

These may look like 'political' questions. In fact, they are six questions that speak to the customer–supplier relationships between schools and government agencies. For some things, schools are supplying government with services for which they pay and have expectations. For other services, schools are customers of government. These questions need to be asked if a strong, reciprocal customer–supplier relationship is to be built. Without them, the choice of strategy for the school may well be poorly informed.

### Social and demographic trends affecting schooling

The children who will leave school aged 18 in the year 2000 were born in 1982. Their teachers were born sometime between 1935 and 1973. We know a great deal about these people. We also know a great deal about population trends by geographic area and by economic region. While some events can have a dramatic impact on these demographic features – natural disasters, major shifts in the economy – almost all demographic trends are slow to develop and are very discernible to those who will keep a constant watching eye on them.

Those seeking to understand the communities they serve or the business environment in which they must compete need a systematic understanding of the demographics of their area. In general, the currently discernible trends that affect schooling are:

1 More divorces and single parents leading to wider social roles for schooling.
2 Increased car ownership, which extends the ability of more parents to transport children to a wider range of schools.
3 Children, through television and electronic games, experience a whole range of home-based interactive stimulation against which schools' teaching methods have to compete.
4 Parental performance expectations now tend to be based on the standards they see portrayed by mass communication rather than by 'local significant others'; the performance standards are being increasingly globally set.
5 Ageing population with fewer people in work being asked to support more people in school or retirement.
6 Increase in the number of women in the workforce, creating further 'childcare' demands on the education system.

Few schools require one of their own management team to be vigilant about changes in the demography of their area, yet a great deal can be discerned from careful reading of census and trend data. In market-based systems, understanding demography is a critical task.

What questions about demographic trends would affect the choice of strategy in the area in which your school is based? Some suggestions are:

1 What is the birth rate in this area and how does this translate into numbers for this school over a ten-year period (a spread-sheet analysis is essential for this work)?
2 What has been the enrolment in the various schools with which your school (in realistic travel terms) shares a parental choice over the last five years. That is, do you know what share of your potential market of children you are getting?
3 What are the characteristics of the total student body (i.e. across all schools in this area) in comparison to our student body (e.g. gender mix, racial mix, language skill mix, ability range, family income, etc.)?
4 What is our parent profile and how does this relate to the parent profile of other schools in this area?
5 What is the nature of local industry and employment available and how has this changed over the last decade?
6 What other demographic trends are pertinent to our understanding of our place in this community?

Some of these data are difficult to find. Some are difficult to interpret. What is important is that you begin systematically to seek out and understand these data in a way that helps you identify possibilities and opportunities, while at the same time recognize the reality of your school. The more you consider radical change in the strategy of the school, the more important demographic analysis becomes.

## Changes in the competitive environment between schools

In many countries, the changes made by government to the educational system for the control of the individual school and the access to it by parents, means that schools cannot stand still in relation to their environment. For many years schools had a concept and reality of a more or less fixed catchment area. This is now not the case; to varying degrees, schools must now operate to some extent in a market environment. They are becoming increasingly concerned with marketing their schools (Marland and Rogers 1991), with enrolment levels and with performance. While some agreements between schools within an area about how marketing may be undertaken are beginning now to emerge – what some have called a 'status quo cartel' – others are aggressive in the marketplace. In some countries, there is strong competition between church schools and public schools for students. The key developments in the market environment, which affect the competition between schools at this time, include:

1 Open enrolment and open boundaries policies, enabling parents free choice of schools.
2 Publication of performance indicators in local and national newspapers affecting parental thinking about the performance of the school.
3 Development of a code of practice for marketing schools by professional bodies.
4 Competition between public and private schools on an increasingly level playing field.
5 Competition between schools for teachers with special skills.
6 Competition between schools on 'focus', e.g. sports, science, links with industry, music, academic performance.
7 Competition between schools for scarce public resources (money, capital equipment).
8 Competition between schools for industry support and partnering.
9 The public's image of the particular school as mediated by the press and important opinion-forming local figures.

Some schools regard themselves as actively engaged in a competition with others, while others see this competition as much more passive. These views can be contrasted between 'hussling the market' and 'let our achievements speak for themselves'. Many more schools are in between these two positions. Over time, as formula funding becomes the sole base for funding schools, the element of between-school competition is likely to grow. It should be noted that much of this between-school competition for students and resources is urban in nature – rural school systems have different kinds of problems. Their primary area of competition is in the field of teacher employment – securing, training and sustaining a teaching force over time can be a significant problem for rural schools, which may be made worse if pay differentials between schools in urban and rural areas are introduced.

### Questions for senior managers and school governors about promoting the school

What are the questions your school management team should be asking about promoting your school to the parental consumers of schooling in your area who have a choice about where they will send their children?

1 Which local schools attract the students we could be serving? (include in your listing schools of any kind – private, special or organizations offering additional services).
2 What features of these schools, which we do not offer, attract students?
3 What is it about our school that 'puts off' these students and their parents?
4 Who do we attract to this school? What is it about this school that attracts them?
5 What steps have we taken to market this school? What are the outcomes of each of these steps – what numbers can we attribute to specific marketing activities?
6 What steps have other local schools taken to market themselves and how successful have these steps been?
7 What are the six features of our school that are distinctive and mark us as different from other schools in this locale?
8 How can we involve each of our stakeholder groups: the parents, the governors, the students, the staff, etc. in assessing our present effectiveness and in giving news of and promoting the advantages of the school?

### Conclusions

What has the analysis we have presented in this chapter to do with applying TQM? Our first objective was to help you understand the dynamic environment in which your school has to operate. All of the forces we have described (and others which you can add) are acting to shape the nature of your school. The second objective was to provide a framework from which you can make clear strategic choices. The key questions heads and senior managers in schools must be asking are:

1 What local developments have implications for how we do things in this school?
2 What national developments, in terms of new service providers, could have an impact on how we do things in this school?
3 In what ways do new providers of educational services have an impact on how our stakeholders think about the work of our school?

4 Given our level of control over budget resources, can we make use of these local services to better our performance as a school?

These are the questions to be explored by the senior management team in your school as a specific focus for discussing the elements of strategy. In Chapter 2 the generic nature of the strategic choices available to you will be considered.

Quality is a function of strategy and strategy depends on your decisions about the way in which the seven forces affect your school. As this text unfolds, you will come to understand the ways in which strategy and quality are interrelated. The key point here is that until you have defined the strategy your school is pursuing (following a careful analysis of your marketplace), quality is secondary.

# CHAPTER
# 2

# Choosing a generic strategy: Four choices for a customer-conscious school

In Chapter 1 we examined the seven major forces which, through the dynamics and the relationship between them, have an impact on the nature of schooling in a particular location. We outlined a process through which a management team within a school could examine the impact of these seven forces on their decision-making and remain proactive in planning and developing a strategy.

The whole focus, then, of the approaches we discussed in Chapter 1 was to understand the context in which the school will need to make a strategic choice regarding placing and promoting itself within the communities for which it wishes to provide its services. Put in the language of industry analysis, this means 'what strategy will be chosen to market the school against the competition of others?'

In this chapter we outline four strategies that appear to have the qualities of generic strategies – underlying strategic frames from within which critical decisions taken day-to-day and month-to-month are driven. We present these as providing a basis of choice for a school as to how it wishes to position itself in the marketplace for educational services.

We are suggesting that, for the immediate future, schools have a choice of one these four strategies, and that an explicit proactive strategy will work, whereas the lack of a distinctive educational role strategy or pursuing a mixture of a bit of all approaches will not.

Many educational leaders find it surprising that schools can be thought of as having strategic choices. After all, the argument goes, they are required in law to provide services to a certain standard to meet the curriculum specifications of government. The law prescribes equal rights to parents in terms of the education of their children. The law also makes specific provision for the way in which special needs children shall be treated and provides a statement of service expectations. While local management practices vary between one area and another, schools appear to vary only slightly in the way in which they offer these services.

Many recognize that this is not the case in the private sector of education, where schools compete for students in terms of their special offerings – place, people skills, product (specific curriculum focus), price – the so-called 4Ps of the school. But schools in the public or state sector of education are assumed to be grossly similar in comparison with the private or independent schools, even though, as we have argued earlier, they are increasingly providing their services in a context that has many of the properties of a competitive market.

Yet schools of whatever kind pride themselves on their uniqueness. Some schools, such as Hartridge in Bristol (Great Britain) have a reputation in the field of sports and intend to use this specific competitive advantage in sports both as a vehicle for marketing themselves and as a focus for dealing with disruptive students. Others, such as Cheetham School in Manchester (Great Britain) have a world-class reputation in the field of music and are primarily music educators who fulfil their across-the-curriculum requirements in addition to training quality young musicians who will develop into professional musicians.

This goes further than just reflecting the specific interests of a collection of teachers. We know from research in the area of school effectiveness that a school's culture – its uniqueness, its sense of commonality around an agreed focus for its work, its 'academic press' – has a major influence on performance outcomes, i.e. schools that choose a strategy and then work systematically within this strategy frame to build loyalty, commitment, understanding and ownership of the strategy are more likely to produce successful students than those that do not have this strong sense of cultural identity.

As we elaborate the four generic choices of strategy, we will provide examples of schools that represent them. In doing so, we wish to stress three points. First, one generic strategy is not intrinsically better than another. They each represent viable, acceptable and potentially success-driven choices that a school could make. In looking at the four strategies, the critical question is which strategy best suits the environment, resources, management skills and people competences available for your school. Second, the choices between generic strategies are not just choices about the nature of the market – what the customer stakeholder groups expect – they are also choices about the way in which resources can be focused, management exercised, curriculum objectives attained and students selected.

The choice of strategy ultimately depends on decisions about four areas – access, resources, curriculum and management.

Finally, strategy is not a matter for annual determination. Strategy takes time to secure and sustain. Success generally follows from maintaining a strategy consistently over time. Failure will often be the result of switching between generic strategies.

## Key dimensions to generic strategy

Strategy choices revolve around access, resources, curriculum (which we define here more broadly in terms of the service mix) and management. Let us define these terms a little more carefully so that the underlying assumptions of the generic models we are about to build are clear.

### Access

Access refers to the extent to which students have free access to the school of their choice. While the law clearly establishes the right of parents to apply to send their child to any school, there are questions of whether the school is required to accept all children. A school dedicated to music and musicianship is able to select only those students with certain levels of competence in music. Equally, there is a move to reintroduce ability streaming in certain schools so as to relate ability to the curriculum demands of the school. How many pupils can be accepted for a given curriculum programme will also depend on judgements about the effective size of teaching groups (and some schools are now radically revising previous assumptions about this, with the wider use of open learning media, etc.) and the limits that the safe usage of the accommodation imply. The access issues come down to the school asking 'Who do we want to take in and who can we take in?' Finally, schools must manage the balance between able-bodied students and students with special learning needs or with physical disabilities. All of these represent access decisions that the school is making.

### Resources

Resources refers to not just the financial resources available to the school, but also to the people resources, learning resources and new technology resources the school has available. Equally important here is the ability of the school to secure new resources through industry partnerships, user fees, special one-time contributions of time, money and skills and new funding. Schools will become increasingly differentiated, one to another, on this dimension. The resources issues behind determining strategy come down to 'What categories of resource do we need to deliver a particular strategy, and what do we possess and lack in these respects at the present time?' It should be noted that this approach is different from that which asks 'What can we do within the limits of our existing resources?' The TQM approach asks that strategy be driven by an assessment of the needs of customers and, when these are expressed in terms of one of the generic strategies we discuss below, it follows that the institution must 'tool-up' for the strategy and not the other way around.

## Curriculum (service mix)

Curriculum (service mix) refers to the processes of pedagogy in the school as well as the learning outcomes intended from this pedagogy. In both Britain and North America, governments are increasing the extent to which learning outcomes are specified. Schools have opportunities, however, to design the delivery strategy, to create learning resources or the mix of resources appropriate to achieving the learning outcomes and to balance the mix of people, skills and new technology in the delivery of learning programmes. In addition, schools can manage the extent to which academic curriculum objectives are balanced with the social learning objectives embodied in such areas as social skills development, sports, drama, music and extracurricular activities. We might refer to these opportunities to create an appropriate blend of activities within the school as the *service mix* in the school. The primary element in this mix is curriculum, but the balance between subject learning and self-development is a critical variable in strategic choice.

## Management

Management refers to the ability of the school staff to provide an appropriate service mix to the students who have gained access to the school within the limits of available resources, and to achieve high student performance through doing so. It also refers to the internal organizational structures, roles and management working processes, which will need to be conceived to deliver the chosen strategy. It is likely that there may need to be drastic changes from hallowed and traditional practice. As we shall explain later, the whole concept of the management arrangements will need to be redesigned to an inverted triangle, in which those nearest to the customer are regarded as key to successful achievement of strategy.

These four factors lie behind each of the four generic strategies we are now about to introduce. Two of them – curriculum and access – are the prime determinants of the four generic strategies. We are here extending the scope of what has traditionally been conveyed by the word curriculum to include those curriculum programme responses to clients in the areas of

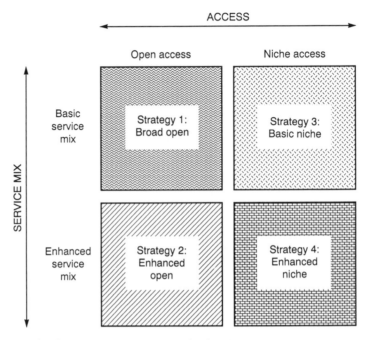

*Fig. 2.1*   The four generic strategies of schooling.

health or wider personal and social development that we discussed earlier. Because of this we shall use the term 'curriculum service mix' to convey the enhancement in scope. While it is the curriculum service mix and access that determine the main form of our generic strategies model, it is the other two factors – resources, and organization and management – that are critical in their implementation. Each available strategic choice among the four depends on a balance of these four factors.

**The generic strategy model**

The two key dimensions that drive the model of generic strategy for schools within the new customer-oriented or TQM context are curriculum service mix and access, with each of these offering alternative choice position to clients. The curriculum service mix dimension could be either: (i) broad basic curriculum mix; or (ii) enhanced basic curriculum. The access dimension could be either: (i) open; or (ii) niche. Figure 2.1 represents these four generic strategies. In looking at the model of strategy, the point to think through is that schools can make choices between these four strategies depending upon the needs and expectations of the stakeholders they are best able to serve, the resources available and a realistic assessment of their management competence. As all strategies carry equal promise of success in their own terms, the choices are real and important. What is more, a generic strategy choice carries significant and substantive implications for: (i) how a school presents itself – image and culture; (ii) how a school recruits staff and sustains them; (iii) the objectives of the school; (iv) the criteria for evaluating the success of individuals, programmes and the school as a whole; and (v) management. We shall examine the implications for each strategy in turn.

A *broad basic service mix* would require the school to offer a broad-based programme of activity (curriculum, after-school activity, sports, music, etc.). It would not seek to be a specialist in any of the areas of the curriculum or social programmes, but would seek to achieve standards of achievement that were satisfactory across the board. In short we call this strategy *broad open*.

An *enhanced basic service mix* requires the school to develop a service mix that gives emphasis to some particular aspect of the services it provides. For example, a school may chose to emphasize its work in the area of science and recruit and develop a cadre of expert science teachers, building a leading reputation in the field of science education and securing a high performance from its science students. The school will still offer all of the basic curriculum (it is required to do so), but it is seeking to have a reputation for being 'good at science'. The same could apply to a school that gave emphasis to sports, drama, music, mathematics, social skills, or liberal arts. In short we call this strategy *enhanced open*.

The terms 'broad' and 'enhanced' are not intended to imply that one is better than another – they are different. Both kinds of service mix may meet the needs of a community and its students. Both may attract quality teachers who are successful in their work and enable and encourage high performance. Both are to be regarded as possible and appropriate strategic choices for a school. In terms of an analogy, an ice hockey team that is strong all round is just as likely to win tournaments as one that is strong in defence. Both are strategic choices a team's general manager can make when recruiting players and determining strategy for the team's development.

*Open access* refers to the school that has no limitations in recruiting its student base. It accepts all students who apply to join the school without discrimination by ability, competence, gender, race or language skills – it is open in its admission policies. In contrast, *niche access* implies that the school recruits some (if not all) of its students on the basis of one or more of the following variables:

1 Ability or competence – a school that seeks to specialize in advanced music education at the post-16 level is likely to select those students who have already demonstrated a particular level of competence in the playing of an instrument or in some other musical skill.

2 Language – some schools in Canada, Wales, Scotland and Ireland, for example, use the minority languages of those countries as the prime teaching medium. Such schools are increasing in number because parents want this curriculum niche and all that goes with it. These schools are restricting their access to pupils who have accepted they will be taught in the language and participate in the various cultural activities associated with that language.

3 Gender – while the number of single-sex schools is not high, there are, none the less a number of schools that exercise gender-based selection.

4 Ethnicity – some schools are intended for students with a similar or the same ethnic background, for example, Ukranian or Polish schools, so that the culture of the 'old country' can be preserved through education.

5 Religion – this constitutes the defining niche market of some schools. They are chosen by parents because of their explicit religious conviction (Catholic, Quaker, Jesuit, etc.); the parents want the ethos and teaching of that religious perspective for their children even though they may not necessarily be committed members of that church themselves or want their children to be in the future.

6 'Free-spirit' – an important niche type of school in some countries, particularly England, has been the school that declares a discipline regime of an avant garde or highly experimental nature. Given that expectations for multiple choice and the goods to satisfy that choice are everywhere on the increase in the advanced countries it seems very likely that there will be substantially more niche differentiation in the access policy of schools in the future.

As with the service mix dimension, the access dimension can either be basic or enhanced, so that the other two generic strategies become *broad/basic niche* or *enhanced niche*. Again, these two access strategies do not carry the implication that one is preferable to the other – they are different strategic choices that carry different implications for who attends the school, and therefore for the work of the school. Before looking at each strategy in turn and examining the full implications, let us make some general points about the strategies we have outlined here.

First, generic strategies can be pursued with varying degrees of vigour. The more vigorously the strategy is pursued, the more emphasis is given to outcomes, as more people are able to examine the claims of the school against its performance. An enhanced niche school (strategy 4) specializing in sports, which continually failed to produce success in the sports in which it claimed strength, would soon find: (i) its stakeholders concerned about relative expenditures on sports versus other subjects; (ii) its staff in sports being concerned about the selection of students for sports; and (iii) would have difficulty in sustaining its position. Maybe parents and governors would also be asking whether in fact the staff were right for the specialist sports approach?

Second, generic strategies are not likely to be changed often. Each takes time to establish, nourish and sustain. Strategy matures over time. Organizations that fail have often switched between these strategies very quickly over time and have not maintained their strategic focus for long enough for the strategy to establish itself as the frame from within which all activities of the organization will be undertaken. W.E. Deming, one of the leading advocates in the quality movement, refers to this point as 'constancy of purpose'. By this he implies that organizations should decide what strategy they are pursuing and become relentlessly good at the work this strategy implies. They should not get blown into another strategy because of temporary changes in conditions, minor setbacks or changes in personnel. Any decision to change a strategy is a very major one indeed, which should be contemplated only after substantial analysis of all the trends suggesting that such an option should even be put on the agenda.

Third, some organizations seek to secure the 'best of all worlds' by being in the middle of the four strategies. They see themselves as hybrids – working across all four strategies. In the service economy and the manufacturing sectors of the economy, there is strong evidence that a failure to work within a particular generic strategy frame produces failure, either in terms of significant under-performance or (more likely) deficits (Porter 1985). The only way in which a particular company can succeed while occupying more than one generic strategy position is by managing these different strategies as different business entities under the same umbrella. That is, management of strategy 4 is so different from the management of strategy 2 that it requires managers to focus on different aspects of the organization, on different objectives and on different ways of working with stakeholders – it requires a different management team. The same is true for any combination of strategies. Most schools would be unable to sustain separate and distinct management support for separate and distinct strategies (as is the case in most service organizations), so it is almost inevitable that a school would seek to occupy just one strategic position.

Finally, the task of management is to determine the strategic frame from within which the school wishes to operate and to be relentlessly successful in achieving the promise of this strategy. Strategies do not 'just happen' or 'emerge', they are managed. It takes vision, commitment, culture-building, leadership, trust, empowerment and communication to build a successful, strategically focused organization. The skills emphasis for management will differ between one strategy to another in terms of emphasis, but each manager in each school can be remarkably successful in terms of their strategic focus.

## Strategy 1: The broad basic service mix with open access – broad open

The resource level of some schools does not permit them to offer a service mix enhanced by a marked curriculum specialism, but they concentrate on ensuring that their students get the best possible broad and basic education at a level commensurate with their abilities. They are what might be called 'solid' in their provision of an all-round education. They do not select students, they accept all who wish to come (provided they have the physical space to accommodate them). The critical determinants of this strategy are resources and people. From time to time the school may find itself having some special success in music or sports or some other field, but this is more because of specific people in the school – individual talents – than the school striving to achieve this success.

Resources are a key determinant here. Typically such schools are in modest income catchment areas and do not have any significant level of additional resources. They have little access to 'soft' money (user fees, donations, partnering resources from business and industry – known as 'soft' because it cannot be relied upon over time in the same way that 'hard' base funds can be). They are unable to offer local incentives to teachers to join the school because the local negotiation component of salaries and benefits have few additional resources to bargain with. Investments in information technology are limited, although such schools are likely to be very creative and imaginative in the use of the limited resources available. Because the school is a ' broad basic' school in terms of service mix, it is unlikely to attract and retain 'high flyers' as teachers in a particular subject area, who are more likely to be attracted to enhanced basic schools that seek out their special skills. While the school can be of any size, subject choice in specialist subject areas is restricted because teachers are recruited on the basis of their ability to offer support in both core and related subjects: advanced work in a particular area requiring specialist knowledge and skills presents a continuing challenge.

The other critical variable here is the people within the organization. Because facilities and resources are 'basic', the teaching staff of the school will be those who are able to make best use of these facilities to work with the ability range of students. In an elementary (primary) school, for example, the teacher needs to be skilled at using a variety of teaching methods with the same resource base to meet the learning needs of students of widely differing abilities. They will have little recourse to alternative materials, new technologies, teacher aides or specialized assistance. Such teachers are self-reliant, show a great deal of hardiness and are well able to handle a variety of student learning needs.

It is important to recognize that this school type can produce high performance across the board. Indeed, being a least-cost provider does not, of itself (the data shows) impair school performance. It could be very successful in providing a broad/basic education to a large number of people. It is likely to secure pass rates in scholastic achievement tests (SATs), which are similar to other schools in the core curriculum. There is nothing inferior about the school strategy of 'broad basic quality' for this is what many parents want.

### Greenfield High School: Broad open strategy

A typical example of this type of school would be the British secondary school Greenfield High (not its real name).

Greenfield High is an 11–18-year-old comprehensive secondary school of 1200 pupils and 70 teaching staff situated in a new town of very mixed economy but with an emphasis on light manufacturing and assembly and service industries. The children come from middle- to lower-income homes, with the majority in the latter category. It has something of a natural catchment area on grounds of distance of four primary schools, although some children attend it from further afield.

Greenfield has aimed to serve effectively all ability groups of children and to give equal attention to the social needs of children from the sub-groups of one-parent families (about 17 per cent), those with unemployed parents and children with special learning difficulties. More generally it has adopted a pastoral and counselling policy aimed at minimizing truancy and out-of-school social problems. It has always asserted its achievements across the board, pointing out that all children are intended to reach the statutory school leaving age with some qualification of value in the employment market. For years all parents have been the targets of requests for their involvement and this has received a high response in the attendance at parents meetings, concerts and school drama. Parents believe that their children will leave this school with a good broad and basic education, which has market value in the outside world, and this has been proven by experience for the majority of parents. Those who have gifted children have not been disappointed either. They have seen as many of this category of child reach the older more famous, universities as any other school in the county, many of which are in much more affluent and advantageous areas. The only problem the senior managers of this school have at the present time is that the school governors, largely made-up of parents and local community leaders, want to be more assertive and outspoken in promoting the school's qualities than they would wish. The senior managers are worried the governors will make outrageous claims, which the school will not be seen to have met, and that they will lose their hard won reputation for being solid and successful for all children.

## Strategy 2: Enhanced basic service mix with open access – enhanced open

The second generic strategy extends the one just described. The school is offering a broad-based service – it is not seeking to achieve a reputation and standing in a particular discipline or service activity, nor is it seeking to recruit its students on one of the criteria we outlined earlier (ability, language, gender, race or religion). What it is seeking to provide is a broad-based education to as many people as possible with the service mix being enhanced by 'added value' qualities deriving from additional activities and resources.

Imagine a school offering the required French curriculum to students in a particular age group. In addition to being offered the programme in the school, the school may also arrange a two- or three-week visit to France or Quebec, arrange for the school to be twinned with a school in France or Quebec and exchange letters (possibly by electronic mail) between the students of the twinned schools. It may have a video library of French video casettes, a special programme to help parents of children having difficulty with the language support them better at home and may arrange links between the school and local companies that do business with either France or Quebec. Students having difficulty with the language may be directed to some computer resources designed to support remedial work. While we have described these 'added value' activities for French, similar 'added value' activities are also taking place across the broad curriculum – in science, history, geography, social studies, language arts and so on. The school is not seeking a leading reputation or niche in a particular subject, but is seeking to go beyond the basics in all of its activities and to be regarded as an enriched learning centre for all that it does.

Once again, resources play a central part in this strategy. To provide these enhanced or added value services, the school has to be able to use its base budgets and 'soft' resources to ensure that the provision of these services can be sustained over time. Typically, this occurs because stakeholders are more willing to volunteer time and resources and make commitments to meet the costs of some additional services, either through user fees or direct full-cost payments. In addition, business partnering is so managed as to support specific initiatives over longer periods of time so as to make the strategy sustainable.

Teachers in this school are expected to be fully engaged in designing, managing and enacting 'added value' strategies for the services of the school. They are recruited because of their imaginative skills, their commitment to their discipline and their ability to work well in an environment where there is a great deal of interaction between the teacher and stakeholder. Demands on such teachers are different from those in the previous strategy (although the level of demand is similar) – there is a greater focus on managing a range and variety of experiences.

*Steephill School: Enhanced open strategy*

An example of such a school is Steephill Secondary School. This is a comprehensive secondary school of 900 pupils situated in a small, green-belt commuter town, which houses many middle and senior executives from industries based within a radius of some twenty miles. It is a very pleasant town in which to live and bring up children, with good re-creational activities and near open countryside. The parents are mainly from the upper–middle income group, with a significant percentage of top earners who live in the open countryside. A large number of them are upwardly mobile and move on to even better things by leaving the area. When they do so, however, they are known to tell their successors moving into the area that there is no need to send their kids to the private schools in the city some twelve miles away because the Steephill school is 'quality plus' across the board.

The senior mangers of Steephill have enhanced the annual budget by a factor of 5 per cent of total annual budget – a considerable figure – by telling the parents 'We will provide a work experience anywhere in the country for your child/all children will get a foreign country curriculum-related experience before they are fifteen/your child will have a personal computer work station, etc. if you help us get the funds for this.' The parent/teacher association (PTA) is given a target figure to reach every year, which they invariably do by regular whist drives, olde tyme dances, summer fetes and by organizing quality music concerts of the type these affluent parents would otherwise need to travel some distance to attend. Financial contributions are also contracted by way of a whole range of compacts with the parent managers from the local companies. These range from direct sponsorship of a school department and advertising on exercise books, to senior students working within their course programme require-ments on projects jointly determined with local companies, and which may have results of interest to the local companies.

## Strategy 3: Basic service mix with differeniated access – basic niche

Imagine a school that has made a decision to be a strong science school. While it continues to offer the broad and basic provision across the curriculum, its special energies are reserved for science. Special efforts are made to recruit and keep high quality science staff, to equip laboratories and libraries with the necessary hardware and software to offer a modern science programme and a reputation is being built around the quality of science education in the school. The school does not neglect other subjects, but seeks to integrate science across the curriculum, as well as developing specialist skills in the science subjects. Parents send their students to this school because they want them to have a good basic education and receive a special education in science. Its niche and reputation derive from the quality of its science teaching.

Imagine another school, which is a Catholic school. It remains concerned to provide a broad-based education but has a focus on the religious basis for its work. Some of its activities will result entirely from this focus – services, religious education, prayers, retreats – while all other activities will be informed by this focus. Culture and commitment in this school depend on this focus. The 'niche' in the science school depends upon interests and abilities, in the second it depends upon religious belief and commitment.

The critical difference between a strategy 1 school and a strategy 3 school is the extent to which the strategy 3 school has differentiated itself by a niche profile in the eyes of the consumer stakeholders. If they perceive that, in comparison with other schools, such a school is achieving a reputation in science, then this will inform their decision about which of several schools their own children should attend.

Critical to the success of a niche strategy are people investments and facilitative management. People make the difference. In the examples we have provided here, the science school depends upon a core of staff who can make science successful to the broad range of students to which it is taught. It also depends upon the remainder of the staff supporting fully the position of science in the school and seeking to work collaboratively with the science staff so as to ensure that other subjects – history, social subjects, languages and arts – can build on the work of the science team and connect to it directly. Building a reputation in science that is resented by other staff at the school is hardly likely to be an effective generic strategy that is sustainable over time.

Facilitative management is important in that it is constantly seeking to both resource science appropriately without denuding other subject areas of needed resources and seeking to facilitate the links between science and other areas of the work of the school.

### Georgetown School: Basic niche strategy

Georgetown School is situated in part of an inner city that has seen much better times; it is, in fact, in decay at the present time. The pupils are from homes where the wage earners, if they have employment, are in low-paid service roles in the inner city. There is a very high percentage of single parent families and many children have been in trouble, mostly for petty crime, but some more seriously. The Georgetown School Head, appointed a year ago, has been a prominent and successful footballer; the chair of the PTA is a former member of the country's Olympic running squad and, prominent among the local magistrates court officers, is another well-known former footballer. In response to pressure from the parents on the

PTA to do something to keep their children away from crime, in addition to teaching them well enough to get employment, the school managers and governors have decided to emphasize participation in 'sport for all whatever your body shape'. They have created a sports niche strategy that encompasses sports kit provided by some of the biggest restaurants and office complexes in the inner city (and carrying the firm's logo) and a range of training programmes using well-known local sports personalities, who are happy to be photographed for the press doing these 'good works' and are happy to become part of the publicity slogan 'sport is a substitute for crime'. All children are made to feel that there is some sports activity they can achieve in and each has the opportunity in the first place to attend the sports supermarket on Saturday mornings, when exponents of an incredible range of sports give demonstrations and advice on what best suits the individual. Each student has a sports mentor and counsellor from among the staff or from outside the school, who will lead them in their personal sports, health and personal development programme. The sports niche strategy involves all teaching staff in a considerable amount of extra work from the large number of teams taking part in competitive fixtures. These need organization and frequent supervision outside of school hours. Georgetown High is finding their niche policy is paying dividends in the classroom; test performance has not suffered but improved, and the number of children coming before the courts has more than halved. The staff are finding that the children are easier to teach now because there is less classroom disruption. They are even attracting some pupils from areas away from the inner city by their sports reputation. They see this niche strategy as enlightened self-interest for all – everybody wins something out of it.

### Strategy 4: The enhanced basic service mix with differentiated access – enhanced niche

A school pursuing this strategy seeks to create a very distinctive position for itself in the education services sector. It seeks to have a unique role in the market for schooling by becoming 'leading edge' and very successful in a particular field. It seeks out, recruits and trains expert teachers in the field it wishes to develop a reputation in and is often looked to for innovations in pedagogy in relation to its specialism.

Imagine a school that has chosen information technology as its niche focus and chooses to teach through the medium of computing technology across the curriculum once certain minimum standards of writing, literacy and numeracy have been reached by its students. Using industry partnering, user fees from parents and 'soft' resources, it builds a massive resource of computing power and software, which permit students to self-pace their learning post-14. Teachers, adapting to their role as mediators of self-paced learning, focus increasingly on individualizing learning and developing remedial-loop teaching for those struggling with the programs available on-line. Parent volunteers and industry supporters are engaged in developing software and support services for students. Learning, because it is individualized, becomes defined through individual learning contracts between the parents, the students and the school, and certain service guarantees are offered in terms of these contracts. The school frequently secures performances from students way beyond the levels they thought they were capable of in a variety of subjects. The niche position is attained through technology. All students leaving this school are very sophisticated users of information technology and computers.

To be successful, this school relies on an element of selection of students, a large technology resource base, the enthusiasm of its teachers to harness the technology and their willingness to change their roles as teachers, the support of stakeholder groups in terms of the learning contract process and the development of appropriate learning systems by provider stakeholders and intellectual property developers, which permit such a strategy to occur. In fact, such a school does exist at Saanich (British Columbia, Canada) supported by AT&T.

Such a school also relies crucially on the vision of management, the ability of management to recruit and keep committed staff, the constancy of purpose for this work and the ability of management to facilitate this work in creative and imaginative ways without imposing undue stress on all concerned.

### Dymond Wyke School: Enhanced niche

Perhaps the most common example of schools with a dedicated niche policy are those with a specialization in a branch of music. Many private-sector schools in Britain are linked with cathedral choirs, for example. To gain entry to these schools pupils must audition for a singing test and be prepared to spend the out-of-school time on the commitments that go with singing in the cathedral choir.

A similar example from the public sector is Dymond Wyke High School, which has a niche reputation for a commitment to brass band and other instrumental music, as well as for an enhanced curriculum across the board. It does not ask for any formal test of the pupils who come to the school but, as the school prospectus says, 'all pupils are expected to take an interest in the school brass band and are given every opportunity to learn a brass or other musical instruments.'

A consequence of this policy is that the staff accept (some more willingly than others) that a disproportionate amount of the money available for internal distribution across departments goes towards instrumental music pursuits and that they must amend their teaching regimes to allow for students being withdrawn from normal scheduled lessons for music practice and concerts, etc. The school boasts that its academic results are excellent across all subjects, equivalent to the best in the whole region, while it also has a national and international reputation for instrumental music. All teachers are expected to facilitate this niche strategy, as well as the whole 'enhanced' reputation, and this is pointed out to them prior to appointment.

This explicit niche strategy is, however, self-reinforcing in that teachers apply because they share this interest or want to be in a school with a specific reputation, and many children come to the school from outside its natural catchment area because their parents want them to be able to play an instrument – an opportunity some of them never had, but wish they had. What Dymond Wyke has done by pursuing this niche strategy is to create its own sector within the 'enhanced niche' marketplace, one in which there is no competition. There is no other school within fifty miles offering such a niche prospectus and enhanced quality across the curriculum provision.

## Some implications of strategic choice

Outlining these four strategies makes some things very clear. First, it is not possible for a school to be successful by being all things to all people. This means that the school must not only determine its strategy, but it must also work to educate its stakeholders in this strategy and create a sense of ownership of the strategy. If it fails to do this it will find itself under pressure to adjust its strategy. Expectations management is as important to success as performance management. Many attempts at a specific strategy fail because of the inability of senior management to secure prior consent for the strategy from the rank and file of teachers, and to talk through and agree the sort of additional commitments the strategy would impose. In short, ownership of the strategy by all key stakeholders has not been secured.

Second, all aspects of the school must be designed in such a way as to fit this strategy or reflect it. This includes recruitment and training of teachers, purchase decisions for learning and service resources, equipment purchases, marketing of the school, the design of communication systems within the school and between the school and its stakeholders, the development of pedagogy, the work of management, links with industry and government and so on. It is important that the school regards itself as active in its pursuit of strategy, so that everyone connected with the school will sense the commitment of people to the strategy. This takes vision, communication, culture building and teamwork.

Third, the strategy must be related to available expertise and resources. A recipe for failure is for the strategy to depend on resources that are either only partly available or available but unsustainable. So as to meet Deming's 'constancy of purpose' requirement, strategy must be based on a firm understanding of how that strategy can be resourced and sustained over a long period of time. 'Resources' here also includes an appropriate and available pool of people with appropriate expertise, not just in their particular subject or skill area but in their ability to implement the strategy within the resources of the school.

Finally, the success of the strategy depends critically on the ability of the leadership within the school to build a sense of commitment, communicate the strategy and vision on a constant basis, manage the resources in support of the strategy and upon the selection and sustenance of staff.

Interestingly, research on school effectiveness points to these kinds of variables as critical in determining the difference between high and low performing schools. Of particular importance, according to this work, is the role of leaders in the school system in shaping vision and strategy, communicating that vision to all stakeholders, engaging stakeholders in the work of the school, engendering commitment and sustaining performance outcomes associated with this strategy over time (Rutter *et al.* 1979; Reynolds *et al.* 1987; Murphy 1992).

## Making your strategic choice

The critical question for your management team is 'Which of these generic strategies do you wish to pursue?' and the prior question is 'Are you pursuing a strategy at all, or are you going along in the "here and now" on a day-to-day basis, travelling joyfully and hoping to arrive safely?' In some schools it would certainly be true that if half a dozen teachers were stopped at random and asked what strategy the school was following, the answer would not be given in consumer or marketplace terms, but in philosophic and very general terms such as 'to do the best for all our children'. Nevertheless, some of the readers of this book will already be pursuing a strategy – few will be making choices from scratch.

Another version of this critical question might well be 'Are we pursuing a strategy that is right for us?' This question can only be answered following a careful analysis of your current position and the environment in which you are working. The previous chapter provided a tool – industry analysis – for you to review the environment. We now provide a basic tool that will be helpful in examining your current position.

The tool is known as a SWOT analysis. The term is an acronym for Strengths, Weaknesses, Opportunities and Threats. With your management team and stakeholder groups, you should explore these questions:

*Strengths*

1 What resource strengths does this school have?
2 What are our people strengths?

3 What are the strengths of our management team?
4 What strengths are evidenced by our performance in a consistent way over time?
5 What strengths are evident in our relationships with our stakeholders?
6 What strengths derive from our relationships with our provider stakeholders?
7 Is there a niche focus to our work that is especially strong?

*Weaknesses*

1 What are the resource weaknesses of this school?
2 What are the people weaknesses of this school?
3 What weaknesses exist in the management skills within the school?
4 What weaknesses are evident in our relationships with our stakeholders?
5 What weaknesses are evident from our performance standards over time by area of work?
6 What weaknesses do we have in terms of the way provider stakeholders see us?
7 What weaknesses do we have regarding resources, equipment or management systems, in terms of what we are aiming to achieve?

*Opportunities*

1 Given our resourcing (and reasonable predictions about resources), what opportunities do we have to make changes in our strategy?
2 Given the people we employ, or could employ, what opportunities can we see arising from the way they work with us?
3 Given our managerial skills and insights, what strategy could we really see as maximizing the fit between resources, people, stakeholders and our skills as managers?
4 What opportunity do our stakeholders want us to pursue?
5 What opportunities do our stakeholders present to us if we start to change our relationship with them?
6 What opportunities exist for this school if we change the way we work with our provider stakeholders?
7 What opportunities exist for us, given the decisions being made by other schools in this area?
8 Given the industry analysis we completed, what opportunities stand out for us?

*Threats*

1 What barriers exist from within the school to the effective implementation of strategy?

2 What are the potential danger signs already in the industry environment that could eventually derail the strategy we choose?

3 What are the threats from our consumer stakeholders that could damage the effective implementation of strategy?

4 What potential threats exist from our provider stakeholders?

5 What actions of government are likely to occur that could pose a unique threat to this school, given the strategy we are looking at?

6 What threats to effective strategy implementation are there from other sources?

This analysis frame is commonplace in education, industry and non-profit organizations. What distinguishes the above version from others is that it focuses attention on strategic choice, and links this analysis to that conducted under the heading of industry analysis.

For some of the questions (such as those involving stakeholder groups), you should collect as much data as is reasonable and possible from the stakeholder groups themselves. Take them through this complete analysis in group discussions that focus on the issues. Survey them on particular points of concern to your management team (telephone surveys are far more effective than postal or send-home surveys). Engage them in the process of strategy development. Use the very process of such development to engage them in better understanding the options and implications. You can never know enough about the perceptions, attitudes and values of your stakeholders.

When all responses to the questions we outline above (and others that may occur to you) are in, the choices are on the table in front of you. The management team has to make a choice between the four generic strategies and be able to provide a justification of this choice to stakeholder groups. In doing so, it is useful to go back through the analysis of public policy choices (see Chapter 1) and see how the strategy can be understood in terms of the four critical dimensions – equal opportunity, individual rights, effectiveness and efficiency.

Having done your SWOT analysis and considered the further questions we have just discussed, there is one other crucial area to be checked before you make your decision on strategy, it concerns the others in the your educational marketplace. This should take the form of answers to the following questions: 'What strategies are our competing/opponent schools adopting or likely to adopt?'; 'Are we likely to be the sole supplier of a particular curriculum service strategy in this area or will we be competing with someone else who is following the same strategy?'; 'Assuming that we have the will and resource to do so, do we want to differentiate ourselves markedly from all others or not?'

Making a choice of generic strategy is a critical task of management in the TQM school. Without a strategy commitment, culture and communication are weakened, teams within the school are unsure of the direction of the school, decisions will not be fully integrated into a strategy, recruitment decisions might change the strategy rather then reinforcing and developing it and resource allocations will not be well directed.

Strategic choice is a relatively new notion to many charged with the responsibility of managing school organizations. Yet the choices, as you can see from our description and examples, are very real indeed. Strategy drives quality and the implementation of total quality management requires the exercise of a critical management skill: the skill of making a choice of generic strategy that engenders commitment and ownership on the part of all stakeholders.

# Definitions of quality and their implications for TQM in schools

Just as the industrial revolution created new ways of working for manufacturing in the 1800s, so the quality revolution is creating new ways of working in all organizations in the 1990s. Whether the organization is a manufacturing company making cars, a service company offering transatlantic flights from Europe to North America, a government agency offering social benefit payments to qualified claimants, a non-profit organization working to better the lives of the disadvantaged or a school, they could all be engaged in a quality re-evaluation process and changes intended to lead to quality management improvements. However, whereas the new ways of working brought about by the industrial revolution were essentially about the use of a new technology – steam power – the new ways of working associated with TQM are essentially about how people are managed at work, and not technological systems.

Some companies are seeking managers for TQM. Others are asking their staff to recommit to quality. Many are sending their staff to courses on quality management and are reconfiguring their organization so as to better respond to quality initiatives. Some management teams in schools are even beginning, in the words of one British headteacher, to make active use of the 'Q-word' (Samuels 1991).

In this chapter we will examine the meaning of quality, the implications of a focus on quality for the work of the school and define the key constructs that inform the practice of quality management in organizations.

Throughout, examples will be given of quality in action – successful implementations of quality initiatives in various organizations.

## Three definitions of quality

There are a great many competing views of the nature of quality. Some see quality as implicit and indefinable – 'you know it when you see it'. Others take what might be termed a 'measurement view' of quality – it is satisfactory conformance to some predefined standard. Still others claim that quality is simply a matter of reputation. How can we make sense of these different, somewhat opaque, and often opposing views of the nature of quality?

There are three basic definitions of quality – quality assurance, contract conformance and customer-driven. Let us examine each of these in detail.

### Quality assurance

Quality assurance refers to the determination of standards, appropriate methods and quality requirements by an expert body, accompanied by a process of inspection or evaluation that examines the extent to which practice meets these standards. For example, in deciding whether a new drug can be sold to the public a period of testing according to predetermined standards has to be completed and certain information provided before the drug enters the market – it has to conform to a standard determined by experts in drug testing. In permitting an aircraft to move from manufacture to public service, the aircraft is tested and examined under the rubric of an independent authority. So as to ensure safety, reliability and durability of the aircraft, standards are enforced through periodic inspection.

Critical to the quality assurance process is the publication of standards. In psychological services, for example, there are published standards for quality and these can be audited and evaluated as part of a quality assurance process. A framework for developing published standards is provided by various national bodies, most of which are variants of the Quality Systems ISO 9000 Series defined by an international standards agency.

### Contract conformance

The second definition of quality is that of contract conformance, where some quality standard has been specified during the negotiation of forming a contract. For example, in building a garage the builder might indicate exactly what the garage will be like – size, materials, completion date, type of door opening and lighting. Quality would then be seen to be linked to these specific commitments on the part of the builder. A psychologist might offer a stress management programme over a period of time and specify that they would work to provide a diagnostic assessment of stress levels and sources for each member of the group, would train the group in five methods of coping with stress and would then seek to establish an individualized programme, using these methods, for each person in the group following some individualized counselling. This specification of what this stress management programme will be becomes the specification, which becomes the definition of quality within that contract and forms the criteria for the assessment of quality.

What is distinctive about contract conformance (as opposed to quality assurance) is that the quality specifications are made locally by the person undertaking the work, not by a panel of experts. The psychologist is not offering a stress programme that meets some requirement for such a programme that has been determined by an accreditation panel – they are providing a statement of intent and then performing according to that statement of intent. This 'intent statement' constitutes a 'contract', even though it may not be a written contract or a contract in law. Some have called this quality through integrity – doing what you say you were going to do.

In our examples, the contract specifications were supplied by the person offering the service, not by the person receiving the service. Another way of thinking about this form of quality is to see it as provider-driven quality. The provider determines the meaning of quality conformance. While the provider may be informed by quality assurance standards for the kind of service they are offering, quality is locally determined.

## Customer-driven quality

Customer-driven quality refers to a notion of quality in which those who are to receive a product or service make explicit their expectations for this product or service and quality is defined in terms of meeting or exceeding the expectations of customers. For example, hotel guests may have very specific requirements for a hotel stay. As a business traveller you may wish to have a fax machine installed in your room, a modem hook-up for your notebook computer, a wet-bar to entertain guests to your room, specific messaging and paging services during your hotel stay, delivery of certain newspapers, access to meeting rooms and so on. A hotel that is unable to meet these expectations will fail to meet your quality expectations, and is unlikely to be used again. One that meets these expectations, and does so at a price you are willing to pay, is likely to receive a return visit. This market-driven quality – quality defined in terms of fitness for use (Juran 1979) – is at the heart of the quality revolution and is requiring organizations to look again at their own procedures and ways of working so as to better meet the needs and expectations of customers.

## Schooling and quality

How do these three types of quality relate to the work of the school? Let us examine each in turn and look at the ways in which schools currently look at quality.

### Quality assurance

Quality assurance (QA) is currently practised in a number of different ways. First, teacher evaluation methodologies are largely QA methodologies. For example, where a panel of experts on teaching might develop evaluation instruments that seek to itemize the characteristics of effective teachers. These have then been tested and validated. Individuals are then trained in their use and are asked to apply their training in their use of the instruments in the field. In use, the instruments become devices by which the behaviours and actions of teachers are evaluated in terms of a model of teaching defined and specified by experts.

Historically in Britain, the work of Her Majesty's Inspectors of Schools (HMIs) has been a QA activity. While standards were not published and defined in a way that would conform to ISO 9000, HMIs were selected on their ability to undertake a careful observation of teaching and schooling so that they could discern whether or not appropriate standards of teaching and education were being met. While they collected some data, they relied much more on their expert judgement. During the late 1960s and throughout the 1970s, 'inspecting' developed further and codifying instruments were introduced for systematic inspection and comparison. This codification took the Inspectorate further into the QA process.

The public examinations systems in North America and Europe can also be seen as QA systems. Students sit examinations set by a national or regional body, with all students from different schools sitting the same examination. The idea is that students will have an equal opportunity of succeeding in the examination and that the results will reflect standards set by the national or local body for conformance to their expectations. The examination is set by a curriculum panel – experts in their field. Marking schemes are designed by experts. Marking is monitored to ensure reliability of marking within a marker's portfolio and between one marker and another. Results are seen to reflect an appropriate statement about quality achievements by the student on an 'objective' set of criteria which are not influenced by local conditions.

One final example. Curriculum standards set by governments at the local and national level can be seen as an attempt to develop a statement of QA standards for all students in school by age group. By specifying and publishing the expectations of governments, based on expert panel recommendations and other considerations, schools are able to strive to meet the performance standards required of them. This is a very basic QA framework for defining the work of schools.

These examples of QA at work in education suggest a number of features of QA that need to be made explicit:

1  QA standards are set externally by experts.
2  QA standards are presented as a set of codified requirements or expectations that the school strives to achieve (the conformance expectation of QA).
3  QA standards are evaluated by some objective criteria.
4  QA standards may account for local variation only if this is a requirement of the quality assessment being undertaken.
5  QA usually involves some form of inspection, formal evaluation or examination.


### Contract conformance

Quality set by contract conformance occurs in a number of ways in schools. For example, when a student with special needs is enrolled in the school some assessment of need is undertaken and agreements are made between the school and the parents, the school and psychological services (and sometimes the school and other services, such as health, occupational therapy and/or social work) about the provision of support to that student. The 'contract' is local, specific and usually written (although not always). Conformance to this contract is evaluated on an ongoing basis, and quality is defined in terms of meeting or exceeding contracted requirements.

Homework assignments provide another example of contract conformance. Teachers set a homework assignment to students, outlining exactly what is expected of them and when this work is to be completed. They also usually indicate when this work will be marked and what place this work has in determining overall marks for a course or programme of study. Conformance is assessed by the teacher in terms of on-time performance (meeting deadlines) by the student and an assessment of the student's ability to meet the requirements of the task. Conformance is assessed by the student in terms of the teacher's on-time performance in returning the assignment (marked and commented upon) and on the teacher's reliability in marking from one student to another. Quality means meeting agreed deadlines in appropriate ways.

A final example concerns teaching assignments. Teachers, at the beginning of each school year, are assigned specific duties and tasks. These duties may be the same as those they performed in a previous year, or they may be different. The assignment of duties represents a contract for work between a teacher and the school. Quality is assessed in terms of whether and how well the duties were performed.

We can discern some basic properties of quality through contract conformance from these examples:

1 Contracts are best negotiated, written down and agreed to before conformance assessment begins.
2 Contracts are local and involve those who will actually be undertaking tasks associated with that contract.
3 Conformance expectations can be built into the contract.
4 Conformance can be mutually assessed by the parties to the contract.
5 Conformance is assessed on an ongoing basis rather than through inspection.

### Customer-driven quality

Customer-driven quality is more difficult to locate in the work of the school, although it does occur. For example, many 11–18 schools have Student Councils. These bodies are intended to represent the interests of students and have been involved in a variety of aspects of school life – social activities, curriculum development planning, timetable discussions and so on. One Student Council sought and secured a major timetable change, which involved changing the structure of the school day. The Council was the major advocate for this change, although they were supported by some key teachers. In responding positively to the proposal, the school reflected a response to the requirements and expectations of its customers and changed its working practices. In general, though, many school managements do not see the perspectives of the students as relevant and worth taking into account. They have not started thinking of their pupils as customers whose views can be valid inputs to improving the quality of school performance.

In another school, parents were unhappy about the way in which parents' evenings and consultations were conducted. One parent described it as 'queuing and viewing' and another said it was an empty process. The Parents' Advisory Council in the school established a task force of parents and students to design a new way of looking at advising parents about the progress of students and suggested a re-design of all progress reporting around portfolios of work, monthly recommendations sheets and a completely different style of parent evening in which there was a combination of training sessions (on such topics as 'how to help your child with study skills', 'six key skills in mathematics for January through March', 'four key project management skills for parents and their children') and individual consultation with parents. The school agreed to these developments and parental involvement has risen from 49 to 76 per cent of parents in two years.

In introducing an AIDS education programme in a school, the management team consulted with parent groups and students about what they expected such a programme would contain and how it should be presented to students. Although there was a variety of views, it was clear that the staff's initial intention to use a standard programme designed by health education workers would not be well received by the 'customers' for this programme. They formed a panel of three – one parent, one student and one teacher – to specify what the programme should look like across the age ranges of the school, and who should be involved in presenting it. The panel designed the programme and offered it in the school. It was regarded by parents and students as successful, although some remained unhappy that the subject was being raised at all. This is a case of the consumer redesigning a product so as to meet their expectations and requirements – in this case the product was curriculum and pedagogy.

A number of characteristics of customer-driven quality (also known as market driven quality) can be discerned from these examples:

1 Customers can define (if helped and encouraged to do so) their expectations clearly.
2 Customer expectations and requirements sometimes differ from those assumed by the providers of services.
3 When providers and customers work collaboratively to define requirements, and the services that will meet these requirements, performance can be improved (e.g. the parents' evening example given above).
4 Not all customers think alike about their expectations and requirements (e.g. the AIDS example) but initiatives that satisfy the needs of significant numbers of stakeholders can be taken.

Customer-driven quality requires providers of services to be constantly enquiring as to the needs of stakeholders and to do so in such a way that stakeholders can see their ideas, concerns and suggestions being implemented on a regular basis. We discussed earlier (Chapter 1) mapping who your stakeholders are. Your stakeholders are your customers and, in the belief position of TQM, only they can define quality.

## The quality revolution

We have suggested that a systematic focus on quality is beginning to revolutionize the work of organizations, and we are not alone in suggesting this (Oakland 1989; Atkinson 1991; Berry 1991). We have also suggested that such a focus is an imperative for organizations to survive in an increasingly global marketplace (Zeithaml *et al.* 1990), whether they are schools, universities or companies. But what is the nature of this revolution?

The basis of the new focus on quality is a move to balance quality assurance, which has been well established for many years, with contract conformance and customer-driven quality. Rather than relying on quality

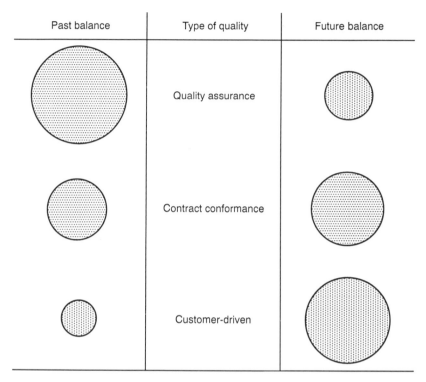

| Past balance | Type of quality | Future balance |
|---|---|---|
| | Quality assurance | |
| | Contract conformance | |
| | Customer-driven | |

*Fig. 3.1*   Balancing quality – past and future.

assurance with some measure of contract conformance, the new quality revolution places emphasis on customer-driven quality supported by contract conformance and quality assurance. We show this diagrammatically in Fig. 3.1. Each circle represents the amount of emphasis on the quality type.

Another way of expressing this is that consumer stakeholders in organizations are becoming increasingly sophisticated and demanding about the products and services provided by the organization at just the same time as governments are moving to an increasingly market-driven basis for the economy, public services and social services. As these two forces coalesce, stakeholders expect more say not just in what an organization provides but in how it does so, when it does so, where it does so, with what skills it does so and with whom it does so. This gives more emphasis to customer-driven quality than has been the case in the past. To meet minimum expectations, organizations are increasingly required to meet quality assurance standards and to add value to these through contract conformance developed at a local level. This changes the emphasis in our thinking about quality away from quality being determined within the professional body or by expert opinion towards balancing the three kinds of quality so as to better meet the expectations and requirements of stakeholders. This is a major change in thinking, requiring major changes in the culture of organizations, especially those managed and run by professionals (Atkinson 1991).

### The internal customer – the new key component in quality

But the revolution in quality thinking does not stop with this realization. It also embraces a key concept: the idea of the internal customer.

Let us look at this concept of the 'internal customer' within the school context, by taking the situation where students make subject choices for the forthcoming term or academic year. Their choices are recorded and a team, or senior role holder, looks at the data generated by this process and allocates students to teachers and classrooms. The teacher is then informed of which students are in which group and which rooms are to be used by which teacher. The teachers then make arrangements for their students to be provided with some basic information about the programme they will be studying (objectives, basic readings, skills expected to be developed, etc.) and asks the school secretary to make sure that these student's receive this as soon as possible. The school secretary asks for these materials to be distributed through the student's home teacher (or alternatively the form teacher, housemaster, subject adviser, guidance counsellor) and the student is advised that their programme selection has been approved, who their teacher will be and what the expectations of them are in terms of this programme. Here then we have a chain of interactions (Fig. 3.2):

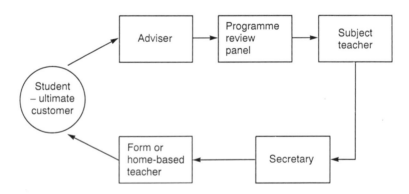

*Fig. 3.2*   A chain of customers and suppliers.

Each person is dependent on both the last and the next in the chain for the successful completion of an important transaction. By regarding the next person as a customer in this chain, we build the idea of a chain of customers (Schonberger 1989). Only by meeting the expectations of each customer in this chain can we meet the expectations of our ultimate customer – in this case the student. The end product received by these students has therefore derived from the work of a chain of customers and suppliers.

This example is a relatively straightforward one. Let us look at another, which involves far more elements of the chain. The mathematics department at Highbridge School has decided to use a text by Hinson as the basis for teaching a particular year group. They have been able to review this text in proof form, as the publishers of this text appear very co-operative. The text is being written to conform to the government's curriculum objectives which, at the time the text was chosen (February of the year before use) had just been finalized. Although the text was reviewed in substance (pending modifications in the light of government specifications of curriculum objectives), the teachers accepted the assurance of the publishers that publication of the text would naturally be accompanied by the publication of a teacher's handbook, practice assessments and examination questions.

In mid-August of the year of use, the textbooks have still not arrived from the bookseller and the librarian informs the staff that they have been delayed because the government made some last-minute adjustments to the curriculum objectives of the mathematics curriculum of this age group in the light of strong objections it had received from university mathematics departments about the emphasis on algebra versus problem-solving. This required more significant reworking of the text than had been intended by the author and changes in the production schedules of the publishers. They could guarantee the book by the first day of the school year, although they were not sure that the teacher's handbooks would be ready at the same time.

In fact the books arrived in the third week of the school year and the teacher's handbooks came in the tenth. To make matters worse, the distributors of the books had a two-day strike, which further delayed the delivery of the books to the school. The teachers had 'survived' these difficulties by using a combination of an old text (which did not fully meet the curriculum objectives required by government) and work-sheet materials developed by the staff working as a team.

This complicated chain of customers and suppliers failed to meet expectations of teachers, resulted in students receiving a poorer service than either was intended or had been led to expect and complaints from parents that students were receiving a 'second rate' education. To make matters worse, the nearby Morgan Williams School had chosen another text, from a rival publisher, which had been distributed on the first day of the school year, together with computer diskettes for those students who had access to computers at home.

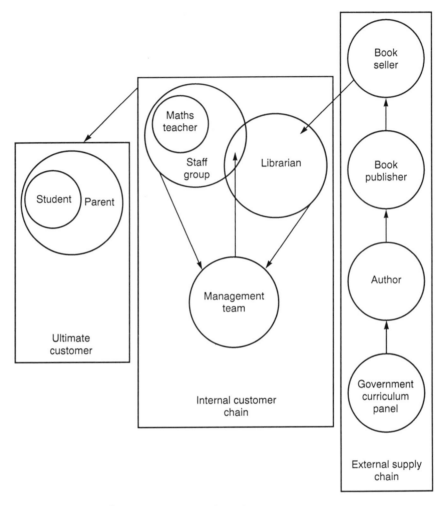

*Fig. 3.3*   A complex customer–supplier chain.

One reason this chain is complicated is that it involves customer–supplier relationships between external suppliers (government, publishers, distribution companies) as well as internal customers and ultimate customers. Let us map this chain of customers in the same way as the last one (Fig. 3.3).

### Implications for management of the internal customer–supplier chain

Quality learning experiences are a function of everyone in this customer–supplier chain (internal customers and suppliers, external customers and

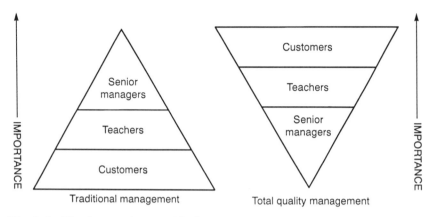

*Fig. 3.4*   The inverted pyramid of TQM.

suppliers) ensuring that commitments are met and quality is assured. This means that quality has to be managed, it just does not happen by chance. It has to be managed at all stages of the customer–supplier relationship if it is to be effective and sustainable. It has to be based not just on quality assurance, but on contract performance and the meeting of the needs of all internal customers in the chain so that the product for the ultimate customers receives their approval as meeting their expectation of the quality they desire.

When looked at in terms of the chain of customers, there is an assumption here about the nature of organizational design and structure, namely that the organization we call 'school' will increasingly be designed around the inverted pyramid.

In the traditional picture of the authority and status patterns of control in running the school (or any other enterprise for that matter), 'the management' is seen to be at the apex of a triangle, with the rank and file of teachers forming the base. In this pattern of management control it is the apex that is seen as being closest to the customers in terms of knowing about their needs and how to achieve a quality product, whether it be learning or a motor car. In this model the 'workers' are seen as supporters of what the management is striving for.

The inverted pyramid concept of management, on the other hand, which is an essential prerequisite of TQM and the need to focus on the detail of the internal chain of customer–supplier roles, puts the rank and file of workers closest to the customers (Fig. 3.4). In the context of the school this means that the classroom teachers are seen to be the only ones who can deliver quality improvement to the customer stakeholders. Hence, it is the job of management to support the 'front line' workers by understanding the detail of their internal customer–supplier working practices and problems, by analysing the obstacles to improvement and by listening carefully to the rank and file workers' ideas on improving quality for their customers. This view is very different from the traditional practice of schools in many countries, where control is very hierarchical to say the least, and where the practice of listening to and supporting those in the 'front line' does not, in reality, take place to any extent.

Consider, for example, the data on the experience of stress and over-work experienced by staff in a large secondary school in the United Kingdom, collected in 1991. This school, like all others in England and Wales, had been going through a period of intense innovation connected with the implementation of the national curriculum and a range of other government requirements. The survey showed that the staff group declaring least stress or increase in work was the senior management, and that increases in stress, etc. were inversely proportional to the status position of the teacher in the hierarchy and the amount of pay received. Those paid the least, and closest to the customer, were the most over-worked and stressed. In effect,  the senior managers had passed the buck to them. This school was very clearly not organized on the principle of the inverted pyramid, or aware of the internal customer–supplier chain. If it had been, then the senior managers (suppliers) would have better served their class teacher (customers).

## Quality and strategy

The previous chapter provided a framework for strategic choice through the selection of an appropriate generic strategy. The selection is based on a view of access, service mix, management competence and resources. What is the link between your chosen strategy and the assumptions made here about the quality revolution, the chain of customers and the nature of organizational design?

The generic strategies suggest very different points of focus for management in determining the nature of quality. All four strategies assume a balance between the three forms of quality – quality assurance, contract conformance and customer-driven – but the balance will differ between one strategy and another. All four also require a focus on managing the chain of customer relationships and performance, with a concentration on both process quality and outcomes meeting expectations. All four require the organization to be designed in such a way as to be both commensurate with the strategy and quality focus adopted.

But quality is a function of strategy. The quality strategy adopted will be a mix of quality assurance, contract conformance and customer-driven, according to the particular generic marketing strategy chosen. Let us now examine these differences between the four strategies in terms of quality.

## Strategy 1: Broad open

In this kind of school, the focus is upon providing sound quality across the broad range of the required curriculum and in social activities associated with schooling. Quality is determined largely in terms of quality assurance (meeting specifications of the government-specified curriculum) with some locally determined contract conformance around social events, social learning and non-curriculum activities of the school. Only to a very limited extent are the specific elements of the curriculum service mix provided by this school driven by the expressed needs of the customers, although the delivery of perceived quality and customer satisfaction across the broad and basic curriculum provided by this type of school is.

## Strategy 2: Enhanced open

This strategy depends on a much higher standard of quality assurance achieved through seeing national standards and requirements as minimum requirements for performance. While the broad-based curriculum and service mix remains the core of the work of the school, the work is enhanced by a variety of means suggesting a strong emphasis on contract conformance. Many of these locally determined elements – the added value services – will be driven by customer needs, so there will be a stronger balance between contract conformance and customer-driven quality.

## Strategy 3: Basic niche

This strategy requires the school to develop a reputation in one or more niche areas – a specific curriculum area, religion, gender, race, sports, etc. To do so means that the school must also achieve satisfactory standards across the board for curriculum work, with additional contract conformance in the niche area, supported strongly by customer-driven quality in this niche. For example, a school that gives special emphasis to sports needs to ensure that its quality standards for sports activities exceed the minimum through contract conformance, and that consumer stakeholder expectations for success in the sports programme and its relationship to other aspects of the work of the school are fully realized. It also needs to ensure that its performance in sports (outcome of the sports programme) meets or exceeds parental and student expectations.

## Strategy 4: Enhanced niche

This strategy leads the school to seek leading-edge status in a particular niche while securing good performance across all other aspects of its work. Because of its leading-edge reputation, consumer stakeholder expectations will be high and it is critical that these expectations drive a great deal of the strategy. In addition, the school will be seeking to secure futures for their students in the niche area of work – students at a specialist School of Music expect to find themselves entering appropriate programmes or training for a career in music. This leads them to ensure that the quality assurance expectations of others – examination boards, professional associations, postsecondary institutions – are both met and exceeded. Finally, so as to ensure that the leading-edge niche strategy is effective, it is highly likely that individualized learning contracts will be negotiated with students, or that the school will develop ways of working with students which can be regarded as local contracts, thus giving emphasis to contract conformance. In its niche area, then, the school will balance equally the three forms of quality. Across its basic curriculum provision (the other aspects of the work of the school), the emphasis will be on quality assurance and meeting customer-driven expectations.

The obvious question that follows from this brief exploration of the nature of quality and the key points of the quality revolution is 'how do we achieve quality?' Chapter 4 will introduce the key ideas behind total quality management for schools, and all of the chapters that follow will examine strategies, tools and techniques for implementation.

# 4

# A model for TQM in the school

Chapters 1, 2 and 3 have examined the complex environment in which schools have to operate and suggested some devices that can aid our understanding of the way in which these developments affect the work of a particular school. We have outlined the nature of generic strategy and indicated the basis for choice between strategies for a school. Finally, we have examined the nature of quality and its relationship to strategy and have suggested that quality can best be understood in terms of balancing three kinds of quality work – quality assurance, contract conformance and customer-driven quality. Now we wish to examine how all of these ideas and frameworks can be translated into action through the practice of total quality management in the school.

## Defining TQM in the educational context

TQM is becoming increasingly used to describe a variety of different initiatives in organizations. It refers to the systematic management of an organization's customer–supplier relationships in such a way as to ensure sustainable, steep-slope improvements in quality performance. In this chapter we will discuss the five components of TQM, the 3Cs of TQM implementation and the three 'keys' of the TQM environment.

The key word in TQM is management. Quality performance does not occur by happenchance or accident, it occurs because it is designed into the way the organization works; it permeates all aspects of the organization.

The essence of total quality management is leadership – the kind of leadership required to ensure that everyone in the organization is working in a way that ensures consistently high performance and constant improvement is different from the kind of leadership we have experienced in many organizations, as we shall see. Leadership in the TQM context is visionary, in that it embraces empowerment, performance and strategy. From the TQM perspective there is the need to see leadership as a systematic basis for facilitating the work of others (empowerment) so that they can achieve challenging goals (performance) that meet or exceed the expectations of stakeholders (strategy). Management, in terms of TQM, refers to this kind of visionary leadership.

Empowerment, performance and strategy in terms of stakeholders' expectations, are not topics that have been discussed a great deal by educational management at institutional level. Teachers are automatically considered to be empowered in the classroom and considerable professional autonomy in this role has long been recognized. However, we are referring here to empowerment in the sense of devolving the resourced freedom to set challenging goals for the processes they themselves control.

Total quality means what it says. All aspects of the organization have to be dedicated to the goal of achieving the highest possible standards of performance as required by their customers (internal or external), given the strategy they are pursuing. This dedication is not to be merely a rhetoric, but defined by specific required standards of performance. It is total, in that it affects all who work in the school and in that it affects all activities undertaken in the name of the school. This requires everyone associated with the school to understand their quality commitments and obligations and the goals they need to meet to make quality a reality – it requires the commitment of all employees to high performance and quality and the alignment of these staff around challenging goals.

We indicated that TQM requires a systematic management of customer–supplier relationships (Table 4.1). You will recall from the previous chapter that the organization is comprised of chains of customers who manage processes that lead to outcomes.

The customer–supplier relationships within the school and between the school and its consumer and provider stakeholders are the basis for all activities. If these processes and chains are managed well, with a constant focus on high performance and improvement, then quality achievements follow. What is important here is that attention is given to the managing of *processes*, because processes produce outcomes. Far too much attention has been focused upon securing outcomes, no matter what the process looks like – yet it is process quality and effectiveness that leads to *sustainable* quality outcomes. Process here refers to the way in which people work to achieve results.

Let us discuss this point a little more, because it is critical. If we want to

*Table 4.1*    Teachers as customers and suppliers

| Teacher as customer | Teacher as supplier |
| --- | --- |
| Work completed by pupils | Teaching and learning outcomes for pupils |
| A working environment | A customized working environment for pupils |
| Information on previous pupil performance | Assessment and testing of pupils |
| Induction and training in expected roles | Reporting and giving feedback on pupils |
| Evaluation and appraisal data from inspectors, evaluators | Counselling and mentoring of individual children |

achieve the goal of zero truancy then there are a variety of processes we can set in place to achieve this objective. These processes may need to be different for different kinds of truancy (Murgatroyd 1988) and may need to be different for different age groups. We may even need to create customized processes for specific individuals. What matters is how these processes are defined and enacted. By focusing on how the processes become defined, shaped and lived in experience the outcome will follow. If we simply create a process for getting the result and focus solely on the result, we are unlikely to achieve the goal of zero truancy.

The message here is important: make absolutely clear what the goal is and remind people of the goal (zero truancy in the example here) frequently; then focus on managing the processes for achieving that goal exceptionally well. Outcome follows process. Enhanced outcomes follow from the quality of management being applied to the detail of the processes of the many internal customer–supplier relationships within the school.

The definition we offer also refers to sustainable, steep-slope quality improvement. These words are central to the ideas behind TQM. Sustainability refers to the ability of an organization to sustain quality performance over time. Not all organizations can. Some make significant gains in one year, only to find that they are back to square one in the next. Others go for several years with gradually improving performance, and then have a major 'collapse'. TQM aims to provide the basis for quality improvements that are permanent and constantly developing. The term 'steep-slope' is also important here. TQM aims at significant and substantive quality improvements and performance improvements, not just small, marginal gains. The idea is that TQM, if applied over the whole chain of customer–supplier relationships, can lead to substantial gains in process quality and performance outcomes.

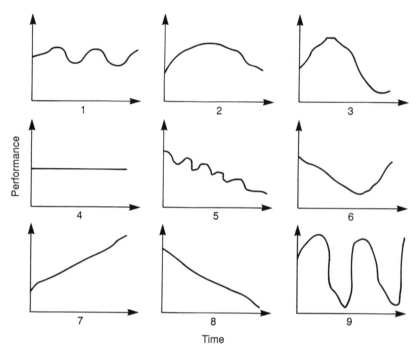

*Fig. 4.1*   Possible patterns of school performance over time.

There are patterns in the performance of schools over time. Reynolds and Murgatroyd (1977), for example, noted the remarkable stability of school performance over time in relation to truanting behaviour. Similar observations were made by the Rutter team (Rutter *et al.* 1979). We can look at some of these patterns by reference to some simple models. Figure 4.1 gives a number of patterns of performance over time – nine in all. The horizontal axis represents time and the vertical axis performance. The first is an uneven pattern, showing roughly similar performance over time, with some highs and lows. Many schools would probably think that this represents their own position, with the troughs representing a 'bad' (below average in range of ability) intake year. The second represents improvement followed by decline. The third is similar to the second, except that the decline – which at the present time few schools (in Britain at least) would know about as they do not collect, organize or analyse the relevant data – is steeper than the improvement. The fourth is the 'if we do what we always do, we'll get what we always get' line – no change in performance over time. The fifth is an uneven pattern of steep decline. The sixth is a pattern of decline followed by the beginnings of a steep improvement. The seventh is a steep-slope improvement line. The eighth is a steep-slope decline line and the ninth is a 'now you see it, now you don't' line. When looking at an organization's history, these patterns become very evident. Only one is sought after in TQM (pattern 7).

Steep-slope quality improvement across a number of performance indicators (student and parent satisfaction, learning performance, social behaviour, attendance, self-esteem) can only be achieved by a consistent and focused commitment to quality performance.

One criticism we have heard is that, if TQM carries the potential of substantial gains in the outcomes of schooling through process improvement, why is it that established working methods have failed to find these gains? There are three responses to this question. First, when used in other settings, TQM has produced very significant gains indeed. In these other settings – hospitals, financial services, service companies, manufacturing companies, etc. – armies of professionals and managers were also hard at work. It took a systematic focus on quality for them to realize that process improvements, involving structural change, could lead to significant gains.

Second, we do not yet know what is possible in achieving steep-slope school improvements, only what has been achieved to date. We do know, however, that some schools outperform others, i.e. that all nine patterns outlined above are visible in school systems. It is possible for all schools to achieve at the level of the schools that are currently high-performing, and for the high-performing schools to make further gains. Of course, when we talk about achieving the level of the high-performing schools, we mean achieving the level of their 'added value' not their absolute gains, for TQM like any other rational approach to the measurement of performance, recognizes that children and schools begin with absolute differences, which are remarkably stable over time, so that it is the amount of 'added value' to the initial position that counts as performance. Finally, the converse of this argument is that it implies that we already know everything we need to know about managing schools and that 'if we do what we always do we will get what we always get'. Examples abound of modest changes in the work of teachers or in the organization of schooling producing significant gains. The three response or rebuttal arguments to the sceptics of TQM, which we have set out, certainly suggest that TQM holds out as much promise for performance gains in schooling as it has achieved in other endeavours.

## Implementing TQM – the five tasks

If this establishes what TQM is intended to do, what steps need to be taken to make TQM a reality? We introduce here the basic framework of TQM – in practice, a framework that subsequent chapters will elaborate in detail and in depth. This overview is intended to provide a map for the remainder of the text.

From an analysis of high-performing organizations and those that can be described as permanently failing (Myer and Zucker 1989), there are five critical features of successful TQM organization that are required to achieve sustainable, steep-slope quality improvements. These are:

1 Alignment within the organization (everyone pulling towards the same strategic ends) and commitment to a shared vision.
2 An extended understanding of the customer-driven and process-oriented basis for quality.
3 An organization designed around teams, with investments made in team development and changes made in performance management systems to reflect teamwork as the basis for the organization's activities.
4 The setting of particularly challenging or outrageous goals, which commit the organization to significant increases in performance outcomes.
5 The systematic daily management of the organization through the use of effective tools for measurement and feedback.

Where all of these elements are strong, provide the focus for the work of the organization and are understood by all employees, TQM has proven remarkably successful. Without these elements, TQM is likely to be ineffective. Each of these features – shared goals, knowing the customer, the primacy of teams, outrageous goals and effective feedback by measurement – can be regarded as a task that the management team within a TQM organization has to achieve if it wishes to be successful.

Let us turn these five requirements for TQM into negatives and describe a permanently failing organization. A permanently failing organization has:

1 No sense of shared vision – people are doing their own thing in disconnected and sometimes contradictory ways; few are committed to the work of the organization and there is a general sense of drift and doubt about where the organization is going.
2 While quality may be the rhetoric of the organization, the reality is that the primary purpose of the organization appears (in the eyes of its customers) to be self-perpetuation, despite the concerns expressed by customers.
3 The organization is very rigid in its hierarchy and has many levels of authority, decisions come down the line about what the goals are and about how they should be achieved, there is little sense of team – too many organizational godfathers – and a great deal of internal competition between staff for promotion, recognition, project responsibility and other forms of reward.
4 The goals set are simple and modest, based on small-step improvements on last year's performance – they are set annually and most often relate to outcomes rather than processes.

5 Employees receive little (if any) feedback about the effectiveness of their own work or about the way in which their work fits into the overall strategy of the organization. Although there is an appraisal system, it is based on competition between people, rather than on clear data and performance indicators for process improvement. The organization may perform at the same level as last year and is satisfied with this – the idea of constant improvement or transformation appears alien to this organization. Mediocrity and conformance are satisfactory states of affairs.

If this latter description sounds like your school, then it is critical that you look to change the way it is designed, focused and structured. If the former description sounds like your school, the question for you will be 'How can I improve on the way the school is performing?' Most schools, however, are somewhere on a continuum between these two models.

This description of the effective TQM organization has hinted at some implicit qualities (so-called 'soft' qualities); it will be useful to make these explicit. They can be thought of as the 3Cs of TQM.

## The 3Cs of TQM

The first 'C' in the soft side of TQM is culture – the implicit rules, assumptions and values that bind an organization together (Ott 1989; Mills and Murgatroyd 1991). A successful TQM organization is one that has created a culture in which: (i) innovation is valued highly; (ii) status is secondary to performance and contribution; (iii) leadership is a function of action, not position; (iv) rewards are shared through the work of teams; (v) development, learning and training are seen as critical paths to sustainability; (vi) empowerment to achieve challenging goals supported by continued development and success provide a climate for self-motivation. This culture minimizes the control role of those in leadership positions and maximizes the power of the employees nearest to the customer. It gains energy from achievement and a sense of ownership of the problems and future of the organization. In the case of schools, the culture just discussed would be revealed by teachers' answers to the question 'How would you describe management in this school and the extent to which rank and file teachers know about and are consulted in what is happening?' Many schools at the present time would be similar to the one recently surveyed by one of the authors, who found that 32 per cent were not put in the picture about what the school was hoping to achieve and 27 per cent were never consulted.

The second C of TQM is commitment. A successful TQM organization engenders such a sense of pride and opportunity for development among its people (staff and customers) that there is a great deal of ownership for the goals of the organization among and between all employees. Commitment extends to taking risks so as to achieve goals, as well as working systematically to keep others informed of the opportunities that exist for innovation and development. Commitment becomes normative, rather than something that is exceptional and due to some event of special personal significance. In the case of schools there is, of course, plenty of commitment about. Teachers are very committed to their own subjects and to the work of their own departments, but the extent to which they are committed to shared goals for the whole school is problematic, unless they have become committed by the sort of processes TQM advocates.

The final C of TQM is communication. A successful TQM organization is one in which communication within and between teams is powerful, simple and effective. It is also one based on facts and genuine understanding, rather than rumour and assumptions. Communication flows freely from one area of an organization to another and between levels of the organization – the stamps (actual or symbolic) 'confidential' or 'for your eyes only' are used rarely; the stamps 'now you've got to see this!' or 'here's something we should all know' are used often. When suggestions are made and communicated, or improvements are being tested out, the issue is not who gave permission or who is doing the work, but what the work does for process improvement or quality performance. Schools are particularly challenging places in which to achieve effective communication. Because of the 'egg box' or 'rabbit warren' nature of the workplace, organizational members are widely distributed into separate occupational worlds, and aware management compensates for this by a whole range of devices: some familiar ones are a 10-minute updating session in the staff room every morning by the Head; a newsletter distributed to every teacher before school ends on Friday giving 'what's on next week in our school'; a video explaining any special projects that affect only part of the school and that is available for play in the staff room. This list is not exhaustive, merely indicative of possibilities.

So far we have suggested that successful TQM implementation depends on five key features (vision, strategy, outrageous goals, teams and tools for daily management) and the 3Cs (culture, commitment and communications). We can show these in a simple diagram intended to help you remember the elements of the model; it encapsulates all that has been said in this chapter so far (Fig. 4.2).

## The TQM approach to leadership

Just saying that these things are critical and important does not make them happen. This requires three other ingredients: (i) trust; (ii) leadership; and (iii) empowerment, the features which unlock the difference between effective and ineffective TQM initiatives.

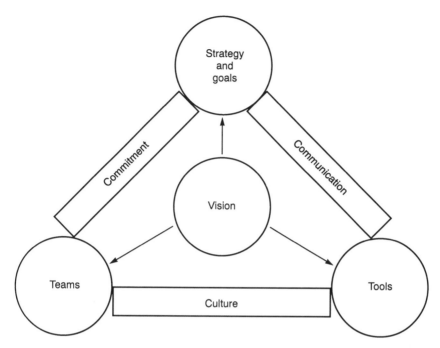

*Fig. 4.2*   The TQM model for school leadership.

The first of these three – trust – has to be earned. It is not something that can be bought, secured through 'deals' or retained automatically. It has to be earned and then kept through a continuous commitment to integrity. Trust, once earned and then lost, is very difficult to secure again. There are very significant differences between the statement 'she has yet to gain the trust and respect of her colleagues' and 'she won and then lost the trust and respect of her colleagues and is now regarded as not trustworthy'. In the first case, colleagues are 'waiting to see' whether the person concerned can command their respect and trust. In the second case the person concerned first won and then lost the respect and trust of colleagues and has an almost impossible task of recovering from this loss. Trust is the basis on which a great many aspects of the 3Cs of the culture of the organization depend.

The second ingredient is leadership. We have already indicated that leadership is not generally to be viewed as a matter of status in the organization, but a matter of respect: 'managers do things right, leaders do the right thing' (Bennis and Nanus 1985) and are recognized for having done so. Leaders who hold positions of responsibility in the organization – headteachers and principals – need to demonstrate their commitment to TQM and its implications in all of their actions all of the time. This means that they have to do what the job requires – mentor, guide, coach, counsel, educate, train and enhearten their staff to see TQM as a way to increase the opportunities they have to succeed and increase their own job satisfaction. They have to see leadership in terms of inspiring, provoking, confronting and challenging people to work to the limits of their ability and to constantly press them to improve their ability. Rather than interpreting the function of leadership as controlling and ensuring the implementation of a given policy, they need to secure a sense of visionary possibility in the organization.

This kind of leadership is very different from the traditional leadership we have witnessed in schools and that has been documented in various studies of school administrators (Hall *et al.* 1986; Morgan and Morris 1989). Traditional forms of leadership in schools have often been characterized by:

1 Solving problems quickly – making sure that the day-to-day work of the school proceeds in as 'problem-free' a way as possible. Seeing problems as potentially disrupting the 'normal flow' of work within the school.
2 The assumption that change is modest and moderate and should not affect the basic work of the school has dominated a great deal of the work of managers – 'Do what we always do and we'll get what we always get.'
3 Planning after the event for the next occurrence – waiting for something to occur before we fully understand the problems and the necessary actions we should take.
4 Maximizing being rational – the task of management requires the exercise of rational, problem-solving, logistical skills – omitting emotions, creativity and excitement.
5 A submissive posture by the majority – leave those in charge to worry about the big picture, our job is to focus on the details.
6 Acceptance of the system – we are the victims of history and decisions taken elsewhere; there is little we can do to shape our own strategy.

TQM leadership requires a very different set of assumptions about management and the work of managers:

1 TQM leadership is about imagination, enabling and empowerment of the rank and file – not about status.
2 The role of the TQM leader is to activate, coach, guide, mentor, educate, assist and support his or her colleagues so that they focus on a shared vision, strategy and set of intended outcomes.
3 TQM visionary leaders realize that it is cost-effective to empower those nearest to a process to manage that process themselves.
4 TQM leaders concentrate on the whole picture and to keep it at the forefront of people's thinking.

5 TQM leaders also search for the small things that can make a critical difference.

6 TQM leaders believe that challenge and fun go together – laughter is healing.

These differences, encapsulated in these two lists, are substantial. They constitute different philosophies of leadership and management within organizations and represent what some have seen as a major change in leadership styles and assumptions (Sergiovanni 1990) from one generation to another. We shall say more about these features of leadership in subsequent chapters of this text.

Now let us briefly position the five critical components of TQM – each of these is to be explored in depth in subsequent chapters.

## Elaborating the TQM model

### TQM component 1: Alignment and commitment to a shared vision

When faced with the challenge of leadership within an organization, a critical question for the school Head is simply 'How can I secure the support of all staff for the work that we have to do?' Put another way 'How can I align the interests of all staff so that we are all working towards a common goal?'

There are various ways to do this. For example, many have adopted mission statements that outline the broad purposes of the school and its critical tasks. Such statements tend to be long and complex, and are often the result of compromises among a staff concerning competing and different interests. Many are not inspiring, but are rather 'mixes' of statements that 'match' the interests of various groups within a staff. More significantly, the mission statements that have been developed are rarely 'owned' by anyone and, even less often remembered. To make the point, we give below the mission statement of a Catholic School system in Canada – a mission statement not untypical of those of schools and groups of schools in many countries.

*Example of a mission statement*

Policy 100, Green Lake Catholic Schools

Catholic schools, as agents of Catholic parents, have the responsibility to help all children to develop their unique individual capabilities to learn and to live, and thereby experience humanity and the world as created by God and redeemed by Jesus Christ.

Catholic schools and Catholic parishes are complementary to the family, which is the primary agent responsible for the child's formation.

*General objectives*
Education must be based on the Christian concept of the individual. The objectives and purpose of education as stated by the Alberta Department of Education must be set in this total Christian concept. The general objectives of the school system are then:

*Growth in academic and interpersonal skills*
Catholic schools will strive for excellence in education for all students to develop their academic and interpersonal skills. In this way, students will be prepared to use their God-given talents to live and work effectively in society.

*Growth in personal values*
Catholic schools will assist all students to choose and develop a hierarchy of values consistent with human nature and the teachings of the Catholic Christian faith.

*Growth in Christian faith*
Catholic schools, in co-operation with parents and parishes, will strive to develop the gift of Catholic Christian faith by assisting all students to:

1 Perceive faith as a personal, free and joyful response to the gift of God himself.
2 Experience the person of Christ in his/her own life through relationship with others and the community of believers.
3 Pray and celebrate his/her faith as a source of strength in daily life.
4 Become aware of their religious heritage and to acquire a better understanding of the various rites of the Catholic Church.

*Growth in social responsibility*
Catholic schools will help all students realize their responsibility to transform the world by practising the Catholic Christian faith in a pluralistic society.

*Growth in physical and mental health*
Catholic schools will foster the mental and physical well-being of all students through:

1 Appropriate programmes which emphasize physical, aesthetic and leisure activities.
2 A respect for the worth and dignity of the individual.

This mission statement is comprehensive and is pretty typical of the way many schools have set out their aims and objectives. It is not memorable though, none of the students or staff could remember this statement in any kind of detail when asked to do so, although many understood its message.

While such statements would have usefulness to outside enquirers wanting a fix on the general aims of these schools, it is unlikely to produce alignment for those involved internally in a school. There are so many areas for interpretation (for example, the meaning of 'excellence in education' or the nature of the 'hierarchy of values consistent with human nature') and so many different ways in which the balance of this statement could affect the way in which a particular school in this system works. A great many activities and possibilities are embraced by this statement, which is part of its intention. As a general statement, which frames the work of such schools, it is perhaps helpful. It is very likely, though, that the document will be filed under 'mission statement' in the drawer of each teacher and rarely referred to. Mission statements such as these do not meet the requirements of TQM component number 1 – indeed we see them as largely irrelevant.

To achieve alignment and commitment to a shared vision, the statement that is produced needs to be something that is used daily by all staff to justify their actions to themselves and to each other. It is the statement by which all in the school wish to be judged. It is a statement that becomes so dominant in the thinking each person brings to their school that all activities and decisions become justified against it. The statement is not only remembered and used frequently each working day, it is also lived out in experience.

We shall examine such visioning statements and how they are arrived at in Chapter 5. The point to note here is that ownership of the vision statement and the frequent use of the statement in the day-to-day processes of the school as a basis for actions and decisions are hallmarks of effective vision statements. Without these, alignment will not occur. Without alignment, there are competing energies in the school, which will detract from a consistent focus on achieving a particular range of goals. Where this focus is 'fuzzy', there is a danger of the energies of the school being dissipated. When this occurs, performance is affected. High performing organizations – those that achieve steep-slope quality improvement – are those with a powerful, widely owned vision that is enacted daily. That is, the vision creates alignment, and alignment is about everyone singing the same hymn from the same hymn sheet, because they have agreed and committed themselves to do so.

## TQM component 2: An extended understanding of customer-driven process and strategy

We have outlined in detail the nature of generic strategy and the link between these ideas and the customer–supplier chain within the organization (internal customers) and between the organization and its consumer stakeholders and provider stakeholders (see Chapters 2 and 3). We have also discussed the precept that to achieve commitment to a particular generic strategy and to achieve steep-slope quality improvement, the units of measurement are the daily transactions in the internal and external customer–supply chains.

Many in education tend to focus their energies on major policy questions and look to those things that they have little ability to influence as the basis for their future hopes and aspirations. In TQM organizations, a systematic attempt is made to draw distinctions between three levels of process influence:

1 *Level 1*. Those matters that you can affect by direct action, that do not require the permission of others and where actions can be justified against the vision statement.
2 *Level 2*. Those matters over which you can have an influence by making suggestions and proposals to those who have responsibility for the process.
3 *Level 3*. Those matters over which, at best, you have only a vague influence and that will take a considerable time to have an impact on those processes for which you are most responsible.

At the first level of influence, you are the process owner and carry responsibility for the quality of the process and for the alignment of the processes to the vision of the organization. You are therefore able to manage the process in such a way as to ensure that those who are the customers for this process are more than satisfied with their experience.

At the second level, you have access to the process owner and can make suggestions to him or her as to how the process for which they carry responsibility can be improved. Your ability to influence this person will depend strongly on how flexible they are and upon how you present your suggestions.

The final level of influence is marginal and cannot be depended upon for process development – they are things that could happen (and maybe should happen), but your role in shaping the coulds/shoulds is marginal. If you focus your energies on those things for which you have level 1 or 2 influence, it is likely that processes within the organization will gradually improve.

By focusing on process ownership at a level that can be affected, and by requiring process managers to align their processes to both the vision of the organization and the generic strategy of the organization, significant performance gains can be achieved. If the energies of the organization are over-diversified, process ownership is weakened and the desired outcomes will not be achieved.

Notice again that we focus here on process quality and process alignment, and assume that outcomes will follow. The tenet and clear experience of TQM is that improvement in the detail of the processes of customer–supplier relationships (internal and external) leads to enhanced outcomes. Hence, constant improvement of processes within the organization is the best way to achieve the enhanced product or service for the customer, which in the case of schools means enhanced learning achievements for students. By dedicating energy to process improvement, and looking at how processes can be improved between one process owner and another, the organization can meet its performance requirements.

**TQM component 3: Teams as the focus for organizational design**

Most schools are hierachically managed. In Britain, there is still a strong tradition of what Schein (1984) refers to as a 'type-b' organization, where:

1 Truth comes from those with positional power (usually the oldest and most experienced but not necessarily the wisest).
2 People need to be directed in the carrying out of instructions and supervised to enact commitments.
3 Relationships are basically lineal and vertical.
4 Each person has a niche in the organization that cannot be invaded.
5 The organization is responsible for taking care of its members.

By the early 1990s, commercial organizations and a great many public sector organizations had changed their organizational design to revolve around self-managing work teams responsible for key processes within the organization. In part, this is a response to declining employee loyalty, but it is more strongly linked to the realization that those closest to a process have a greater understanding of these processes and are therefore better able to improve process performance (Moss-Kanter 1991). This is especially the case in New Zealand, Austria and Finland, where the 'empowerment through teams' movement has its strongest hold.
    Teams are seen to be desirable because:

1 They maximize the creative talent within an organization and promote learning.
2 They are learning units in that they encourage the transfer of knowledge and skills.
3 They promote problem ownership.
4 They encourage a wider range of problem-solving than can be tackled by a single individual, especially when the teams are cross-functional.
5 Team work is more satisfying (when managed well and associated with team development and training) than working alone.
6 Team work carries lobbying power in terms of support for proposals that will lead to change.

All of these features are conditional on four things: (i) a commitment to team working from the top of the organization; (ii) investment in training and development to help teams to master the skills of effective team working; (iii) that teams are the basic unit for dealing with all activities within the organization; and (iv) teams being given very specific mandates, deadlines and resources to perform their tasks responsibly and efficiently.

Some of the organizations that have adopted team work as the basis for their organizational activity and have invested in team development have been astounded by the results. For example, Motorola secured significant quality improvements through team work, cutting the defect rate from 2,732 to 3.2 per million opportunities (a reduction of 854 per cent). The 3M corporation secured three major quality and service gains through team work – a 35 per cent reduction in cycle time (the time taken to complete a process from beginning to end), a 35 per cent reduction in the labour content of all work activities without requiring job loss and a 35 per cent reduction in the costs of quality (inspection, checking, repair, warranty service). At the Open University in Britain and Athabasca University in Canada, courses that are internationally regarded as excellent and high quality are produced by multidisciplinary teams. The government-sponsored TVEI initiative in British schools between 1982 and 1990 produced many teams for curriculum development and innovation.

The TQM approach does not simply establish teams and let them loose within the organization, as we shall see. The teams are given a great deal of latitude to perform excellently in terms of the customer-driven strategy the organization is pursuing, the vision it has and the goals that are considered central to the organization. Indeed, the team is empowered to determine how it will achieve the goals it has been given in a context of a shared vision and understanding – in a climate of trust.

### TQM component 4: 'Outrageous' or 'challenging' goals

The TQM perspective requires organizations to regard themselves as being good at what they do, and to be able to exceed their own expectations about their performance. All the examples of outstanding organizational performance, i.e. those that have demonstrated steep-slope quality improvements, have in common the fact that at one point in their history extraordinary goals were set, which represented a major – almost revolutionary – challenge to all in the organization, yet the organization responded and met the challenge.

Perhaps the most obvious outrageous challenge was that from President John F. Kennedy, who challenged the US scientific community, through NASA, to put a man on the moon within a decade. At the time it was made, the possibility of meeting this challenge was low but the sense of accomplishment that would follow from achieving it was also perceived to be very real. People were not sure it could be done, but developed the 'can do' spirit in response to the challenge.

In the corporate sector, we have mentioned two companies – Motorola and 3M – who achieved major sustainable steep-slope performance improvements. They did so by setting challenging goals, which everyone in these companies had to respond to. These two companies are not alone; Milliken, a New York-based carpet manufacturer, secured a 99.2 per cent on-time performance record (moving from 84.2 per cent) over three years; Hewlett-Packard, the computer and instrument manufacturer, secured a 70 per cent reduction in the size of their inventory and a 50 per cent reduction in labour costs without job loss; Warner Electric, a computer products manufacturer, cut the time taken between having an idea approved and getting the finished product into the marketplace from 36 months to 36 weeks – a change of huge proportions and enormous commercial significance in a highly volatile and fast-changing industry.

These goals, set by top management and responded to by teams across the organizations concerned, have a number of features in common:

1 For success, teams have to undertake a great deal of new learning so as to make the achievement of the goals possible – simply doing the old things faster or working harder are not appropriate responses to the challenges set.
2 The goals focus primarily on process outcomes (completion of learning targets in less time, increased percentage of pupils meeting a particular performance target, new learning activities, new modes of teaching, etc.) rather than profitability or market share.
3 The goals apply to all in the organization, not just some.
4 The goals are directly measurable on a frequent basis – usually weekly or monthly (preferably daily).
5 Investments need to made in learning for all in the organization if the goals are to be met and sustained. Those who are customers for the processes concerned need to be involved in the re-design of processes if they are to both meet and exceed the customer's expectations.

An educational example of the application of these principles in recent years can be drawn from the home institution of one of the authors of this book. Athabasca University is a distance teaching university, similar in many respects to the Open University of the United Kingdom. In 1985 its completion rates for courses was around 44 per cent. In 1987 the top academic management team of the University set the goal of achieving a completion rate of 65 per cent by 1990 without any loss in quality of courses or any rigour in marking. By 1990, the completion rate across the University was 67 per cent and in some areas (notably the professional schools) it was higher. At the time the goal was set, few knew how it would be achieved. It was not the task of management to propose ways in which this would be achieved; rather, the task of management was to support efforts to achieve the desired result; these efforts came from the academic and professional staff of the University working in teams, clusters and as individuals. By creating a challenging goal and supporting efforts to meet it (empowerment), the University was able to meet an important goal and achieve significant gains from doing so.

One side-effect of the achievement of the goal of enhancing completion rates was that it would lead to a greater rate of student retention. As it does so, this in turn will lead to a higher rate of students graduating. As this occurs, the ability of the University to secure new resources (both from government and from other sources) increases, which means that more students can be admitted to the University to study more programmes. This one outrageous goal has many valued consequences.

This single goal harnessed the efforts of a great many people – academic staff, administrative staff in student-related areas, instructional designers, tutors and students. Many experiments to secure gains were tried, some of which succeeded. Others failed and were used as an opportunity to learn. Systematic studies were conducted of the practices of other similar institutions to examine how such gains had been made elsewhere. Think-tanks and other methods were used to brainstorm ideas. The goal was used frequently to remind people what the task was.

This example demonstrates the power of such a goal within an organization. It also shows that goals that challenge the organization for measurable and significant performance gain can be achieved.

**TQM component 5: Tools for systematic daily management**

When the organization has two or three outrageous goals and a strong collection of teams working systematically to achieve them in their own process areas, the organization can be highly energized – a great deal is going on. The danger is that no one keeps track of what is happening and of how the organization as a whole can learn from its experiences.

A critical aspect of a TQM-run organization is, therefore, the systematic recording of what is happening and the use of these records to feed-back information about what is happening to the members. Recording and managing TQM changes are essential activities of the management team, and focus on the following aspects of the organization's work:

1 Agreed-upon indicators of performance in relation to the goals set. For example, if a school has a goal of 'no discipline cases sent to the Head's office' then a chart can be shown in the staff room of the number of cases sent to the office each day. When this chart reaches zero and stays there for a period of time, the goal can be seen to have been met.
2 As milestones are reached on the way to achieving a goal, the processes used to achieve these milestone are written up so that all can use

them. This is known as 'standardizing the knowledge' or 'codifying best practice'.

3 As achievements are made, processes that link to these achievements are examined, systematically with a view to 'fine tuning' the improvements. The idea is to ensure that the underlying learning that has occurred in making the improvements is not lost.

In schools and other organizations that have adopted TQM as their basis for working it is not unusual to see walls covered in performance charts and achievement boards. It is also not unusual to see flow-charts of processes, with red lines and marks indicating areas where changes have been made. Nor is it unusual to see members of the organization carrying data on performance indicators in their diaries – the idea of systematic measurement in terms of outrageous goals permeates the organization.

But there is another point here. By insisting on measurable gains and frequent use of indicators and 'success' charts, people in the organization are being asked to make decisions and judgements on the basis of facts and data rather than anecdote, guesses, instinct or rumour. As W. E. Deming, a major figure in the quality movement, has cited 'In God we trust – all others must use data!' How many times have decisions been made on the basis of very little (if any) information, guesses about consequences and no data about the history of the problem being tackled? How many attempts are made to collect systematic data about a problem before action is taken to 'fix' it? How many 'fixes' backfire because the assumption on which the fix was based turns out to be false?

Systematic data on achievement needs to be subject to critical analysis on a systematic basis. New analytical and thinking tools such as systems archetypes from systems thinking or de Bono-like thinking and problem-solving skills coupled with systematic data analysis tools such as Pareto charts, run charts, matrix analysis and statistical process control charts (SPCCs) can be used. These tools enhance understanding of the dynamics of a problem and, at the same time, can build stronger, better informed and more knowledgeable teams. Without the daily use of these tools, problems will be poorly understood and incorrectly adjusted. When this occurs, the 'fixes' used will be unlikely to produce sustainable, quality improvements with long-term benefits and no unintended side-effects.

## Putting this together

When we look at these five components – the 3Cs of TQM and the nature of TQM leadership – it becomes clear that we are describing ideas about leadership and organizations that are both pervasive and powerful. They carry a variety of implications for people (appointment, training, work patterns, rewards and recognition), structures, roles, performance expectations and the engagement of stakeholders in the work of the organization. More importantly, the successful implementation of TQM in a variety of organizations has shown that TQM leads to higher morale, lower staff turnover and reduced levels of stress and job dissatisfaction.

# CHAPTER 5

# Vision, ownership and commitment: The starting point for TQM in the school

Vision without action is merely a dream. Action without vision just passes the time. Vision with action can change the world!

Barker (1990)

This chapter is about an important concept in TQM – vision. Before any success occurs in an organization it is preceded by a great deal of hard work, which is motivated by a powerful sense of vision. In this chapter we wish to examine the process of vision building and the development of commitment to a vision within a school. The key word throughout will be 'ownership' – whose vision is it and what does having a stake in the vision represent in terms of action? The key idea here is that 'significant vision precedes significant success' (Polak 1973). By vision we mean the overarching concept or guiding force to which the school is working and aiming and which finds expression in an economical vision statement. The vision concept and statement should be seen to embody two components: a guiding philosophy and a tangible image (Collins and Porras 1991).

The underlying assumption of this chapter is that all successful TQM implementations involve key persons in an organization – usually those with designated leadership roles – having a strong and compelling shared vision, which they encourage others to regard as their own. Once the vision for the future of an organization is widely shared and begins to penetrate all aspects of the organizations' activities, then the vision begins to be a reality. A vision of a school dedicated to exceeding the expectations of consumer stakeholders in such a way as to achieve recognized standards for quality and success can be a powerful motivator for just these things to happen. For example, the parents and community leaders of Marshtown Primary School have always indicated the importance they give to ensuring that the children are good readers. Consequently the school has worked to the target that satisfies consumer expectations, namely that at seven years of age no child should be unable to read and that all should meet the normative reading age of a well known reading test. Among the staff, there is the shared determination that 'we'll show them by doing better than they (parents and governors) expect'.

Behind the development of a visioning community, which shares and owns the vision for the school, there are also the qualities of 'translation' – being able to convert ideas into action – and commitment – being able to stay with the vision, whatever the problems. We will examine here the ways in which vision becomes action through translation and commitment.

## Visioning the future

When a school seeks to become powerfully effective in achieving objectives it does so by creating a climate or culture in which the range of shared values is high and commitment to these values translates into innovation and the effective use of scarce resources. There are few hidden agendas and cliques in such organizations (Stein 1986). Risk-taking occurs because teachers and administrators within the organization know what it is they are each trying to achieve and how these individual achievements will fit into the vision for it as a whole. Those who use the school as consumers or provide it with resources and services each have the same understanding of what it is the school is working towards and what this represents for them. The vision is a shared image of fundamental purpose. If we take examples of industrial organizations we find that, in most cases, the powerful vision that shapes their future is a very simple one.

Toyota wants to be the biggest car company in the world; Sony wants to 'entertain everybody everywhere'; Ford (USA) wants to build the best quality cars in the world, which is why their vision statement is simply 'Quality is job #1'. The simplicity of the vision is the key to its importance, as we shall see.

What is important is that the vision statement embraces the hopes and aspirations of all associated with the organization. The Japanese words for such vision statements are 'kaisha hoshin', meaning basic challenge, which is similar to the definition of fundamental purpose that we offered earlier. Others have used the similar notions of 'compelling guiding force' or 'the spark'. The vision statement should become the basic challenge for all within the school – the force that shapes and energizes all its members. The school mottoes that were so much in vogue earlier this century – often combined with the school badge – might be seen as an early form of vision statement. Take, for example, the motto of a school that was founded as a Grammar School in the days of British Empire and is now a comprehensive school: 'Serve and Obey'. This speaks volumes about the type of product the school in those times was aiming to achieve. What is now needed are new school mottoes i.e. vision statements that embody the contemporary philosophy and tangible vision to which the school is working. A good example of a contemporary school motto that conforms with our definition of a vision statement and that we like very much belongs to one of the more recently established Welsh language medium schools in West Wales. It is 'Oni heuir ni fedir', which in English means 'If you do not sow, you will not harvest'. The vision statement should become the basic challenge for all associated with the organization, for all of their efforts all of the time.

What should a school vision be like? It should be defined as a vivid picture of a challenging yet desirable future state that strongly meets the needs of students and is widely seen as a significant improvement on the current state (Whiteley 1991). To be effective, vision statements need to be:

1 Challenging – always in sight but not out of reach.
2 Clear – not open to conflicting interpretations.
3 Memorable – a statement that is no longer than 20–25 words is ideal.
4 Involving – a statement that enables and empowers.
5 Value-driven – there should be a strong tie to the values of the school.
6 Visual – it should be something that can be represented or pictured visually.
7 Mobilizing – it should demand a response from all.
8 A guideline – it should be something by which all engaged with the school can measure their actions against daily.
9 Linked to the needs of students – the ultimate test of a vision will relate to the actions and achievements of students.

One example will show why these features are important. Bill Maynard was appointed to lead a High School in Seattle. The school had the largest multi-ethnic mix of any school in the city. It also had the highest rates of juvenile delinquency, police cautions, absenteeism, staff turnover and burn-out. It had the lowest levels of academic achievement and sports success. The school football team had not won a match in four seasons. On his appointment, Bill asked the Superintendent of Schools to outline the basic criteria by which he would be judged (as Bill says, he'd just been on a management course so knew to ask this question). The reply was unambiguous and precise: 'no riots!' The previous Principal had lost control of the school and the students had rioted, overturning police cars and staff cars, as well as causing significant property damage. Some students were also injured.

Bill had no previous experience of being a Principal. He approached the task cautiously, seeking to develop friendships with all in the school and to 'bring back a sense of humanity and commonness'. He re-instituted full assemblies of the school and encouraged open dialogue between staff and students. He encouraged the sports teams to think of themselves as heroes. He began monthly ethnic evenings – dinners and entertainment reflecting the different cultures in the school offered by students and their parents. He stumbled on the vision statement the school adopted – 'We've Got Pride!' – during a full school assembly called as a pep talk before the first football game of the season. He asked each pupil to touch the one behind or in front of them (this would usually be someone from a different ethnic background) and say simply 'hey, we've got pride'. Within twenty minutes all 1,200 students were chanting this statement. That Saturday, the football team won. Within months, the walls of the school were full of representations of this idea painted by students in symbolic forms closely associated with the cultures in the school.

Over a period of three years, the school improvement was significant. Not only did ethnic tension within the school rapidly decline, so too did the incidence of violence. Attendance improved, as did academic performance. The school's football coach was named Seattle's Coach of the Year after the team won four games in a season. Although all was not plain sailing – there were tense moments – the school was transformed because a vision was shared (We've Got Pride!) and acted upon by all in the school.

Another successful vision has been that of the founders of The Open University of the United Kingdom, and most notably of its first Vice Chancellor, Lord Perry of Walton. The idea was committed to in 1966, planning began in 1967 and the university admitting its first students in 1970 (who began their studies in 1971). Despite the scepticism of the established academic community and objections from some universities at the time, the Open University has been a remarkable success story. Its vision is to bring university education to all, irrespective of age, geography or prior learning. From the start the Open University was to be equally accessible by all inhabitants of the UK, however far they lived from the metropolitan areas. In setting out this fundamental purpose at that time to all staff, Walter Perry frequently used the image of bringing university education to the isolated Scottish crofter and Welsh hill farmer. Using audio, video, text, computer-aided learning and support, local seminar tutors and counsellors, the university serves in excess of 125,000 degree students a year and offers degrees in a variety of disciplines from the baccalaureate level to the doctorate. With a regional structure that now spans all of the major countries of Europe for certain programmes, the University is now a major source for educational development and innovation in Britain. In addition, it has been the inspiration for the founding of sister institutions all over the world. The vision of an open and flexible university using all available technologies to provide education to all who wish to pursue learning has inspired students and staff to create something that is seen to hold a leadership position in the world of adult education and development.

In both of these cases – the school in Seattle and The Open University – vision was the harbinger of success.

Notice that vision, as outlined here, is not the same as strategy (see Chapter 2). If strategy is seen as a blueprint for success, then vision is the artist's creation, through pictures and models, of what this blueprint could become when finished. The artist's impression inspires all associated with the blueprint to make the blueprint live and fulfil the artist's vision of what is possible.

## The three functions of vision

Outlining the nature of a vision statement and its characteristic features is often a helpful first step to clarifying the power of vision. But there is more to vision than simply inspiration. What a vision does is more important than what the vision actually is (Senge 1990). Nevertheless, the first function of a vision is to inspire. As Whiteley (1991, p. 28) suggests:

A truly integrated and permeating vision energises people and can resurrect disgruntled, routinised, burned-out employees. It provides true challenge and purpose. It makes each person feel that he or she can make a difference to the world. It becomes a rallying cry for a just cause – their cause.

The key question is, then 'Does your school have a vision, for without one how are the teachers inspired?' To achieve this outcome, everyone involved with the school must be included in the development of a sense of vision and should be encouraged to articulate the meaning of the vision to them personally once it has been developed. The vision should become a basis for encouraging, enabling, empowering and developing the staff of the school, and should also be regarded as the cornerstone for all actions in the school. If the vision is in daily use and occasionally treated to a 'special treatment' intended to re-invest everyone's understanding of the vision, its power and its importance to their individual future, as well as to that of the school, then it can be a 'lived' experience. By 'everyone' we must stress that this includes the pupils – has the vision been shared with the pupils?

The second function of a vision statement is to act as a cornerstone for decision-making. In normal day-to-day decision-making, the question to ask is 'If I agree to this proposal, what value am I adding to the work of this school in terms of achieving our vision?' Put simply – will doing this help our vision become more of a reality today than it was yesterday?

Another way of thinking about this particular function of a vision statement is to think about every action taken in the school every day. In looking at each of these actions, can each person concerned justify their action in terms of the vision? Could changing the actions move them nearer to making the vision a reality? Could involving others in the actions make a difference to the way in which the vision is understood and experienced within this school? As each student or staff member leaves the school each day, can they look back and ask what they contributed to the attempts by the school to turn vision into reality today?

Behind aspects of inspiration and ownership for decision-making is the very simple assumption about vision: if everyone in the school shares the same understanding of what the school is seeking to become, then more independent actions will be taken to make the vision a reality. All who work in the school – whether as teachers or learners or supporters of teaching and learning – need to know where they are headed so that they can modify their actions daily to help the school travel on its vision journey. If we take a hypothetical school, which we shall call Beacon Primary, we could ask the same question (and hope to get the same answer) of teachers, parents, caretakers, teacher aides, governors and local community leaders 'What is the vision of Beacon School?'

The third function of a vision statement is to enable all in the school to find common points for focusing energy to achieve sustainable steep-slope quality improvements, i.e. vision is the primary vehicle for creating alignment of energies within an organization. Teams working together to achieve common goals, clusters of individuals working cross-functionally to achieve new objectives or several persons' energies being directed towards achieving a common learning objective for all students, e.g. learning about AIDS, or about a particular event in history or a particular process in science or mathematics, are all examples of alignment within an organization. People focusing their energies together to make the vision become more of a reality today than it was yesterday.

These three functions (inspiration, decision anchor and team alignment) of a vision statement do not happen by chance. They take time to develop, although once engaged they are powerful functions. To trigger these three functions, school management teams need to:

1 Bring about the existence of a vision.
2 Communicate the vision constantly in all aspects of the work of the school.
3 Set outrageous goals, which are clearly and strongly vision-related, and show how these goals link to the achievement of the vision.
4 Embody the vision in their day-to-day behaviour as a team (called 'walk the talk' in North America).

Once the institution's vision is in place and owned by staff and students, the power of the vision to shape the school and its actions will become very real. Without vision, the school will end up somewhere else.

## Commitment – the real challenge of vision

In this section we shall be dealing with a whole range of issues concerned with people committing themselves to an agreed vision. Getting commitment to a vision and related strategy is not a matter that can be taken lightly. Commitment is a difficult quality to elicit and secure from the members of a complex organization like a school. In this section we explore the nature of commitment at two levels: at the level of the school as an organization (the macro-level) and at the level of the individuals within the school (the micro-level). The argument behind the ideas here is that vision is the binding force that engenders commitment at the macro- and micro-level of the school.

Commitment at an organizational level arises from a small number of reasons:

1 The organization is locked in to a strategy and cannot back out of it, even if it wants to – to survive, the organization must pursue the strategy to its successful conclusion.
2 The organization has so delimited its options that it is locked-out of alternatives because of prior decisions.
3 Because of time lags between starting a strategy and its effects, the organization has to hold to its strategy so as to reap the benefits of its investments in people, equipment, marketing and buildings.
4 Inertia – the organization is unable and unwilling to respond to changes in circumstances and, in any case, sees itself as insulated against them because of historic factors (Ghemawat 1991).

Many schools, faced with the opportunity to make strategic choices or revisions of their vision for the future will find themselves constrained by one or more of these four commitment factors. The impact of these constraining factors vary. Let us examine them by reference to case examples from school systems.

### Macro-level commitment

*Lock-in*

A school in Canada 'locked into' computers as a basis for teaching all mathematics and science subjects in 1983. Using resources provided by one of the major manufacturers of hardware, it created seven individualized learning laboratories, each with thirty computers. All science and mathematics teaching was geared to these resources and to a demonstration laboratory. Science staff were hired on the basis of their ability to write and develop software for the teaching of science and mathematics, using computer-aided learning write-wear and on their ability to work to facilitate individualized learning. The skills of a nearby University were harnessed to help develop the appropriate courses and several studies were undertaken to show how effective these methods were in comparison to 'traditional' methods. These studies did indeed show that individualized, self-paced learning produced greater levels of achievement than other methods when matched subjects were compared. By 1989 the hardware supporting these developments was almost exhausted and replacement of virtually all of the equipment was required. The original manufacturer was no longer in business, but several alternative manufacturers offered to supply the school with the needed equipment at discounted prices. The cost of doing so would be (approximately $200,000 (£100,000)). The school needed to find this money to continue its strategy.

What complicates this story is that several other departments within the school – notably the Modern Languages and English departments – had started to use the hardware extensively, to support the teaching of their subjects, and the history staff were hard at work writing the software needed for individualized learning in history. The whole school was beginning to see and use the technology to change the process of learning so that students could work at their own pace. What is more, the school had developed an international reputation for its work in computer aided learning (CAL) and was known as a demonstration site for CAL. Many of the science and mathematics teachers indicated that they would find it very difficult to return to 'traditional' teaching methods given the success that CAL had shown, especially in working with students who found these subjects difficult. Parents also were committed to the use of CAL as a basis for teaching, because the results demonstrated that the methods were effective. In addition, parents had found that their children found these methods to be more interesting than the traditional ways of teaching and would often bring computer work home to work on compatible machines at home.

The school was 'locked into' this strategy and needed to find the new investment to sustain its strategy. It did so, after a tremendous effort by all staff and students, and raised enough funds to replace four of the labs in 1989 and the remainder by 1991. Many who gave funds noted that the dedication and commitment of staff and students to this project was a key factor in their donations. Some companies who sponsored equipment (it now carries the company logo) noted that it was a pleasure to provide resources for a school 'which is so clearly committed to making learning effective as their various research studies show'. This is clearly an example of a 'locked-in' commitment.

### Lock-out

A school in South Wales in 1984–5 was just beginning to develop its own ways of working when it was required to merge with another school in an adjacent community. All of the decisions about the 'new' school were being made by a small team of senior staff who had been designated to leadership positions in the combined school. Although they had the opportunity to transform the way in which the previously separate schools operated by the decisions they made, they chose not to 'risk' anything, but to build on the perceived strengths of the two schools. In doing so, they took the available capital resources and dedicated them to extending existing facilities in the style of these facilities. They did not seek to look at creative designs or to imagine any alternative options for the use of these scarce, one-time capital resources. By their decisions, they simply made the old schools bigger and therefore better able to do 'more of the same'. These decisions 'locked-out' others, most notably a proposal to develop a sixth form regional college complex with these funds. By committing these resources in this way, the strategy for the school was largely determined and various alternatives were 'locked-out'. It would not be fair to suggest that the leaders concerned committed themselves by default – the decisions they made were taken in full cognizance of alternatives.

*Time lag*

By 1992 about 150 schools in Britain will have 'opted out' of the control of their Local Education Authorities (equivalent to School Boards in North America) and changed to grant-maintained status (GMS), so that in effect they receive their funds directly from central government. Strategic management of the GMS school is in the hands of a school-based governing body, which has elected representatives of each of the stakeholder groups. The decision to 'opt out' and become a locally managed school is taken following a referendum of parents and staff. There are some immediate benefits of opting out – schools receive a higher per capita grant, as fewer costs are taken out of the grant for 'central' administration, the school experiences a sense of what might be called 'opportunity for renewal' in that all concerned can renew their commitment to the school and its vision (which has to be articulated) and the school takes full responsibility for its own financial resources of every kind (including those for staff salaries and for equipment and building). However, there is a significant lag between the decision to take this option and its full consequences being realized – a lag of some several years. In part this is because it takes some time to change the working assumptions and practices of an organization and in part because the results will be seen first in the cohort of students whose only experience is of a school that is managed in this way. We know from studies of industry that major changes in human resource practices take between four and seven years to be effective (Skinner 1981) and longer if the organization is large and complex and requires restructuring (Donaldson 1989). The literature of experimental schooling shows, time and time again, that time is needed to make effective and operational the ideas of the experimenters. This time-lag requires those within the organization and associated with it to show commitment to the principles and strategy they are pursuing and to stick with it. The failure of Risinghill (Berg 1968) is an example of what happens when those with authority over a school fail to permit the organization to 'live through' its growing period and work through the lag-time to achieve the promise of the strategy. What these examples show is that some things take time – to get commitment the leaders need to stick with their decision.

*Inertia*

The final source of commitment is inertia, 'It is better to do nothing than to do something and get it wrong' was the way one British headteacher expressed this to one of the authors during a 1975 study of innovation in the pastoral care and counselling provisions within schools in a given region. It is a widespread belief, especially among politicians and business stakeholders, that schools have a built-in bias towards inertia and that the dominant posture of many school Heads is that their schools have been doing OK, so 'If we do what we always do then we'll get what we always get'. Many politicians see the school system as such a large beast that, if you twist the tail vigorously, nothing happens at the other end for years. But how does inertia occur in schools?

We can think of examples, in all countries, of the 'locally rooted' low-turnover schools, which have a clear majority of their staff born in the community and who have returned to teach there. In such a rural American school, known to the authors, all but two teachers were pupils of the school and many of the staff were related to each other. The mutual reinforcers of tradition and social expectations among these staff are high. They are, to use the analysis provided by Murgatroyd (1984) and developed by Mills and Murgatroyd (1991) enmeshed and structured in their response to challenge and the threat of proposals for change. They act as if they were one body and respond to new circumstances by reinforcing old patterns of transactions. The two 'outsiders' are outnumbered and have chosen to conform rather than rebel, as this offers the most psychological comfort and is a way of developing job security in this system. The Principal of the school has her own daughter as Vice Principal.

This is an extreme example, although others with similar historical patterns can be found in Canada, Britain and Europe. In other schools, inertia comes about for a variety of reasons. First, school is comprised of sets of routines. Teaching a particular construct at a particular point in the school year can be a routine. Arranging for school photographs, running the Christmas concert, planning the school summer trips and conducting the end of year examinations are all routines. Routines, once learned, become second nature and it is difficult to change them. Second, the power to change the principles by which the school operates are felt to be limited at the level of an individual staff member. Changing the way a particular construct is taught is not difficult, but changing the methods of teaching or the structure of the curriculum or the links between one department and another can be. Rather than face the risks and challenges of these changes, many back-off and stay with what is most comfortable and familiar: they stay in their comfort zone. But the most important reason for inertia in terms of vision and strategy is that decisions and agreements reached at the level of individuals compromise collective work towards a vision. Putting this another way, 'on-the-spot' transactions and coalitions between individual teachers and the leadership of the school can hamper vision-work and strategic development: a degree of inertial commitment is intrinsic to organizational coalitions.

These four kinds of macro-level commitment – lock-ins, lock-outs, lags and inertia – dominate the reality of vision development within a school. There is a need to overcome some of the limitations these factors impose on the ability of the school to change and develop over time. The development of a strong and powerful vision for the future coupled with the setting of outrageous goals and the systematic recognition of the importance of total quality within the school are powerful ways of overcoming these potential barriers.

It is worth noting that schools vary in their commitment to current strategies and operating practices and can vary considerably in their adaptability. Indeed, Ghemawat (1991) has proposed that commitment is the only general explanation for sustained differences in the performances of different organizations. What differentiates one school from another is the extent to which commitment to a definite strategy exists and the reasons for this commitment. By engendering positive commitment to a strategy intended to make a vision real, the leadership of a school can make a sustainable difference to performance over time.

## Micro-level commitment

In looking at the nature of commitment at the level of the school as an organization, certain models of commitment were drawn to your attention. In looking at the commitment of an individual to a vision, the framework will be different. Rather than focusing upon generalized patterns of action, here we look at the required ingredients for individuals to make a commitment to action. The ideas in this section are derived largely from studies of personality, motivation and conformity.

To make a commitment to a vision and strategy, an individual teacher needs to be presented with the following features:

1 A feeling of choice – that they have a voice in the decisions being made and that they are not being presented with a 'take it or leave it'/'my way or the highway' choice.
2 An ability to contribute to the symbolic importance of the choice being made – they need to recognize that the choice is not just a routine decision, but a decision of major and symbolic importance.
3 The final choices made of vision and strategy must be choices they can identify with.
4 The implications of the choice made should require the individual to use their existing skills to the full and should encourage the development of new skills for a flexible response to the vision and strategy.
5 The choice made should increase rather than decrease the opportunities for recognition within the school of the teacher's work and importance.
6 The rewards of the vision and strategy should be made clear and explicit – in doing so, realism about time-frames for success and obstacles to be overcome need to be made clear.

Many of these points should be self-evident. They all suggest that it is important to engage and involve all on the staff of the school in the process of determining vision and strategy and that the consequences of making choices should be understood in terms both of the organization as a whole and in terms of each person in the organization.

The one idea here that may require explanation is the idea of symbolic importance. We will take some time to describe this idea and its significance in the task of turning vision to reality, as it is often misunderstood or not recognized in other accounts of this process.

The critical question for leaders in an organization is whether, through the clarification of the vision for the future and the careful delineation of strategy, individuals within an organization can be encouraged to modify or transform their taken-for-granted assumptions about the organization and its processes so as to be in alignment with the vision. The question is 'can beliefs (significant meanings about what is) and values (significant meanings about what ought to be) be changed intentionally by leaders?' This is a complex question, involving a great deal of understanding of individual psychology, the sociology of organizations and an understanding of organizational behaviour. We are not going to explore all of these facets in this short chapter (see Mills and Murgatroyd 1991 for a detailed examination of the relevant ideas). Here our concern is with the practice of gaining commitment to a vision or strategy at the level of the person.

We have presented the idea of a generic strategy in terms of choices a school can make that will bring medium- and long-term advantages if appropriate choices are made and committed to over time. The essential idea of generic strategy is to match internal resources and competences to environmental opportunities so as to maximize the potential for success and competitive advantage. Such a view of strategy is largely instrumental.

Vision and strategy, however, also carry social functions within the school and between the school and its stakeholders. By the deliberate choice of strategy and making strategic assumptions explicit through both vision-work and strategic delineation, the leaders of the school are seeking to articulate a set of values and meanings that they wish others to share. Indeed, the very functions of vision and strategy are to achieve this at all levels of the organization so as to create alignment of effort and a communality of commitment. Vision and strategy define the future; in so doing, they establish an agenda for the present and re-define the past. Vision and strategy provide a language and context for discussing current actions and plans.

Vision and strategy are thus to be seen as vehicles 'for generating and encapsulating significant meanings about the nature, direction and purpose of an organisation, which enables members to make intelligible their organisational worlds and explain to others why what they are doing makes (collective) sense' (Green 1988). They become devices for promoting a sense of belonging, of shared goals and of developing an understanding of how the actions of individual teachers or support staff contribute towards the fulfilment of the vision. They also become the focal points for the work of teams within the organization, as they provide a rationale and a set of common values from which the team derives its meaning.

To achieve the kinds of commitment implied here, the leaders of the school must continually 'finesse' the symbolic meanings within the school. The decisions leaders make about structures, technology, rituals, routines and even stationery, are all indicators of the symbolic meaning of the vision and strategy of the school. Each decision provides an opportunity to remind all in the school of the strategy and the vision that informs it. In looking at these opportunities to constantly tune, nudge and reinforce symbolic meaning, leaders in schools need to recognize that all messages carry both intended and unintended meanings. Often, it is the latter kind of meaning – unintended meaning – that has most power.

For example, consider the school Principal who disciplines students for arriving late to school, but is frequently late in arriving at the lessons she teaches. Or the teacher who penalizes students for handing in homework late but has yet to return the homework on time to students. Or the school business manager (bursar) who is fastidious about cutting costs, but always travels to conferences and meetings at the highest cost and stays in the most expensive hotels. The implicit messages here are not what these individuals say, but what they do. The first rule, then, of effective symbolic management is for those in leadership to 'do what they say they are going to do' and to examine all opportunities for tuning symbolic meaning carefully. To reinforce the declared vision and the strategy requires constant attention to these two points.

There is a second rule for symbolic management, which is critical in terms of developing commitment to a vision and its related strategy. It is that changes that are proposed and that challenge the *status quo* need to be legitimized in terms of a more forceful set of shared meanings than those that reinforce inertia. This requires interpreting strategy in terms of links to existing values and assumptions or in terms of a realistic response to new external circumstances. What is important is that those in leadership positions in the school seek to legitimate the vision and strategy by their choice of metaphors, words or models. After all, strategy and vision need to become part of the culture and language of the school, as well as part of its business strategy.

Leaders can influence a great deal of thinking in a school through tuning and finessing symbolic meaning, but the other critical variable in terms of engendering commitment concerns recognition. If the rhetoric of the school changes, but the rewards and recognition systems for individual and team performance remain the same, then the natural tendency of the staff and students will be to follow the rewards and recognition system, not the rhetoric.

What does this mean in terms of commitment-building? It means that every act of recognition for a student or a staff member, every promotion decision, every appointment decision, every 'favour' handed down in the staff room must have a link to strategy and vision. Of all the powerful symbols that a leader can manipulate, none are more powerful than recognition and reward symbols.

The difference between working conditions for a teacher in one region and another are not major determinants of a teacher's decision to stay in one school rather than move to another. The major determinants after pay are job satisfaction, the extent to which the contributions being made by that teacher are valued and recognized and the extent to which their ways of working are producing success for students. One teacher told the authors 'sure the money's important, but the big reward I get is seeing those kid's faces when they move one step nearer to achieving their ambitions . . .'. There are hundreds of ways in which the work of a teacher, support staff member or student can be recognized in a school. What is important is that the recognition is linked to the school's strategy and that those receiving recognition do so for their contribution to making the vision and strategy live. Through recognizing staff and pupil implementers and achievers, the strategy and vision will be reinforced.

A most important recognition act and symbol is promotion – from teacher to Head of Department or to a position of special responsibility or leadership in the school. Often, promotion is based on the wrong criteria, such as:

1 Long service and due recognition.
2 Paying-off old debts.
3 Rewarding those who do not 'rock the boat'.
4 Adding another clique member to the team.
5 Technical competence in their current job (which may have no bearing whatsoever on their next job).
6 Because some sporting, political or cultural activity they do outside the school is admired.
7 Success at playing school politics such that the 'boss' thinks that they are achievers, although the staff recognize window dressing when they see it.

There are many others, all of which have frequently been seen as the basis for promotion decisions within a school or to leadership positions in another school. The criteria perceived to govern promotion are powerful determinants of what the rank and file of teachers see organizational reality to be.

To be effective in sending symbolic messages to all in the school, promotion decisions have to be based on demonstrable competencies essentially linked to the new job, and which would include the criteria of commitment to the vision and strategy and real (rather than imagined) achievements in relation to this strategy. In announcing a promotion, these points of decision need to be articulated so that all can see and examine why a particular person was promoted at a particular time and can understand the message being sent by the fact of this promotion. Promotion decisions (and hiring decisions) carry profound implications for strategy implementation. In the TQM approach to school management, the link between the abilities and performance of those appointed to leadership posts and the school's declared vision must be evident to all.

### Ownership as the voice of commitment

When the staff of a school take ownership and command of the tools of a vision and related strategy, there will be no stopping them from making the vision a reality. The task of leadership is to make the vision and strategy speak through facts, actions and achievements so that those with a vested interest in the school can see tangible consequences arising from their investment of labour, emotion and commitment. Owning the vision and making it live through daily action is what will make a vision translate to reality. A key question then, is how to bring about ownership? There are six steps to achieve this. They will be dealt with briefly here because they receive extended treatment in Chapter 10. These steps are presented in the sequence in which we have used them in school organizations, but there are other sequences, which may work equally well.

*Step 1: Vision talk – presenting the idea of 'Vision'*

Before a vision can develop, the leaders of the school need to talk-up the importance of a powerful vision. Staff and students need to understand the power a vision can have. In Britain the Quality Initiative videos from the Department of Trade and Industry have been found to be useful by schools for this purpose, as have the videos developed by the Further Education Unit of the Department of Education and Science. There is also the well known video *The Power of Vision* (Barker 1990), which makes clear the potential power of vision for shaping the future of an organization.

*Step 2: Vision words – obtaining the key words*

Before trying to encapsulate a vision in a single statement, ask every staff member to write down the three words that best encapsulate their vision of what the school could become; each word should be written on a Post-it® note. The staff should be asked to place their words at random on a wall and then to work in small groups to cluster similar words together. What are the key words that come out from this exercise? Are these key words sending a message? Are there conflicting agendas buried in the words that appear on the wall? This activity can be repeated with a cross-section of students, parents and other stakeholders. It may be helpful for the management team to do this first before asking all staff to do so.

*Step 3: Vision images – obtaining the image component*

At a subsequent meeting, ask staff to work in groups of four to use the words generated at the previous session as the basis for completing this statement: In the Year 2020, we want our school to be thought of as _____. This activity can be repeated with a cross-section of students, parents and other stakeholders.

These first three steps have been concerned with bringing some aspects of the mental maps of stakeholders out into the open – a critical process in vision building. Notice too that these processes are open – everyone can be involved and all can make a direct contribution. As a result of these three activities the management team in the school has a lexicon for making explicit a vision and has some beginning points for speculating about what this vision can lead to.

Not everything will be plain sailing. Some staff will not like this process – it may be too open for them. Others may see it as threatening in that their particular vision may be supplanted by others. The management team need to be vigilant in ensuring that these concerns are both heard and addressed.

Before the next stage, the management team needs to articulate among themselves what the vision of the school could be, given the resources made available by the first three steps, they should develop a systematic view of what the vision might be.

### Step 4: Obtaining the values to inform the vision

Using the same kind of process as described at Step 2, ask each staff member to write down on a Post-it® note the key values that should inform the work of the school. From experience, limit each person to three Post-its®. Arrange these Post-its® into like-minded values and develop a list of key values. Remember, values are descriptors of what ought to be. Issue this list the next day and ask other stakeholder groups to propose additions to the list.

### Step 5: Propose a vision – the statement

It is critical that senior management in a school offers leadership around vision. The best way to do this is for the leaders as a group to propose one. This should be in two parts: (i) a detailed description of the management team's response to the incomplete sentence suggested at Step 3; and (ii) a sentence of 5–25 words, which encapsulates this vision. The aim in doing so is not to close the process, but to build into a crescendo. The vision proposed must make as much use as possible of the words and phrases proposed at Steps 2 and 3 and must make use of the values statement developed at Step 4. But it should be powerful. At the end of the vision presentation by the management team (this presentation should use visual images, symbols and stories as well as educational descriptions so that it appeals at a variety of levels, not just at the cognitive level), each team and individual in the school should be asked to look carefully at the vision statement and invited to propose improvements to it. A deadline should be set for the completion of this exercise.

### Step 6: Signing the vision off

In the light of the feedback received, the management team of the school should finalize the vision and values statement and present it as a document. Following some discussion of the changes made (if any) and a further reminder of why the vision statement is important, all staff should be asked to sign the statement indicating their approval and acceptance of this as the vision for the school.

This six-step process achieves a sense of ownership of the resultant vision statement, engenders dialogue around the future of the school and its strategies for success and encourages individuals to articulate their willingness, or otherwise, to enter into commitments. The signing of the vision statement symbolizes acceptance and commitment, and it might then be framed and displayed in a public part of the school.

Some have suggested that these steps are 'gimmicky' and that, although the process looks democratic, the school is being led by those in senior management positions. Our response is that, while the processes may be unusual they work and that it is the task of leadership to create a climate in which things get done and people have a sense of ownership. This is not the same as running the school as a democracy. Leaders are paid significantly more to do the right things at the right time and involve as many as possible in the 'doing'. They do not, however, wait for all to agree before moving on. Ownership of the vision is critical. When the critical mass for ownership is reached (some time between Step 2 and Step 5), then the responsibility of leadership is to act. The credo should be that 'vision with action' can achieve major changes and improvement in the learning goals schools set themselves.

This chapter has examined the concept of vision and its value to the development of a high performing organization. It has also made explicit the conditions under which commitment to a vision can occur at both a macro- and a micro-level and suggested a six-step process for developing a vision within a school. In our model of TQM, vision is a central feature. But vision alone is not enough, the other four components need also to be present to make the vision a reality.

These other elements are:

1 An extended understanding of the customer-driven and process-oriented basis for quality in the school.
2 An organization designed around teams.
3 Challenging or outrageous goals.
4 Systematic daily management of the school using effective tools for feedback and measurement.

All of these are driven by the sense of vision and strategy. Subsequent chapters examine each of these features of TQM in turn, linking them each time back to vision and strategy.

# CHAPTER 6

# Customers and processes as the basis for schooling

In the end, it is important to remember that we cannot
become what we need to be by remaining what we are.
de Pree (1989)

In the USA, the average State expenditure per pupil on primary and
secondary education is $4,243 (£2,495), although the range shows a great
deal of variation between the lowest State ($2,548 or £1,498) and the
highest ($7,971 or £4,688). There is a similar variation in the expenditure
per pupil between the education authorities of England and Wales. What is
interesting is that in these countries there is no relationship between expenditure levels and performance, as gauged by such measures as the
number of students graduating from high school in the USA or by Key
Stage 1 test results for seven-year-olds in England and Wales. In results
published in January 1992 the education authority that was first in the
expenditure per pupil ranking was 81st in the ranking of results, while the
authority that was bottom in the results was 15th in the expenditure
ranking! Further, there is no strong relationship between teacher:pupil
ratios and performance on this same criterion. The absence of this relationship was particularly evident in the findings of the 'World of differences'
study (Lapointe *et al.* 1988), where the performances of thirteen-year-olds
on the same maths and science tests were compared for a dozen education
systems across the world. The country that performed best in mathematics
and came a close second in science, Korea, had the highest average pupil:
teacher ratio – twice that of some of the other countries studied. Some traditional notions of the link between labour, expenditure and performance
in education are therefore in serious doubt. Whereas it was widely assumed
over recent decades that the link between resourcing and performance was a

crucial one, the evidence now suggests that spending more money per capita on education is unlikely to make a significant difference to performance (Coleman and La Roque 1990).

According to the school effectiveness literature (Glasser 1990; Mitchell and Cunningham, 1990; Barth 1991; McGraw *et al.* 1991; Spady and Marshall 1991), the most critical variables in determining what makes a difference between a high performing school and others is not teacher: pupil ratios or per capita expenditure, but: (i) the climate or culture of the school; (ii) the nature of leadership within the school and the system of schooling; and (iii) the support of parents for the work of the school. The argument in this literature focuses upon the extent to which these variables make a difference and the particular weighting that should be given to each of them. There is also some vociferous debate about the most appropriate indicators of performance that should be used in such studies.

Notice something important about these three variables: they are all about ethics and processes, about school culture and the way in which the experience of this culture shapes action and performance in the school, about the dynamics of leadership at every level of the school as a system and about the nature of the relationship between the school and its primary stakeholders – teachers, students, administrators and parents.

Another way to conceptualize the school effectiveness data is to suggest that schools that perform better than others do so because they manage their processes and their 'moments of truth' exceptionally well and in a way that both meets and sometimes exceeds the expectations of the primary stakeholders and translates vision and strategy into reality. That is, the customer–supplier relationships within the processes of the school are managed in such a way as to ensure sustainable quality performance.

In this chapter we will examine the ways in which schools can work systematically to achieve quality through skilful process management. Some key ideas of TQM will be introduced here – moments of truth, the customer's journey, process mapping and the 'House of Quality'. The aim is to develop a set of understandings and skills and to present some tools that are valuable in developing school-wide quality activities and in securing significant quality gains in the processes of schooling.

The underlying assumption of this chapter is that the experience of schooling can be conceptualized as a set of processes in which someone provides services (supplier) to another (customer) for the benefit of student learning in the school. The nature of each of these services is value adding to the experience of learning and the providers of these services are fully aware of the impact their services can have on the provision of value added learning opportunities to students. It is also assumed that many of the processes have become routinized and only become a focus of attention – a moment of truth – when something goes wrong. It is these very routinized processes that hold the promise of improvement when re-examined and reshaped in the light of the school's vision and strategy. As the students pass through the school in their customer journey, they experience the school as a set of processes. Their experience of these processes is the key to unlocking the promise of improvement buried in the routinized processes of schooling. By engaging all primary stakeholders in a vision- and strategy-based re-examination of key processes from the perspective of the customers of these processes, new gains can be made in the quality of the school's achievements.

## Students and parents as primary customers of the school

Students and parents are not the only customers for the process of schooling, as Chapter 1 made clear. But they have a great effect on the way the school functions and operates, on school performance (measured almost entirely by student performance factors) and on its reputation.

### Customer journeys and their moments of truth

When a student begins school, a series of events and processes occur in a sequence. This sequence is known as the customer's journey. Each element of the journey carries symbolic importance, as it communicates something of the culture of the school and a great deal of the implicit qualities of the school are revealed at each stage of the journey.

To examine the nature of this journey, let us look at the sequence of events relating to a student's transfer from a primary (elementary) school to a secondary (junior high) school. We do not offer a comprehensive account, but only an exemplar of the key elements. From the student's perspective, the journey involves these stages:

1 Establishing that transfer will take place.
2 Establishing which school they are to be transferred to.
3 Knowing which of their friends will also be transferred to this school.
4 Knowing something about this school from friends/relatives already there.
5 Visiting the school and getting a sense of its size, shape and feel.
6 Working out the new timings and possibly the best route for getting to school.
7 Finding out what the dress code of the school is like.
8 Getting a list of necessary equipment, books and clothes.
9 Buying these clothes, books and equipment.
10 Packing the school bag.
11 Getting to school.
12 Finding the classroom allocated.
13 Meeting the 'home room' (form) teacher for the first time.
14 Finding out who else is in the class.

15 Getting the timetable and finding out who else will be teaching.
16 Undergoing 'fresher' rituals in the school play areas.
17 Finding out what the lunch arrangements are.

There are many more steps of significance and importance to the student. But we stop at these first seventeen to make some simple points.

First, this journey is being mapped from the point of view of the student – the customer of this process. If we mapped this same journey from the school's point of view, then the map would look very different. What is important in the TQM approach to management is that we examine all of the work of the school from the customer's perspective. In the words of one writer, we need to begin to see the customer (the student in this case) as an 'honoured guest' (Armstrong 1991) who is making, by their very presence, a direct personal and financial contribution to the well-being of the school.

Second, in this journey the school is not physically involved until after the parental choice decision is made at stage 5, although it has been very involved in the mind of the parent as customer for some time. We know from a great deal of related research that, where parents have a real choice of schools available to their children, word of mouth knowledge will be the main determinant. Also, for the majority, the child's preference will not be the most important factor in making the decision. The way the school handles the student's initial journey could be a major influence of subsequent decisions these and other parents will take.

Third, most schools (in our experience as researchers) seek to manage this journey in some way. For example, many secondary schools arrange a visit day for primary school pupils likely to come to them after transfer. In addition, they may send some of their secondary pupils to visit the feeder primary schools to answer the questions of those who may come to their school. Others have a 'buddy' system, so that the incoming student is automatically linked to a senior student and can be helped to adjust via their experience. Almost all issue a student handbook, which is meant to be helpful. The ideas behind these interventions are sound, but the question to ask is 'What do the students think of them and what do they suggest would be most helpful?' Have you in your school ever surveyed your pupils regarding their transfer experience and subsequent journey?

In a focus group the students recently transferred to a junior high school in a Canadian city suggested the following:

1 Instead of hearing it on the 'grapevine', the school should provide a list of students who are 'signed up' on a neighbourhood basis so that they can see which (if any) of their friends will be attending. This would help in terms of both friendship networks and the sense of 'safety', and may also provide practical help with such matters as getting to the school (car-sharing, travel buddies, etc.).

2 Timetables should be issued before the pupils arrive at the school so that they have had time to learn what the pattern of their school week would be like and that they knew when to bring and not to bring gym gear and other 'special' equipment, etc.

3 The school should have a simpler handbook with the things that students needed to know in it. The current handbooks are written for teachers and parents, not for students.

4 The handbook should contain short biographies and photographs of the teachers, so that the student can learn something about the teachers, and can recognize them.

5 More should be done in the first few days of the school year to make clear the expectations the school has about homework, reading assignments, etc.

There were some seventy-five other recommendations, making eighty in all. When we examined school practices, only five of the recommendations could be seen 'in action' in any of this city's twenty junior high schools. When we asked these students if their schools had asked for their ideas, the unanimous response was 'No', followed by laughter. It seemed strange to these students that the schools might look to them for ideas for improvement. When we presented this list to the Principals of the school, without revealing how it was generated, they said it was a very practical list of useful suggestions, many of which were so obvious that they were surprised that they had not thought of them. When we told them who generated the lists, they were very quiet. The TQM approach therefore urges that we ask the students more and that we do this on a systematic basis.

What does this account of customer-focused improvement proposals suggest? It suggests that the major source of expertise about customer satisfaction in the school system (i.e. the customers) are not being used to generate ideas for constant improvement. It also suggests that the processes used to mediate transfer from one part of the system to another are based on taken-for-granted assumptions about what it is that the students need, rather than on specific data collected from students about both what they need and about how these needs may be met. Finally, in view of the remark that many of the ideas were obvious, yet it is surprising how few of them were being acted upon – this strikes at the heart of quality improvement: the ideas are obvious if you are the person taking the journey, but if you are the tourmaster or travel agent, they are not. Only by enquiring in a structured way, listening to the responses of the customers, understanding their needs and their point of view and gathering their suggestions, can customer expectations by fully met and exceeded.

Within the journey outlined here there are some real moments of truth – moments at which either the standing of the school or the student or both is 'on the line'. Such moments occur when expectations are not being met or when a significant failure in communication takes place. All of the legs of the journey could be moments of truth, but this is rarely the case. Usually, one or two become moments of truth because what was expected and what occurs are two different things. The moment of truth in the customer's view of the world is a sense of discrepancy between what is expected or desired and what is occurring. For example, imagine a student arriving at a school that operates streaming – the most able are in one stream and the least able in another. The student has been led by their previous teachers and their parents to expect that they will be in the able stream, but instead they are put in the less able stream. Or imagine a student arriving at school with the expectation that they will not have to take a language (other than their native language), only to find that they have to study a second language. In both of these cases, expectations and experience are significantly at odds – these experiences are moments of truth for the student. It is the same as happens to adult consumers when we register the discrepancy and say 'I am not going there again'. At a recent British workshop some secondary school teachers were asked to give examples of what kinds of event they thought were 'moments of truth' for their pupils. They listed such items as: feedback from parents' evenings, careers interviews, teacher assessments of set work, etc. – the more discrete and dramatic events rather than the micro-detail of everyday happenings in student–teacher interactions. However, even the events mentioned were best guesses, for only the pupils can really provide the data on moments of truth, which means asking pupils about their experience. A school in Hertfordshire, which is applying TQM, has begun by investigating what they see as two key areas of pupil experience – what do pupils experience when their timetabled teacher is absent? And is the homework policy well conceived?

How the school handles such moments of truth is critical for its reputation in terms of both process and quality service. A failure to handle these moments well results in the student becoming more sensitized to other aspects of the school that do not quite fit into their expectations – all of which they will share with parents. This in turn feeds into the word-of-mouth network and can eventually affect the decisions of parents about the placement of their children and contribute more generally to the level of performance. It is well established that a poor experience of service will be shared with between eight and ten others, while an experience of excellent service is likely to be shared with fewer people. In a school we know of some 600 students, there are likely to be some 558,000 moments of truth for the students a year (between five and six a day): the task of leadership is to make each of these a positive experience for the students.

Moments of truth affect the way we think about a great many experiences. Consider your experience of the ground crew at an airport being unable to locate your luggage, or of a restaurant being unable to accommodate your reservation or of a plumber not arriving to repair a leaking pipe when they said they would. These all lead us to talk vociferously about these experiences to others. The students do the same in talking about their experience of schooling. At a secondary school in Wales a teacher completing a Masters degree in educational management surveyed the pupils' view of their schooling and found a whole range of 'disturbing responses', among which were the findings that 35 per cent were constantly worried about bullying and 29.4 per cent admitted that they sometimes stayed at home even when they were not ill (Dyer 1991). A similar survey by another student into the client services provided by a College of Further Education found that most of the amenities provided were seen to be inadequate by the students, and local employers who sent students to the college criticized the reception facilities for those visiting the college (Aga 1991).

Moments of truth are valuable for a school. First, they provide further insights into the expectation of students and parents about the role of the school. Second, they provide opportunities for learning within the school about improvement opportunities. Third, they are powerful moments for making some transformation possible – through a quick and appropriate response to the experience of the moment of truth, the school can not only change the experience of the person but also increase its standing in the eyes of that person.

Every activity in the school, whether it is the teaching of trigonometry, the understanding of space–time relationships, the development of sports skills, engaging in community service or performing in the school Christmas pageant or drama all involve the customers (parents and/or students) in a journey that has moments of truth. Each of the processes associated with achieving the goals of these activities invoke customer–supplier relationships. By managing these processes effectively and gearing them to the needs and expectations of the customers, schools can be remarkably successful in meeting their own and the students' strategic goals and in bringing the vision closer to reality. What this takes is a systematic attempt to make these things happen.

When planning any event or teaching/learning activity, or when considering any new development, the team responsible should examine the customer journey carefully and seek to identify the moments of truth that could make a powerful difference to the experience of the customers for the event, activity or development. Their aim in doing so should be to seek to understand the processes of the event, activity or development from the customer's point of view and to design the process to meet customer expectations.

There are some tools that can help this process. The most simple is to undertake a customer journey analysis for any activity, as we have suggested. The most powerful is a tool known as the House of Quality.

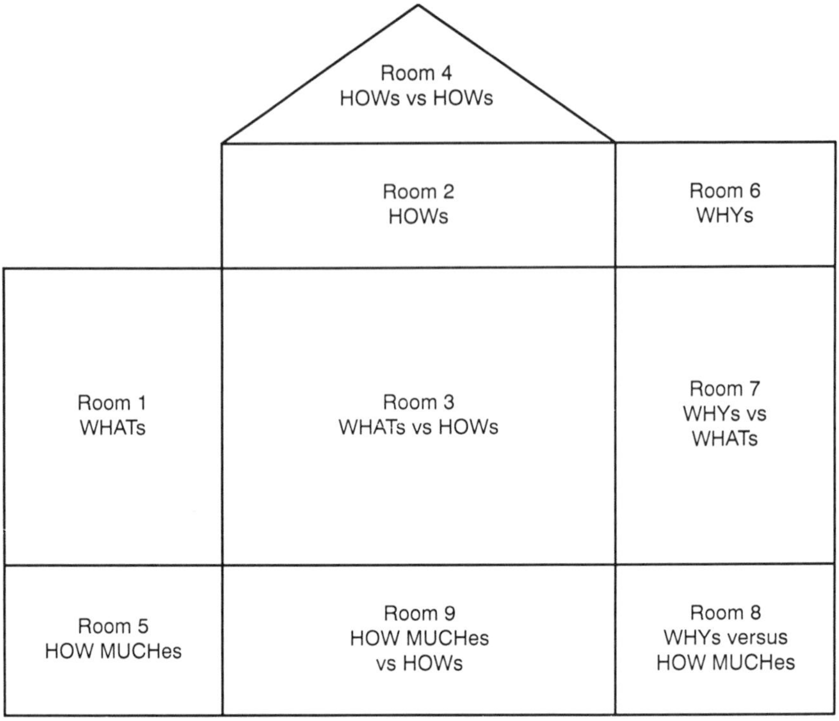

*Fig. 6.1*   Room contents of the House of Quality.

### Using the tool: 'House of Quality'

The House of Quality has its origins in a set of procedures known as quality function deployment (QFD), developed by Professor Yoji Akao of Japan with the Bridgestone Tire Corporation and Mitsubishi Heavy Industries. Although most frequently used in manufacturing industries, it is increasingly being used in service and non-profit organizations. It was first applied to education by Murgatroyd (1991).

The basic idea for the House of Quality is that designers of programmes, services, activities, curricula, organizations and learning experiences should be rigorous in understanding just what the customer needs from an experience or product so that the design of the process can meet or exceed these needs. The 'house' comprises a number of rooms, each of which has their own basic functions. The rooms correspond to information that the team engaged in the design of a service or activity need to collect or create so that the design best matches expectations. Figure 6.1 shows the basic structure of the House and gives names to each of the six rooms it contains.

Now let us provide a description of each room and its role in making the house functional:

### Room 1: The WHATs

These cover the content that customers would expect or request in the service or activity being designed. The WHAT statements are developed following surveys with customers, focus group work, reviews of the literature, discussions with others who have provided these activities or services in the past and so on. The intention is to have a focused but exhaustive list of the critical ingredients for success from the customers' point of view of the activity or service.

A common problem with such lists is that many of the items are often presented in the form of a solution. For example, if the House of Quality is being used to design a curriculum programme, a WHAT may be stated as 'good interaction between teacher and student in the classroom'. Stating it in this way limits the opportunities for design and specifies functions and roles for the teacher. A better item on the WHATs list would be 'quality teacher–student interaction' – the response to this need could be provided in a host of different ways (e.g. peer group learning, computer aided instruction with immediate feedback, teacher interaction, interaction through teleconferencing, use of expert systems and so on). The rule for inclusion is that the WHATs list must be characteristics desired not ways in which the characteristics can be provided.

It is helpful to list the WHATs in rank order. It may also be helpful for complex processes to arrange the WHATs under headings and have sub-categories.

### Room 2: The HOWs

This is a list of those aspects of the activity or service that are in the control of the school and that can be seen to have a bearing on meeting the needs and expectations of the customers for the activity or service. For example, in the case just described of a WHAT being 'quality interaction' some of the HOWs might include:

1 Quality individualized interaction.
2 Fast feedback turnaround.
3 Computer-based feedback, assessment and diagnosis.
4 Learning support from peers.

A common problem with the HOWs list is that the items are often presented in terms of what the organization currently does rather than in terms of the underlying purpose of the action or behaviour. For example, in the list above we might add 'once a week telephone contact with an

| HOWs vs HOWs | | | WHATs vs HOWs | | |
|---|---|---|---|---|---|
| Strong Positive: | ■ | 9 | Strong Relationship: | ■ | 9 |
| Weak Positive: | ◢ | 3 | Medium Relationship: | ◢ | 3 |
| Weak Negative: | × | −3 | Weak Relationship: | ◿ | 1 |
| Strong Negative: | ✳ | −9 | | | |

*Fig. 6.2*   Weights for the House of Quality.

expert on the subject' – this would be a common error. A better statement would be 'regular contact with an expert outside the school', which opens up possibilities of how best this can be achieved.

### Room 3: The WHATs versus the HOWs

This is the 'living room' of the House of Quality. It is the room that reveals the relationship between the WHATs and the HOWs.

The team responsible for the activity or service in question looks at each junction of the WHATs and HOWs and either uses hard data collected from customers (preferable) or uses its best judgement (temporary until data are collected) to determine the strength of the relationship between the specific WHAT and the specific HOW. The aim of this is to build a picture of what is working with what and how well this is working.

There is a convention of using certain symbols to represent strengths of relationships (Fig. 6.2) but numbers can be substituted, or other symbols or colours.

The dialogue within the team around the processes of weighting each WHAT/HOW pair can be quite extensive and very valuable for the insights provided. This is why the House of Quality is both a team development tool and a quality planning tool. The dialogue often leads to additional WHATs and HOWs being identified, and these opportunities for improving understanding of the activity or service should not be lost.

At the end of this process, when all WHAT and HOW cells have been examined, debated and weighted, a number of options are available to the team. We recommend the following steps:

1 Sum the weights for each column (i.e. for each HOW). This reveals the importance of each HOW in the overall work associated with the activity or service. This sometimes reveals that those things that first appear important are not as important as some other aspects of the work of the school in making the activity or service a success from the customer's point of view. In addition, this process also reveals activities that have a weak or poor relationship to the expectations of customers.
2 Sum the weights for each row (i.e. for each WHAT). This reveals how well the school is doing in meeting the expectations of customers for the

service. This will frequently reveal areas where the school needs to improve its services or needs to develop new features of its activity or service to better meet a need. It also often suggests the need to collect more data from the customers themselves to see if the weightings given are accurate.

3 Look through the WHATs versus HOWs matrix and shade in a bright colour those items that score low. Is there a pattern to these items? What is this pattern? What does this pattern tell us about our activity or service?

4 Look at each of the columns as a cost item (if possible obtain the actual cost of this feature of the activity or service you provide). Then look at the column total scores and ask: for this expenditure, are we securing an appropriate level of fit between what we do and what our customers need us to do? Look at the WHATs versus HOWs matrix as an indicator of the added value of the investments being made. Frequently, we find that items involving the most cost have a lower rate of added value than those of moderate or low cost.

5 Look at each column as a staff satisfaction item (if possible, obtain data from staff about their satisfaction with the activities listed on the HOWs list). Then look at the column totals and ask whether those things that produce the most satisfaction on the part of staff produce the most added value in terms of meeting customer expectation? What is the correlation between the HOWs with low staff satisfaction and the scores in these column? What are the implications of these relationships?

These five uses of the WHATs versus HOWs room in the House of Quality are powerful justifications in their own right for the systematic use of this tool in the planning and development of the activities and services within a school, whether they are curriculum-based, social, extracurricular or administrative. Teams engaged in a systematic use of this tool (after the first few uses) soon become skilled in using it as a powerful way to develop ideas and exchange understanding. What is more, it begins the quest for data and hard information to 'get underneath' some of the issues that arise in a first run-through of the House.

### Room 4: The HOWs versus the HOWs

Above Room 2, in the loft of the House, is a matrix showing the relationship between the HOWs and the HOWs. That is, how does one HOW (e.g. quality individualized interaction) link to another HOW (e.g. regular contact with an expert outside the school). The convention for showing these relationships is identical (or similar) to that used in Room 3.

You may wonder why this room is necessary – one management consultant found it difficult to understand and a leadership team in a school found it very complicated, although most see its relevance straight away. The primary purpose of this room is to help a team engaged in reviewing an activity or service understand the interrelationships between one activity within the organization and another.

Imagine that, on the basis of the analysis you had undertaken, your team wanted to delete a column on the grounds that the activity produced little 'added value' and was not well liked by teachers. What would be the impact of doing this on other activities in the school? The matrix in Room 4 helps you understand this. Once you have completed the work of putting Room 4 in place, by weighting each HOW against each HOW, you should again undertake some simple tasks. We suggest:

1 Shade in a bright colour (different from the one used in Room 3) those HOW versus HOW relationships that are weak. Ask 'Is there a pattern here?' If 'Yes', what does this pattern suggest?
2 Look at the HOWs versus HOWs and ask if any HOW stands alone and is not connected to any other HOW? If 'Yes', how valuable is this HOW (look at the column total in Room 3)? Is it really worth doing?
3 So as to encourage new thinking about the work, take out the two most connected items from the matrix (cover them over with a piece of paper cut to size). What is left? What would the activity or service look like without these two? What could you do (other than just restoring the HOWs) that would create the same or more added value?

Too little time is generally spent in this room, yet it is in this room that most 'heat' is lost during debates within the school. You might want to spend more time here.

### Room 5: The HOW MUCHes

The basement of the House of Quality is a place that used to be confusing but, with a clear sense of strategy and a strong vision, is now very tidy. It is where the benchmarks for each HOW are kept.

We shall say more about benchmarks later (see pp. 165–7). Here you need to see them as targets for the scores in each column and as targets for customer satisfaction ratings for the activities. These are two separate items. In the first, the team is saying that, while currently they see a score of $x$ in the future they wish this to be at least $y$. For the second, they are saying that, overall, they wish their customers for this process (the HOW) to rate this as $x$ on a given scale where the scale concerns their satisfaction with the way in which the HOW was completed.

### Room 6: The WHYs

The last room in the House of Quality is the atrium – a room full of light and shade. It is where the customer satisfaction with the way in which their

WHAT is being dealt with by the school is recorded against benchmarks set by the school.

For example, in the WHATs room we had an item 'quality interactivity'. In the WHYs we would have a databased indication of how well the customers for this activity thought the school was doing in providing 'quality interactivity' and an indication of the benchmark that the school is aiming at for this item. Usually, these data are collected from customer surveys or from focus group work and the benchmarks are set by reference to the vision and strategy of the school. The content analyses of the remaining rooms (7–9) are analagous to the comparison made for Room 3.

A team in a small primary school, which we shall call Beacon Junior, used this tool to assess the quality of their handling, from a customer's perspective, of the experience of students transferring into the school from other schools as a consequence of parents changing their occupational location. Prior to using the House of Quality tool, the staff had obtained the customers' perspective of the transfer process by interview and focus group discussions with those who had experienced it in recent times.

From the 'Customer data' the team discerned the six WHATs shown in Fig. 6.3. In a brainstorming process, followed by a process map (see pp. 114–19), the same team identified seven key steps, or HOWs, they currently used in the transfer process. These WHAT and HOW lists therefore provided the design of the House of Quality shown in Fig. 6.3, and were in fact the contents of Rooms 1 and 2 in the way we described earlier. They then decided that they would work on Rooms 3 and 4 only, ignoring Rooms 5 and 6.

The Room 3 task required the team at Beacon Junior to compare and weight the relationship between the HOWs and WHATs. In each case, the question posed was the same: 'What is the strength of the relationship between HOW we do things and WHAT the customer wants?' For example, when they looked at the relationship between the third WHAT in the list – social rules made explicit and clear – and each of the seven HOWs, the most important HOWs were the two concerned with 'mentoring', rather than the issuing of the School Handbook, something they would have assumed to have carried more weight. It will be seen from Fig. 6.3 that this process required the team to analyse 42 specific HOW/WHAT interactions – the most rigorous review yet undertaken of transfer arrangements since the school was opened in 1962.

What did this show the staff team at Beacon Junior? The bulk of the effort had previously been put into the handbook, yet the customers' judgement regarding its value was different. Furthermore the House of Quality analysis clearly showed that the role of the Adult Mentor in the transfer process should be strengthened. In similar fashion the team worked on

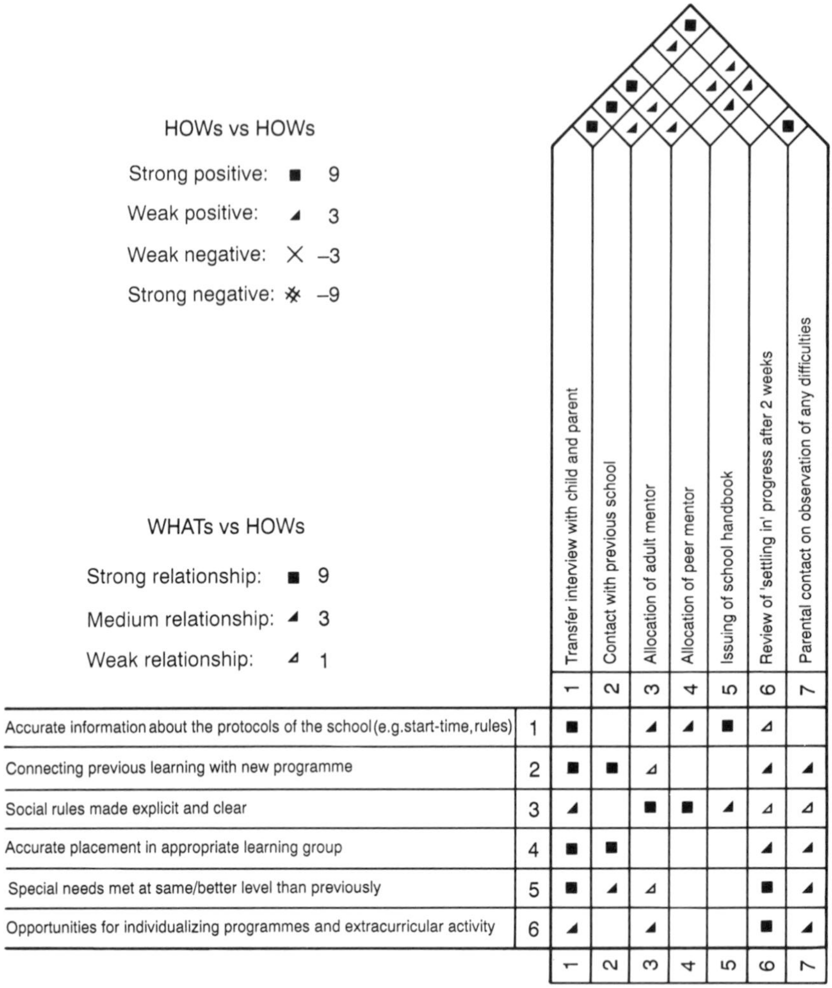

**HOWs vs HOWs**

Strong positive:   ■   9
Weak positive:   ▲   3
Weak negative:   ✕   −3
Strong negative:   ✳   −9

**WHATs vs HOWs**

Strong relationship:   ■   9
Medium relationship:   ▲   3
Weak relationship:   ▲   1

| | | Transfer interview with child and parent | Contact with previous school | Allocation of adult mentor | Allocation of peer mentor | Issuing of school handbook | Review of 'settling in' progress after 2 weeks | Parental contact on observation of any difficulties |
|---|---|---|---|---|---|---|---|---|
| | | 1 | 2 | 3 | 4 | 5 | 6 | 7 |
| Accurate information about the protocols of the school (e.g.start-time, rules) | 1 | ■ | | ▲ | ▲ | ■ | ▲ | |
| Connecting previous learning with new programme | 2 | ■ | ■ | ▲ | | | ▲ | ▲ |
| Social rules made explicit and clear | 3 | ▲ | | ■ | ■ | ▲ | ▲ | ▲ |
| Accurate placement in appropriate learning group | 4 | ■ | ■ | | | | ▲ | ▲ |
| Special needs met at same/better level than previously | 5 | ■ | ▲ | ▲ | | | ■ | ▲ |
| Opportunities for individualizing programmes and extracurricular activity | 6 | ▲ | | ▲ | | | ■ | ▲ |
| | | 1 | 2 | 3 | 4 | 5 | 6 | 7 |

*Fig. 6.3*   Example of a House of Quality.

Rooms 4 and 5, and found, as Fig. 6.3 illustrates, the lack of linkage of the handbook to the other processes, thus enhancing the findings of Room 3.

In the initial use of the House of Quality, a number of common problems are likely to be encountered. Here are the six most common:

*Problem 1: Mixing WHATs and HOWs*

We have already mentioned this problem, but it is worth repeating here. In specifying a WHAT it is important to focus on a specific requirement that is 'solution-free'. That is, what is it that the customer for this process really requires and how can we express this in such a way as not to provide a solution. For example, students often ask for a 'workplan from other students to show how they completed the course', but this is a WHAT that contains both the requirement and the solution. By expressing it as 'work-planning aids' we open it to HOW possibilities.

## Problem 2: Avoiding concept-specific HOWs

In the initial use of the House of Quality, teams will normally define HOWs in terms of how the school currently works, rather than specifying the principle behind the way the school works. For example, at Athabasca University tutors work with students by telephone on a weekly basis. A typical HOW entry might therefore be assumed to read 'weekly contact with home study tutor by telephone', but this specifies a principle, a time-span and a role. The essential element of this HOW should read 'a regular, personalized academic link with the University'. How this is achieved is open to discussion and debate, but the principle of the how is clearly established. The HOW should therefore be written as a generic desideratum rather than content-specific.

## Problem 3: Guessed-at WHATs instead of customer-generated WHATs

The most basic problem is the most obvious. We do not usually know what it is that the customers for each process actually require or expect. Rather than collect hard data, we 'guess', for example by using panels of experts, common sense or some other rubric that favours our current ways of operating. It is essential that the WHATs be generated by real customers for the process. We accept that this is not always easy. But the creative use of focus groups, surveys and evaluation instruments should provide the basis for getting at the WHATs and the WHATs versus HOWs data.

## Problem 4: Confusing apples, oranges and pears

When customers are specifying their WHATs they often do so across a variety of different levels of detail and abstraction. For example, students might specify that, in the teaching of mathematics, they need worked examples, quick feedback, links to be made to 'real-world' problems, a step-by-step routine guide to doing the problem, links to be made to other mathe-matical procedures, an indication of how essential this item is in the syllabus and so on. Not all of these are of the same order of importance and some of them (e.g. the linking items) can be seen to be 'nested' together. It is important to group like-minded items together and to see what they have in common so that the nest can be simplified. Remember, the purpose of building this House is to improve the quality of its functioning.

The same problem arises with respect to the HOWs in the House. Using the teaching of mathematics as an example, we may have the following HOWs: (i) chalk and talk example; (ii) illustration of application to real-life problem; (iii) model of solution strategy; (iv) assignments; (v) worked examples; (vi) detailed feedback on assignments; (vii) practice books; (viii) links made to other maths; (ix) links made to other subject areas and so on. It may be helpful to nest some of these together (e.g. links, practice, feed-back) to simplify the matrix but still to capture the key features of the HOWs.

### Problem 5: Getting in too deep

The first school-based team that used the House of Quality to look at the process of parental involvement in the school ended up with a matrix of 127 WHATs and 57 HOWs – a total of 7,239 potential moments of truth within the WHATs versus the HOWs matrix – the matrix was too big and involved far too many issues.

A helpful set of rules of thumb (for initial work at least) is to narrow the problem down (e.g. parental involvement in student progress matters) and to restrict the size of Room 3 (the WHATs versus the HOWs matrix) to no more than 25 WHATs and 25 HOWs. This still gives some 625 moments of truth cells, but narrows the number of issues to be dealt with down to more manageable proportions.

### Problem 6: Unrealistic expectations for the house

Once mastered, the House of Quality looks deceptively simple. Yet, as you will have gathered, there is a great deal of work to be done if it is to be built well and serve its purpose. It is not an easy task to build the House and it requires a great deal of attention to detail. A school management team often expects the House to be built faster than the process for successful house building permits.

The second problem buried here is that the expectation of management within the school for quick results once the House has been built are usually optimistic. Careful consideration of how to improve Room 3 and of the impacts of doing so on Rooms 4–6 takes time. It may also involve data collection. Establishing a House of Quality team and setting it goals is what is important, not how quickly these goals can be achieved. Sustainable quality improvement in the process of schooling will take investment of intellectual energy, time and patience; there are no quick fixes.

These six problems are the technical/operational problems with the House of Quality tool. But others have raised more important questions about its application to education, and here we address three of these.

A first objection raised regarding the validity of the House of Quality to education concerns the competence of customers to define the work of the school; some see this whole area as a matter for professional judgement because pupils and parents are not experts. The view we hold is that there is both a professional and a consumer domain, and that the consumer domain is insufficiently recognized and used by managers at the present time. The whole approach of TQM in education is not to diminish professional expertise but to enhance it by the addition of what customers can bring to the analysis. There is, in fact, a hierarchy of customers that must be recognized – the government with its experts, the technical public, parents and pupils – all of whom have a right to specify levels of needs that if embraced, enhance achievement. However, responsibility for, and creating the means of, achieving the needs is the professionals' domain. For maximum success the professionals need the input from the consumers.

A second objection is that the work required by something like the House of Quality is considerable – is it worth it? Service organizations that have used the House of Quality have found very substantial gains in customer satisfaction and organizational efficiency. In particular, organizations have found that the House of Quality: (i) is a powerful aid in the development of shared understanding within teams; (ii) helps to identify 'taken for granted' assumptions that need to be re-examined; (iii) identifies key areas for systematic improvement attempts. No one suggests that quality improvement is quick and easy – most systematic attempts to create dedicated TQM organizations have taken several years of consistent effort and item-by-item understanding of what customers need and want and how the organization can best meet and exceed these needs. The kind of detailed work implied by the use of the House of Quality tool is an essential prerequisite for such development, hence this makes an ideal tool for a management team to work with when they are away from the school on a residential basis.

Third, it is suggested that the House of Quality tool gives considerable emphasis to student needs and concerns at the expense of those of the teachers or a school's senior managers. This is in part true: the purpose of the House of Quality is to create a pressure to focus on student (as customer) expectations and needs so that the school can gear all of its activities to meeting them. The working assumption, outlined at the start of this chapter, is that the students (and through them, their parents) are the primary customers for the work of the school and that by meeting their expectations the school can be successful in achieving its vision and making its strategy work. There is no ideological stance here, only the pragmatic experience that 'close to the customer' enhances performance. In any case, the other part of our response to this issue is that customer expectations can be shaped by the school.

This last point may need some explanation. Expectations about schools and schooling are not simply 'sitting' in space waiting to be called upon, but are the product of a variety of influences. The most critical influence is the experience individuals have had of similar services in the past. Other influences include: (i) opinions and suggestions from valued and trusted opinion leaders and friends; (ii) performance measurements supported by testimony from satisfied parents and students; and (iii) clearly articulated statements of vision and strategy, which are in-line with the thinking of the stakeholders. These, and other aspects of stakeholder expectations for a school, can be shaped and influenced by the school working in a systematic and strategic way (Kotler and Fox 1985). The skilled use of personal communications, written material for local newspapers, audio material for local radio stations, audiovisual material for local television and for showing in a variety of organizational settings and at school events can all be powerful ways of influencing expectations about the school and its work. While some object to having to 'market' schools and schooling, those that choose to do so can exert a significant influence over who their students are, what their expectations are and how satisfied they are with the services they receive.

All of the examples we have given so far in this chapter focus on the student or parent as the primary customer for the school's processes. But they are not the only customers for the work of the school. There are other critical customer–supplier chains in the work of the school, as Chapter 3 made clear. The House of Quality tool, as outlined here, can be used to look at any process or service within the school or between the school and some critical supplier, consumer stakeholder or provider stakeholder. By being systematic in understanding the needs and expectations of these individuals and groups, the school can better ensure that it is able to meet them.

### Process mapping

The House of Quality tool requires the management team within the school to look at an activity, service or function as a set of expectations that have to be met. What is being reviewed are the ways in which expectations and assumptions are being met through the performance of the organization. But even the House of Quality tool has limitations, in that it does not look at every specific process in the school in detail or treat each of the processes within the school as problematic. By doing so, we can usually make sustainable performance gains within the organization and support quality improvement efforts significantly. One technique that can help get at this kind of detail is called process mapping – a systematic way of looking in detail at all of the processes used in the school.

We are using the term 'process' in a specific way here. In fact, we are using IBM's definition of what a process is – 'A series of definable, re-peatable, and measurable tasks leading to a useful result for an internal or external customer.' The intention would be to look at every process, be-ginning with those that are most problematic and ending with those that are currently working well but could be improved through systematic investigation, so as to better understand the process, benchmark it and identify improvement targets.

How do we do this? Let us look at process mapping by reference to a simple process, that of inducting a new teacher to the work of the school. We will outline a step-by-step method for mapping this process. To follow this process, you will need a quantity of Post-it™ notes.

**Inducting the new teacher**

*Step 1: Who is the customer for this process?*

The first question is simple: who is this work ultimately for? Identify the customer for this process by placing a Post-it™ note to the far left of a board, table or wall-space.

There are four customers for the process we are looking at here: (i) the incoming teacher; (ii) the immediate colleagues of this teacher; (iii) the students of this teacher; and (iv) the education authority's inspector/adviser in the subject area that the new teacher covers. Recognizing that each of these individuals or groups has a different requirement from this process is an important ingredient in reviewing in a systematic way the processes of the school. Each identified customer should be given their own Post-it™ on the left-hand side of the area on which you are working.

*Step 2: What triggers the process in the first place?*

When you think about the process, what is the first step in this process and how can this best be described? Once you have identified this, write down a description of this one part of the process on a Post-it™ and place it to the right of the customer Post-its™.

In our example, the first point of induction occurs during the placement of the advertisement for the position. What does this say about the school and the nature of the work the person is being appointed to do? How does this advertisement help to orient the person to the vision and strategy of the school.

*Step 3: What happens next in the overall process?*

Once you have identified the start for a process, you then keep asking 'and then what happens . . .?', adding a Post-it™ for each process step that is identified, placing them in the sequence in which the process most commonly happens, one beneath the other.

In our example, the next point of the process relevant to induction would occur at the point of being offered the job: the teacher would be advised (in person, in writing or both) of just what expectations the school has for their teaching work and their initial teaching loads.

### Step 4: Repeat Step 3 until the answer is 'That's it!'

By the end of the iterations between Steps 3 and 4 you may have some 20–30 Post-its™ in a sequence (top to bottom). What you now have is a process description (start to finish) of all of the elements of the process.

### Step 5: Calculate the process cycle time

When you have completed the process map, ask the question 'How long does it take to go from the beginning to the end of this process?' This time-span is known as the process cycle time – the time taken to complete this cycle of activities.

In our example, it may take a whole school year to complete this cycle of full induction to the life of the school.

### Step 6: Count error opportunities in the process stages

When you look at each one of the process items (each of the Post-its™) in the process chain, what potential error points are there? How would you know a problem in the process had occurred?

### Step 7: Record customer satisfaction as a process quality rating

Create a customer evaluation instrument to cover the process steps. Using information gained from the customer, rate the quality of the process on a 10-point scale, where 10 is high and 1 is low. This provides an indication of how well this process meets the needs of its customer – using data from the customer is the only way of getting at this information.

Your process map should now look something like Fig. 6.4.

### Step 8: Audit the process of induction from the feedback

When you look at the items in the process list, for each one ask 'Who is the customer for this part of the process and what is the importance of this item to this customer?'

The purpose of doing this is to look at how each component of the process adds value to the experience of the customer for the process. You will often find that some elements of a process are being done 'because we've always done this', although no one can remember why or for whose benefit this is done. Sometimes, no one can articulate just how the activity being examined adds value to the experience of the customer.

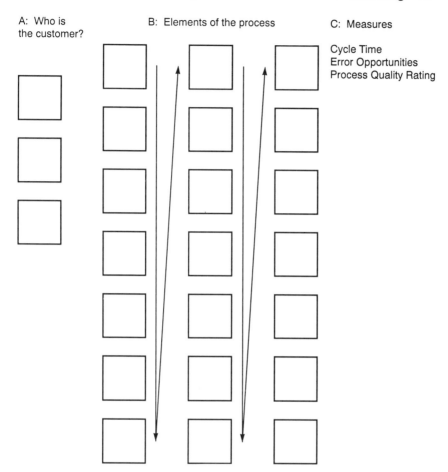

A: Who is
the customer?

B: Elements of the process

C: Measures

Cycle Time
Error Opportunities
Process Quality Rating

*Fig. 6.4*   Components of a process map.

*Step 9: Question the cycle*

Once you have itemized all of the elements of the cycle, estimated the cycle time, identified potential error sources and looked at the value-added audit, it is time to ask some critical questions. Many questions can be asked, but the following are usually very revealing of process weaknesses and potential sources for improvement:

1 Are there too many/too few elements in this process? Are there too many/too few people involved in this process?
2 Do the elements 'flow' well or are there some blocks in the process flows?
3 Are there too many hand-overs?
4 Are there redundant elements?

5 What is missing?

6 What feedback mechanisms are built-in to the process?

7 Is the value of the work done at each point directly or indirectly measurable? If not, why do we do it?

If yes, what do these measures show about how well we are doing in using this element?

1 What *should* be happening at each stage (targeted process and outcomes) and how does this compare with what *is* happening?

2 What are our 'benchmarks' for this process?

The term 'benchmarks' is used here. It refers to a quality target you are aiming at, given your strategy and vision. It is a definition of what you are aiming for in terms of each process within the school.

*Step 10: List the learning*

Look over all of the steps and all of the points you have developed from Steps 5 through to 9. Now list the learning points and action points for this process: what has been learned through mapping the process and what actions need to be taken to improve the process.

Mapping the processes of the school – selecting students for special events, allocating students to particular classes, allocating staff to particular tasks, ordering books, ensuring stakeholder involvement, setting up examinations, teaching contemporary history, selecting new teachers, planning and running a parents' evening or whatever the process may be – is a powerful technique to understand, examine and seek to improve the process, especially when used in a team. The power of this tool arises from: (i) the need to lay-out the process in all of its detail (something rarely done); (ii) the need to look at each element of the process as a potential area for improvement, rather than the process as a whole; (iii) the need to examine each element of a process as a potential error source; (iv) the need to establish benchmarks for quality and speed; (v) the need to audit the process in terms of meeting customer needs; and (vi) the need to review systematically the way in which processes are understood within the school.

There is an added side-benefit to this process. Once the map is completed, the audit undertaken and the learning/action steps identified, the team developing the process map has, in fact, developed a complete entry for the School Manual – How We Work. This 'how we do it' manual becomes a tool-box for new staff or newly promoted staff, helping them understand what to do and what gets done for a range of tasks; it also becomes a book with lists of opportunities for improvement.

Like the 'House of Quality' tool, the process map involves a lot of work. But the results are dramatic and very substantial. The gains in industry have been remarkable. For example, Motorola has reduced the defect rate from 2,732 defects per million opportunities to 3.2 per million over ten years and Air Canada has reduced the time taken to unload baggage at Heathrow Airport from 32 minutes to 12 minutes in three years. These examples may look 'obvious', but look at the gains from using this method in school systems:

1 A school in Canada was able to reduce the time taken to complete the final two years of secondary education (grades 11 and 12) by one-third and used this new time to offer two undergraduate university courses to students.
2 A school in Britain increased by 8 per cent the size of its intake by re-thinking the ways in which it publicized its successes and, as a consequence of the effect of this on its formula funding, will be able to add some teaching staff.
3 A school in Ireland was able to increase significantly the amount of pre-paration time available for each teacher by changing its timetable, having realized the process assumptions behind the timetable.

These gains are real and substantial. They stand in testimony to the power of process analysis and mapping.

Process mapping and the House of Quality are linked. The House of Quality permits an overview of all of the processes related to a particular activity, service or event. The Process Map enables us to look in depth at particular processes that lie behind an element of the House. Both require benchmarking (Camp 1989) and demand that teams and individuals learn more about the dynamics of the processes for which they carry responsibility, and that they share their learning, while at the same time recognizing possibilities for improvement and gains.

At the heart of these two tools – the House of Quality and Process Mapping – is the idea that the processes of schooling should be examined in depth and detail so that their value-added nature (or lack of it) can be identified; also, so that the value of the work that schools do can be better understood in terms of the needs of the customers for these processes, whether these customers are students, teachers, support staff or others. Through this scrutiny of the day-to-day processes of the school – the meat and potatoes of the school day – the school can work at the task of continuous process improvement.

The ideas in this chapter are demanding of a school's managers. They require a great deal of effort and focused work. They require the school to focus on details and minutiae. It is here that the most significant gains will occur. While some may find this a slow process, we believe that the quality of the resultant work will result in sustainable steep-slope improvements over time: the ultimate aim of TQM.

# CHAPTER
# 7

# Outrageous goals and the task of continuous improvement: Performance through challenge and empowerment

Central to the task for leadership in TQM organizations is the challenge of alignment: how do we get all members of the organization to be dedicated to quality performance and continuous improvement in such a way as to ensure that we can meet and then exceed the expectations of those we are here to serve? Another way of expressing this is: how can organizations, through their strategies for performance management, ensure that the TQM mission is fully adopted by all within the organization?

Beneath these questions are some issues about the nature of goal setting within the school, the balance between empowerment and control and the focusing of activity within the school. There are also some very significant questions about the difference between the kinds of goals typically used in TQM organizations and the goals typically used by non-TQM organizations, which need to be examined. In addition to examining these questions, we shall outline a practical process for the development and setting of what we have called 'outrageous' goals (but which are technically referred to as Hoshin goals) – goals that challenge the organization to go beyond that which it currently thinks itself capable of. This chapter is concerned with one of the main characteristics of a successful TQM organization – Hoshin planning. It will also draw particular attention to the role and scope of self-managing work teams, and draws on systematic

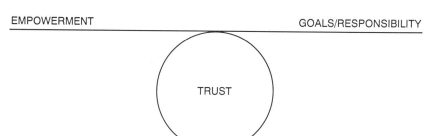

EMPOWERMENT                                                GOALS/RESPONSIBILITY

TRUST

*Fig. 7.1*   Balancing empowerment and responsibility.

fieldwork over a seven-year period of evaluating curriculum development in schools in Wales and Canada and their effectiveness in meeting goals. A case study is presented of a Canadian school, which has systematically adopted TQM as a frame for its work.

Another key term to our foregoing discussion is 'Empowerment': the ability of an individual or a team within the school to work in their own way within an agreed time and with agreed resources to achieve a goal set by the leadership of the school. This definition is different from many of those advanced by others. Empowerment, at least in highly effective organizations, is not an unfettered freedom to determine what goals the team has for the school as a whole, or how they would like the school to be. Basic empowerment begins when the vision and goals have already been set by the school leaders. What a team or an individual is empowered to do is to turn the vision and strategy into reality through achieving those challenging goals set for them by the leadership of the school. Individuals are being empowered in terms of how they can achieve the goals set, not in terms of what the goals might be. The parallel to be drawn here is with classroom teachers, who have curriculum goals and objectives set for them through the national curriculum (in Britain) or through State/Provincial curriculum specifications (in North America). While teachers may have a hand in developing these specifications, most do not: they are received. How the teacher meets the specifications and expectation of the particular school in which they are being pursued is a matter for them to determine, either in their curriculum team or on their own.

Figure 7.1 makes this clear: empowerment is the balance to goals set by the leadership of the school, so empowerment of classroom teachers as to how they teach is the balance to curriculum specifications about what they teach. At the fulcrum of this balance is the trust the teacher has in the leadership.

Our aim in this chapter is to establish clearly a process for schools to become high performing through a focus on a small number of medium term (two to four years) goals that support the strategic thrust of the school while at the same time ensuring alignment of energies and commitment within the school.

## The nature of goals in TQM

Chapter 4 noted that schools normally place excessive emphasis on achieving outcome improvement – better examination results, less truancy, more money, more market share, etc. Each of these items usually attract goal statements from the school. For example, a school in Fort McMurray (Alberta, Canada) has as its goals for the period 1991–4: (i) to reduce absenteeism without cause (truancy) to zero by 1994; (ii) to end all discipline referrals to the Principal's office by 1993; and (iii) to secure an attendance in excess of 85 per cent of all parents at the parents' evenings each semester. These goals are commendable in themselves and involve the staff and students stretching themselves considerably to achieve them. But they are not process goals – they are outcome goals. The TQM approach as was earlier argued is to concentrate on process, and the application of TQM to education sees the translating of certain industrial process terms to the educational context. For example:

1 Defections – not losing a student to another school system or school.
2 Defects – not making mistakes in the way any process or activity is conducted in the school and ensuring that all benchmarked performance criteria are met.
3 Cycle time – working systematically to reduce the time it takes to complete any or all of the activities in the school (e.g. the time taken to register a student, the time taken to teach successfully a particular curriculum, the time taken to complete the school photographs, etc.).
4 On-time performance – to work systematically to ensure that all scheduled deadlines are met 100 per cent of the time for all.
5 Labour content of work – to work systematically and intelligently to reduce a teacher's labour content of work for a given level of achievement while enhancing a teacher's professional activities and to do this without any loss of teaching staff so that more staff are available more of the time for tasks and activities deemed essential (e.g. lesson preparation, curriculum and materials development, additional services and support, working with special needs children, etc.).
6 Plan to action time reduction (P to A) – reducing the time taken between the development, planning and testing of a new service curriculum or activity and its full implementation.
7 Space reduction – reducing the reliance on expensive capital space (e.g. classrooms, laboratories, purpose-built facilities, car parks, etc.) for the performance of the tasks of the school.
8 Customer satisfaction – making significant differences to the levels of satisfaction with the work of the school expressed by all stakeholders – internal and external.

These eight process concepts or areas can, when applied in the school situation, provide substantial opportunities for re-thinking current practices so as to achieve the gains that, in totality, can significantly enhance performance.

## Challenging existing practices

To make these potential areas of process change challenging to the staff of the school, the kinds of goals that need to be set are ones that can only be met in a fundamental and permanent way. For example, if the school sought to reduce a teacher's class contact, i.e. the labour content of teaching by 2 per cent per annum over three years, it would be looking to save the equivalent of (approximately) 3.5 days per teacher of teaching time per year or a total of (approximately) 10.5 days over three years. This does not appear overly dramatic, particularly given the power of peer learning, the potential of new technology and the contributions that can be made to learning by non-teachers in the school. However, the setting of a really challenging or outrageous goal at a level that might permanently change the process of schooling might be something like a 20 per cent reduction in teachers' direct class contact over three years without leading to any staff loss.

Similarly, the cycle time reduction strategy (the time taken to complete a particular programme or activity without loss of quality) could be set at a dramatic level – say 25 per cent – with the 'freed' time being dedicated to new activities, such as co-operative learning, self-managed or computer aided learning, work experience, undergraduate studies at a distance or community service. An example of a cycle time that might well offer considerable savings as a consequence of process analysis in many secondary schools in Britain is the whole process of university (UCCA) and polytechnic (PCAS) applications.

Both these process components – 'labour content' and 'cycle time', and the others listed earlier, have been the focus for work in TQM organizations with dramatic effects. Below we give some examples of these goals from the commercial sector. Our aim in doing so is to provide clear illustrations of just how significant and substantial the process gains are when applied to real-world tasks. While the commercial sector is very different from the school sector in many ways, the examples given here do include the training and support divisions of these organizations. Our aim is to illuminate the extent of the benefits derived by outrageous goal setting in the commercial world.

### Hewlett-Packard

30 per cent reduction in needed floor space (offices, warehouses, etc.).
50 per cent reduction in labour content of work without layoff.
50 per cent reduction in lead time (equivalent to P to A Reduction).

*3M*

35 per cent reduction in cycle time for all processes.
35 per cent reduction in the costs of quality (checking, inspection, evaluations, etc.) without a loss of quality.
35 per cent reduction in the labour content of work without layoff.

*Motorola*

50 per cent reduction in cycle time over five years.
Reduction of defects from 2,732 per million opportunities to 3.2 per million.

*MBNA (America) Credit Card*

75 per cent reduction in customer defections over five years.

*Milliken (carpet manufacturing)*

Percentage increase in on-time performance from 84.2 to 99 per cent.
30 per cent reduction in lead-time and set-up time.

*Warner Electric*

58 per cent reduction in P to A over three years.

As TQM management approaches are only now being applied to schools we do not yet have data of this type for the world of education. However, certain pioneering schools have set outrageous goals, which parallel those in the commercial sector.

In the commercial examples cited above, success leads to considerable reductions in operating costs and hence profitability. In the case of MBNA (America), for example, profit gains have been 16-fold over a five-year period: the company has moved from the 38th largest credit card company in the USA to the 5th during this time. The analogous gain for the educational organization would be significant gains in student learning, demonstrated by hard measures.

All of these industry examples suggest some lessons to be learned about these goals. First, none of these goals is trivial. They each required the organization to dedicate a great deal of time, energy and intelligence to the achievement of new targets. None could be achieved by simply working harder or faster – all require the organization as a whole to be smarter. Second, to achieve these goals, everyone in the organization needed to be involved, not just some. For example, Motorola's long march for massive defects reduction (it took a decade) involved every single activity in the company – from sorting mail, dialling phone numbers, mailing clients, producing cellular components, to managing payroll deductions. No one was exempt from the challenge. Third, these kind of goals were not set

*Table 7.1*   Changing existing practices – a framework for outrageous goals

| Feature | Description |
| --- | --- |
| Purpose | Process improvement and change<br>Team development and learning<br>Ensuring continuous improvement<br>Increased profitability through effectiveness |
| Organization context | All involved are affected<br>Leadership is visionary and supportive<br>Team based |
| Objective | Substantial improvements in process quality<br>Substantial improvements in customer satisfaction<br>Keeping operating costs 'flat', or reducing them |
| Methodology | Team work<br>Flexibility<br>Process mapping and the House of Quality<br>Benchmarking |
| Focus | Outcomes follow process improvement<br>Self-diagnosis leads to self-improvement<br>Learning leads to change<br>Working with customers helps to satisfy their needs and<br>   mould their expectations |

as annual goals (a severe limit on what is normally achieved in organizations), but as medium-term goals. In each case, there was a target date – usually some three to five years after the goals were announced. Fourth, all the goals just outlined are process goals in the way in which we have outlined the processes to be focused upon in this chapter. The underlying assumption is that, by changing the way in which the routines of the organization are managed and experienced, will lead to cost-reduction and increased customer satisfaction if these two things are kept at the heart of these changes. Fifth, no one person was responsible for making these changes – teams had to be involved in the work. While the leadership team set the challenges, they then focused upon mentoring, guiding, coaching, supporting and championing developments that supported these goals. They knew what they wanted, but they did not go around telling the staff how they should achieve these goals.

Finally, to achieve these goals required major investment in learning for everyone in the organization. The goals demanded that staff 'shake-off' taken-for-granted assumptions about what is possible and what works and to look at alternatives through systematic learning about possibilities and expanding the knowledge-base of the organization. These key points are

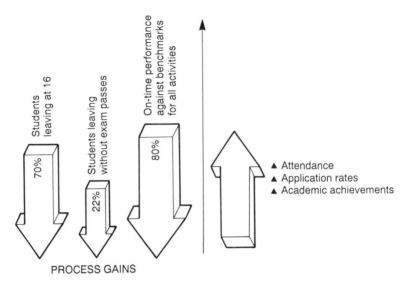

*Fig. 7.2*    Spurred-on school achievement, 1990–2.

summarized in Table 7.1. As we will see, these kinds of features are very different from those traditionally developed in organizations. Goals based on this way of thinking are most likely to lead to significant, sustainable steep-slope quality improvement in schools. These kinds of goals have already been described as Hoshin goals – meaning (in Japanese) 'shining metal' and 'pointing direction' or, more simply, the shining light of good direction. The strategy of Hoshin planning was developed by Yokagawa Hewlett-Packard and the Kayaba Corporation in the 1970s as means for transforming their organizations. Both organizations achieved dramatic results. Here are those at Yokagawa Hewlett-Packard:

75 per cent reduction in the size/cost of the inventory.
30 per cent reduction in needed floor space.
60 per cent improvement in quality (in terms of percentage of work that had to be reworked or scrapped).
50 per cent reduction in lead-time (equivalent to P to A time).
50 per cent reduction in labour costs.

Some years later (in 1985), many of the key indicators had improved by a factor of five.

Translating such achievements into the work of the school, imagine a school which could display the chart shown in Fig. 7.2 as an indicator of its progress to date in quality achievements. Overall, the aim of Hoshin planning and the setting of challenging or outrageous goals is to take the organization beyond its 'comfort' zone and into the area of possible and challenging future. Essentially, schools that adopt this approach are seeking to imagine and achieve certain possibilities. Adapting a set of ideas developed by King (1989), a school using these approaches could reflect the following:

*Imagine this as a statement about your school*

IMAGINE a school that knows what its stakeholders will want 5–10 years from now and what they will do to prepare to meet and exceed their expectations.

IMAGINE a school where each teacher and manager knows what he or she needs to do to make the school system run smoothly. His or her actions are documented, audited and updated daily as changing situations require.

IMAGINE a school where each teacher and manager manages their processes and decisions by facts and knows how to analyse problems by using simple tools.

IMAGINE a school where each teacher and student generates 100–200 suggestions for the school each year (2–4 per working week), of which 95 per cent are implemented.

IMAGINE a school where the Principal/Head sets the two or three most important goals for the year, every stakeholder knows these goals and the most important tasks they can work on to achieve these goals.

IMAGINE a school where each person understands not only how they can do their work but also how they can improve that work on a regular basis.

IMAGINE a school where all problems are regarded as opportunities for improvement that provide opportunities for teams to work to improve their performance.

IMAGINE a school where teams ensure that quality, cost, efficiency, services and achievement are managed on a consistently high level throughout each area of the work of the school.

IMAGINE a school system where improvement efforts occur at every level, so that each teacher, student and manager can be helped to reach their full potential.

Hoshin goals are also intended to overcome some of the traditional problems with planning and organizational development in schools. These problems include:

*Complete absence of planning*

Many schools do not have an organizational development plan. In some schools, activities, tasks and work patterns have evolved over many years on the basis of propose–dispose decisions: teachers propose things and the senior staff in the schools agree or disagree with the proposals. The working assumptions here are: (i) that 'if we do what we always do we will get what we always get'; and (ii) 'no matter what you do or fail to do it will get you there', although we don't know where 'there' is. The school motto for such schools may well be 'no worse than anyone else!' This is sometimes called 'adhocary'; it is unlikely to provide a basis for effective quality development, successful strategy implementation or a basis for engendering active commitment.

*Short-range focus for planning*

Many schools have plans that relate either just to the current term/semester or to the current school year. While mission statements are seen to be valuable for the long-term, goals are usually requested in annual terms and are examined at the end of each term/semester. This is not unlike companies who set goals and measure them in terms of quarterly shareholder reports. Most major, sustainable improvements take time to develop and become established within an organization. The examples cited in this chapter from Motorola, Hewlett-Packard, Milliken, Warner Electric, MBNA (America) and 3M took several years to achieve and continue to be a source of inspiration and work within the companies concerned. Short-range planning tends to reinforce the *status quo* or force drastic but temporary measures on the organization. Such short-term goals also encourage the 'work harder and faster' mentality and not the 'work more intelligently' mind-set. Finally, such short-term goals tend to lead to more cyclical patterns of performance than is the case when a medium- or long-term focus is adopted.

*Difficult-to-measure goals*

Schools and their staff have become expert in offering unmeasurable goals. For example, one school has a goal of 'Developing the whole person by the time they leave Grade 12 (equivalent to Sixth Form)'. When asked what this means, the staff reply in terms of 'rounded self-concepts' and 'core competencies enhanced by a sense of moral well-being'. Asked how they would know if they had achieved these two 'states of grace' they replied 'we know it when we see it'. Staff turnover in this school is well above the average. The number of students graduating from Grade 12 is declining (it is currently 66 per cent of those registered). The goals outlined here are not capable of being evidenced in a systematic way by measurement. It also seems that these goals are not the most appropriate goals for this school, as less than 50 per cent of the age-group register for Grade 12. The point here is that goals become tangible when they are measurable.

### Measurable goals are not measured

One difference between the corporate world and the world of education concerns the extent to which measures are recorded and used. It is often the case that school goals are measurable, but measurements are not taken. For example, in a major series of studies of school absenteeism (Reynolds *et al.* 1980) it was frequently the case that the schools themselves had not examined the available data for patterns of absence over time. In contrast, many companies are excessive in their use of measures – many of which are poorly or inappropriately used. When goals are in place but not measured, and when systematic attempts to learn from performance are not made, then the school tends to begin each new year with a blank sheet and minimizes the value of performance-learning from previous years. By not measuring measurable goals, a school's staff is choosing to minimize the potential of their work for organizational learning and development.

### Opaque goals

It is frequently the case that school goals are written in such loose (unmeasurable) terms that they can either be ignored or interpreted entirely differently by different groups of stakeholders.

### Long-range goals not tied to daily management and the pupil experience

Planning and goal setting are sometimes seen in schools as something that the senior managers do while the rank and file get on with the job of teaching, so that these two groups have wholly separate identities – one does planning, the other teaching. Sound Hoshin planning focuses on process goals that affect all aspects and participants in the daily life of the school. For example, if a school sets a goal of reducing cycle time for everything it does, then every daily event presents itself as an opportunity for systematic improvement in terms of this goal. Look again at the IMAGINE list on page 127 and ask 'How many of these statements translate into daily events and activities?'

### Plans without teeth

Many 'feel good' grand plans are made in educational institutions without the necessary resources to support them. Good plans recognize resource realities, focus on reallocation of existing resources and free existing resources so as to make new work possible. Reallocation budgeting will be a major feature in public service organizations in the 1990s and school planning must reflect this.

### Planning used as a political weapon not a learning agenda

Sometimes the administration of a school will use a planning process and the resultant plan as a way of posing a threat to some staff or stakeholder group. Often the threat is veiled, but sometimes it is overt. One aim of Hoshin planning is to secure alignment (everyone is involved) and commitment (everyone is working to the goals). Playing politics with planning reduces the likelihood of the plan being enacted and owned.

### Excellent planning but poor communication

Some school leaders have developed some excellent planning strategies and have done well to develop measurable goals. But the plan fails. In most cases this is because they have failed to communicate the ideas and essence of the plan and its vision. The plan has been seen as a behavioural plan with little vision. Powerful Hoshin goals are seen to be strongly linked to the vision and strategy the school is pursuing and are communicated directly and explicitly as frequently as possible and in as many ways as possible. Leaders are not 'shy' of their plans, they are 'proud' of what they will represent when achieved.

By setting out the list of school planning defects above, we have at the same time delineated the desiderata of the TQM approach and the features of Hoshin planning. We will describe the steps of Hoshin planning later (see pp. 133–40).

## Management by objectives (MBO) and TQM goals

Management by objectives (MBO), is a conventional method by which performance within a school is managed through the setting of annual objectives for each person and each team within a school.

It was in the early 1900s that Frederick Taylor realized that not every supervisor of every worker knew just how each task should be completed. He experimented with a method he called 'scientific management', in which those responsible for major projects specified in detail just what a subordinate should generally do (job description) and what they should do for a specific task (task–activity listing). Further, each supervisor should provide for each of the persons under their supervision a task–activity list indicating precisely what was to be done, by when and with what resources. The aim of these measures was to improve performance and quality by increasing the control exercised down the line through a set of

statements of work tasks and objectives. This innovation was very successful indeed. At Bethlehem Steel, for example, this method resulted in 200–
300 per cent productivity increases within less than three years of
implementation (King 1989).

Scientific management evolved as everyone associated with the labour
force became better educated, especially following the establishment of
public education as a requirement for labour, which began in earnest
between the two World Wars. One outcrop of these developments has
been management by objectives (Drucker 1954; Humble 1968). MBO has
become widely used in educational systems, as Davies noted as early as
1972 (Davies 1972, 1973). As Davies (1975, p. 339) observed:

> MBO seeks to integrate the organisation's need for growth, fulfilment
> of its objectives and its client's expectations with the individual
> manager's needs to contribute to the organisation, and to develop and
> satisfy himself in the process. To this end, MBO makes the organ-
> isation define its objectives at various levels and assists the manager
> to define his own key results or key effectiveness areas within this total
> framework.

The underlying purpose of MBO remains very much scientific management
or, put more directly, management control. Read the quotation from
Davies again – look carefully at what is said about the manager's need
to contribute and satisfy himself (sic) and define key results. The assumption is that, if only managers could better control what is going on in the
organization and shape more directly what people do and how they react,
the organization would be more effective and efficient. As Palazzoli and her
coworkers observe, this is rather like a manager saying to his or her staff:
'It's not that you should do something different; you should be different.
Only in this way can you help me be what I am not [i.e. a better and more
successful manager], but what I could be if you were not as you are'
(Palazzoli et al. 1978). The problem is that Palazzoli is here describing
schizophrenia, something she claims is endemic in organizations (Palazzoli
et al. 1981).

MBO takes many different forms, but usually involves the Head/
Principal setting annual objectives for each staff member in a school in
such a way as to aid the achievement of overall goals and plans. Such
goal setting is usually focused on observable 'surface' problems (discipline,
teaching competences, curriculum knowledge, special skills) rather than
the 'underlying' problems of values, vision, strategy or process. The goals
are also linked to annual performance appraisals, where these have been
implemented or required. In some MBO systems, teachers self-evaluate and
suggest objectives that are then agreed to, amended or added to by the
Head/Principal concerned. The primary features of MBO are summarized
in Table 7.2.

*Table 7.2*   The features of management by objectives (MBO)

| Feature | Description |
| --- | --- |
| Purpose | Management control<br>Defining appropriate actions for people<br>Securing small gains on an anual basis |
| Organization | Decisions by objectives<br>Task-focused and outcome-oriented<br>Small range of tasks focused on individual, or group-oriented |
| Objective | Outcomes not process |
| Methodology | Politics<br>Social engineering<br>Normally top-down, but sometimes participative |
| Focus | Results through targets expressed in behavioural terms<br>Linked to performance evaluation<br>Salary implications for some |

We would readily admit that an MBO approach to school management is substantially preferable to the 'management on the hoof', 'management by reaction' or 'management by default' modes found in many schools. However, there is a growing realization that many organizations that have adopted MBO are permanently failing as organizations in the sense described by Myer and Zucker (1989). That is, the objectives set do not represent what employees know they are capable of, or indeed what the organization really needs to achieve to obtain outstanding performance. Instead they represent compromises between possibility and 'do-ability', between tradition and incremental improvement. MBO can be seen as the hallmark of gradualism and suboptimization.

Almost without exception, MBO has been focused on maintaining work practices rather than transforming them. MBO is a 'do what we always do, but slightly better' strategy. It has only rarely been used as a basis for transformative process change within an organization, and never successfully.

Perhaps the main argument for thinking beyond the application of an MBO approach to schools and to justify advocating TQM, is that there is evidence that managers set objectives that are too readily attainable and that do not challenge staff to achieve above the level they think is possible – few set challenging goals. This has been explored by Schaffer (1991). Schaffer suggests that the failure to use MBO and performance management systems to achieve high performance is due to: (i) the ability managers have to rationalize past practice as being able to meet future needs ('let's do what we always do so that we get what we always get'); and

(ii) reliance on procedures to solve problems rather than changing processes. These two habits lead organizations to attack performance problems from the wrong angles in the wrong place with the wrong people at the wrong time. MBO has provided a valuable basis for building a strong TQM management performance system.

The nature of performance challenges is important because a characteristic feature of successful TQM implementation is that challenging goals are set for the whole organization. The idea of TQM is not to ask employees for small gains, but to ask for substantive changes in performance. Hoshin planning seeks to set challenging process goals for the organization: Hoshin planning is widely used in TQM developments, such as those at Ford, Dow Chemical, Xerox, some school systems and elsewhere.

## Hoshin planning

The practice of Hoshin planning is very different from the practice of MBO. What is critical is that the whole notion of outrageous goals is shared within the organization in a variety of ways. We now outline a process for developing Hoshin goals within the school.

First, there are some principles we should consider which inform this process. These are:

### Principle 1: Participation

There should be participation by all in the development of the school's vision statement (see Chapter 5). Senior managers provide leadership by defining the vision at the end of the day.

### Principle 2: Individual initiative and responsibility (empowerment)

The leadership of the school sets school-wide Hoshin goals, involving all organizational members and following a process (outlined below). Having done so, each person and each team within the school sets their own goals in relation to these. Leaders then look through each person's goal portfolio to establish: (i) how their goals will aid the attainment of the Hoshin goals; (ii) what learning is required to support the personal goals; and (iii) what organizational barriers might get in the way of goal attainment and what they can do about them. In addition, the leadership of the school sits down with each team in the school and goes through the same process. Notice three things about this. First, having established the school-wide goals the leadership empowers the staff of the school to achieve these goals in their own way: they empower the HOWs. Second, the task of the school's senior management team leadership is to aid and support learning in the organization. Third, one critical issue the leadership needs to examine is the connection between individual and team goals and the overall Hoshin goals, and the nature of the measurements to be used by the individual and the team. Fourth, the leadership of the school must consider how it can help remove or minimize potential barriers to the achievement of personal and team goals.

In autocratic organizations, the boss sets the goals and defines how these goals should be met. In participative and empowered organizations, everyone is engaged in a journey of continuous improvement and learning.

### Principle 3: Root causes are tackled, not just symptoms

The focus of Hoshin goals is to go beyond the 'fix-it' mentality into the 'continuous improvement' mentality. The saying 'if it ain't broke don't fix it' is no longer appropriate in the fast-changing technological and social environments of today. The TQM approach teaches 'if it ain't broke, still improve it and look for the causes that inhibit enhancement.' There are still schools that keep students in unproductive detention or give them purposeless tasks to do if they are often late arriving at school, without ever tackling the causes.

### Principle 4: No tie to performance appraisal

The point of Hoshin planning is to encourage and facilitate constant improvement. This involves some risk taking. Risk means that sometimes things will fail. Peters (1987) has noted that 'if you don't fail some of the time, you're not trying.' Using the possibility of failure to encourage attempts at success will be important, as there will be many false-starts and some failures in the search for quality improvement. If people feel that their own career development within the school or their advancement in the system is irrevocably tied to the ups and downs of improving performance then few risks will be taken.

### Principle 5: Quality before all else

In genuine Hoshin planning systems in powerful TQM reorganizations, quality and process improvement are prerequisites for sustainable improvements in academic performance, attendance and social behaviour. Once achieved, standardizing the process will sustain the gains.

### Principle 6: Communicate, communicate and then communicate some more

Leaders within an organization need to communicate the vision. Team members need to communicate within their team. Teams need to communicate with each other about their work, their successes, failures, methods and ideas. Stakeholders need to communicate their hopes, opportunities, failures, successes and ideas. Communication is the cornerstone of TQM commitment and culture building – we do not mean memos or a surfeit of paper. Communication by walking about, by sharing data, by sharing activities, by working in cross-functional teams. Communication by displays, charts and diagrams. Creative communication.

### Principle 7: Focus on process

Outcomes follow process. To achieve process gains, everyone with goals should review them monthly and ask 'What is helping us develop this process and how is our process for changing the process working?'

In designing a process for the development of outrageous goals, it is important that each of the principles set out above are adhered to.

## The Hoshin planning process

The Hoshin planning process needs to challenge the individuals and teams within the organization to go beyond that which they think themselves capable of and yet be based upon process challenges that the individuals and team see both as powerful objectives to which they can commit themselves and as objectives that will stretch them significantly. How can this be achieved?

Here is a six-step process that has been tried and tested in schools, hospitals and industry as a basis for undertaking Hoshin planning. It starts from the assumption that the school already has made explicit and clear its vision and strategy.

### Steps in Hoshin planning for a school management team

#### Step 1: Imagining alternative circumstances

Ask all teams in the organization to imagine what it would be like and what they would do if the school had: (i) more time available to work with the students; (ii) made fewer errors in working and did more things on time; (iii) had more people-time available; and (iv) could act quickly to implement and test new ideas. The teams should be asked to outline what they would do under these conditions; to imagine that they could make their own situation better by changing what they do.

#### Step 2: Considering the responses

Ask each team to present their response to Step 1 to the school staff at a staff meeting. Listen very carefully to what is being said – there will be three kinds of things to listen for: (i) the ideas that the teams have for what they would do; (ii) the barriers they feel there might be to utilizing the opportunities that exist within the organization; and (iii) the sense of commitment that the teams appear to have. After each team has presented, meet with them to clarify any points of uncertainty and to check perceptions.

### Step 3: Creating the Hoshin team and the outrageous goals

Ask each team to identify one staff member who will sit on a cross-functional team (a between-teams) planning group. This person should both command respect within the team and be committed to TQM and to the vision and strategy of the school. This cross-functional team will have a short time mandate to look at the ideas from every team, to look at the vision and strategy and to help to define the outrageous goals the school will pursue. It will have no more than five weeks to develop the goals and gain commitment to them. The team should be chaired by the Head/Principal and should work to the set of principles we have presented above. It should also recognize that the school needs no more than three or four Hoshin goals over a 3–5-year period.

### Step 4: Declaring the outrageous goals

Once the Hoshin cross-functional team has made its recommendations to the school it should announce the goals. The goals should challenge everyone (they really should be outrageous), but should be goals that everyone can recognize the value of achieving. In announcing these goals, the school leadership team needs to communicate accurately what achieving them would mean for: (i) the vision and strategy; (ii) the development of student and teacher learning in the school; and (iii) organizational well-being and development. Some will react negatively to these goals: it must be made clear that they are non-negotiable because earlier commitment had been given to follow a Hoshin strategy.

### Step 5: Team empowerment

Empower every team in the school to achieve these goals. Make it clear that the goals represent the most significant challenges for the future of the school, but it is up to each team in the school to determine what these goals represent for them and how they will achieve them. Make it clear that the WHATs are non-negotiable, but the HOWs are a matter for the team. This is equivalent to making each team in the school a self-managing work team: they are free to experiment, risk and develop new ways of working and to form new cross-functional teams to get new things done, provided that they are seen to be working towards the Hoshin goals announced by the school. The role of leadership is to communicate the goals frequently, to show how these goals aid and support the vision and strategy of the school and to celebrate successes and learn from failures as indicators of progress made. Chapter 8 will look in more detail at the ways in which self-managing work teams can aid the achievement of Hoshin goals.

### Step 6: Maximize feedback – good and bad

Monitor progress constantly. Require each team to show, in simple terms (i.e. by means of a simple graph, a numerical statement or some measurable device), how they are doing in achieving the Hoshin goals every month. At the end of each semester/term, review the whole school and look at the way in which achievements can be recorded. Display achievement charts in the corridors and entrance ways of the school, so that everyone can look at how the school is doing. Share the feedback (good or bad) with all stakeholders so that they can see how the school is doing what it said it was going to do – make commitment tangible and real. In this stage, work systematically to remove barriers to experiments, risk-taking, innovation and change. Use success as a basis for building strong gains over time.

Chapter 8 will look in more detail at the ways in which self-managing work teams can aid the achievement of Hoshin goals. Underlying this whole process is the requirement that people within the school realize that they are in control of a great deal of their own working arrangements and that, by changing these arrangements, many things can happen. While this may require them abandoning the notion that new activity requires new funds or that 'if we do what we always do we'll get what we always get', it also requires them accepting the fact that 'you cannot cross a chasm in two small leaps'.

### Case study: Dortman School, Alberta, Canada

One school that adopted this last philosophy is Dortman School in Alberta. This is a school which has pupils aged from five to eighteen years (K-12) in a demanding community. It has modern facilities and a very stable teaching staff; indeed, staff turnover is one of the lowest in the province. It has challenged its staff to respond to real issues in a creative and challenging way. What is more, the school has been powerful in communicating its ideas to its stakeholders, most notably the School Board (equivalent to an LEA) and its parents.

This was the process used at Dortman School:

1 In June 1991, at a regular staff meeting, staff identified four outrageous goals in basic form.

2 Later that same month the staff elaborated these goals and conducted an analysis of the value of these goals in terms of their potential impact on wastes in the school, strains on resources and people in the school and the gaps between what the school could/should be doing and what it actually did.

3 The administrative team in the school fed-back to staff the ideas generated in these first two stages, and suggested a process for implementation.

4 Each of the four goals areas would have a minimum of two goal 'crusaders' (with associated parent crusaders, student crusaders and community crusaders). Students were involved at this stage, and the 'crusaders' have the role of championing their particular goal and taking all necessary steps for its achievement.

5 All parents were then surveyed by the staff of the school as to their response to the four goals and gained a significant degree of commitment to these four goals.

6 Staff and parents together presented the four goals to the School Board to gain their support. While the Board was somewhat surprised at the approach, it was supportive.

7 Having secured approval for the four goals, the senior managers in the school then developed baseline data from which gains and achievements could be measured. This essentially involved establishing which dates and what data would be used as starting points for the measurement of gains and achievements.

The four goals adopted through this process for the period 1991–4 were:

Goal 1:  Reduce paper use by 80 per cent.
Goal 2:  Reduce discipline problems to zero.
Goal 3:  Involve every Dortman family in a parenting course.
Goal 4:  Increase the student population from 170 full-time equivalents (FTE) to 225 FTE, mainly through retention strategies.

Other goals were discussed, but these were seen to reflect the dominant concerns of the stakeholders at this time.

The staff did not just simply state the goals above in bold terms and hope that things would happen. Each goal has a championing team and an action plan developed by this team and agreed to by the whole staff. We outline below some aspects of the plan for Goal 2 – Reduce discipline problems to zero by 1994.

*Goal 2: Reduce discipline problems to zero*

For the purposes of the goal, a discipline problem was to be defined as an occurrence or series of occurrences of deviant behaviour requiring intervention by an adult in the school. The event would be of a magnitude beyond the normal socialization of students and imply a failure on the part of the student(s) to comply with normal school rules. Usually, the senior members of staff would be involved. As the baseline for this goal the recorded occurrences of unacceptable behaviour for the 1990–1 school year were used. The goal would be regarded as achieved when, over any consecutive twenty-day period, the number of discipline problems according to the above criteria reaches zero.

Here is the action plan for these goals:

*Positive*

1 Super student tickets – earned for distinctive good behaviour, given by any teacher and deposited in a draw, which is made each week. The winning teacher and student get a luncheon at a local restaurant on the Friday of that week.
2 Phone parents when student does something good – one parent per day.
3 Rewards are given to pupils for achieving 5 (not necessarily consecutive), 10, 15 and 20 'zero' days – most rewards to be in terms of student free time.
4 Big rewards for achieving 20 days of consecutive time (awarded by community organizations), e.g. stereo systems, video cameras, day trips, etc.
5 More staff supervision at the lunch-time break.
6 Teachers to greet students on arrival at school and be on the door for departure thanking 'good behaving' students for their work.
7 Develop and use 'buddy' or pairs system for lunch-time play and assembly.
8 Highlight 'zero' discipline days at the end of each of these days using the school messaging system.
9 Shorter noon hours with more club-organized activities. All students stay for lunch.
10 School rules posted in simple form throughout the school and discussed in a variety of lessons.
11 During 'meet the teacher night', every teacher will hold a session for all parents to explain the strategy the school is adopting and the rules.
12 Students and staff sign individual discipline contracts.
13 Educate some parents about diet (especially sugar intake) and link to hyperactivity.
14 All students will study a social skills unit in the first 2–3 weeks of school.
15 Students will be involved in developing and refining rules. Consistent application of rules throughout the school will be monitored by the student council.

*Punitive*

16 Remove existing privileges, e.g. breaks, access to clubs, to solve small discipline problems.

17 Supervised recess detentions.
18 Ensure due process to all students during major problems. Everyone is entitled to hear what they are accused of, to have a chance to respond on their own behalf and to attempt to prove that a rule is unreasonable, arbitrary, capricious, discriminating or too vague to understand.
19 Parents will be notified of all major rule infractions.
20 Develop a school consequences chart for major problems (If this . . . then this . . .).

As can be seen, this goal (and all the others) involved everyone in the school working towards its achievement. Not all of the twenty items are new to the teachers; what is new is the concerted attempt to use these techniques collectively to achieve the goal of zero discipline.

What is important about these goals and the process used to achieve them is that there is a great deal of ownership and commitment to them at all levels. Further, the goals have been outlined in measurable terms and the school has been involved in determining how these goals can be met initially. Each crusader team will subsequently be empowered to refine the strategy and ideas so that the goals are achieved. There is no doubt that these four goals are important to this school and to all stakeholders associated with this school. As one staff member said 'this process has brought us together in a way that no other ever has.' This is a statement about alignment of energies, and also about commitment.

The purpose of Hoshin planning is to focus the energies of the organization through the creation of challenging goals to which individuals and teams feel that they can be committed. Through the setting of challenging goals, the school can achieve beyond its comfort zone – it can become more like the school of its vision statement and can propagate its strategy.

# CHAPTER
# 8

# Teams, team performance and TQM

The traditional link in many schools between those in the hierarchy with positional power and the opportunity to be creative is antipathetic to the aims and processes of TQM. For reasons already described, all of those nearest the customer – the rank and file of the organization – need to be involved in the effort for continuous improvement. All need to be empowered to work to secure vision-related goals. From this tenet comes the central importance of teams or, to describe its essential nature more directly, the self-managing work team. This chapter begins from the observation that self-managing work teams are the building blocks and innovation sources in successful TQM in organizations. It will consider the characteristics of high performing teams, key work team behaviours, stages in team development and caution about the dangers of 'group think'.

## Why teams?

TQM requires that the school regard itself as a learning organization for all of its members. That is, it is critically important that the adults who work in the school are seeking to learn about and continuously improve their work as teachers, educators and organizational members. If this is not taking place – if there is not a search for continuous improvement (what the Japanese call 'kaizen') – then the adults in the school are in danger of replicating existing performance levels rather than aiming for significant and substantial shifts in the level of 'value added' achieved.

Teams are more powerful learning entities than individuals seeking to learn on their own. Teams provide an environment in which learning can be articulated, tested, refined and examined against the needs of the organization and within the context of the learning of others. To be effective, team-based learning activity needs to be based upon the needs of the team, the needs of the individuals within the team and the needs of the organization. By articulating these three sets of needs within the team, it has been frequently demonstrated that real progress and development can take place within an organization (Liswood 1990).

Teams are, however, more than a learning organization; they are also, in effective organizations, self-managing. This means that they are able to determine their own procedures, subgoals, objectives and ways of working, providing that the goals teams set are commensurate with the outrageous goals of the organization as a whole. Putting this another way, within the parameters of the challenges faced by the organization and set by the Hoshin goal process, teams are free to work in their own way to achieve these goals within an agreed budget and an agreed schedule. Self-managing teams are empowered to achieve the outrageous goals of the organization. These latter conditions would present, as we have already indicated, a particular challenge to those schools where the TQM principle of devolution of power and resource to work teams has yet to replace the ingrained tradition of top-down control over the detail of work practices.

The third reason for encouraging the growth and development of teams within schools is that they can examine cross-functional issues more effectively than individuals acting on their own initiative. A cross-functional issue is one that affects more than one team. For example, an issue about how best to provide pastoral care and counselling within a school cuts across year groupings, discipline interests and specialist interests; by working through a cross-functional team with a clear set of goals, a deadline and a budget limit, the issue can be resolved to the satisfaction of all concerned, because the understanding of the needs and interests of each affected group is available to the team through the way in which the team is structured. Rather than decisions being based on who wins the 'turf' war within the school or on the views of those who are regarded as 'the blue-eyed favourites' of senior management, they are based on an attempt by a team to understand the needs and concerns of all and to reach a satisfactory outcome in the best interests of all.

These are the three primary reasons for seeking the development of teams as the basis for TQM development within the school. There is another, pragmatic, reason. For TQM to achieve sustainable quality improvement over time, it has to be independent of any particular individual: it has to belong to the whole organization and to groups within it. Many excellent initiatives die when their champion leaves the school for another position; innovations which are team-owned and team-sustained are far less likely to be dependent on an individual champion. By working through self-managing teams and by insisting on the development of teams within the organization, the momentum for TQM can be assured, along with its sustainability.

Put together, these four arguments for teams would appear to be very powerful. They are made even more powerful by the evidence available for the effectiveness of self-managing teams in achieving the outrageous goals and possible TQM outcomes. All of the goals listed in Chapter 7 were achieved through team work. Indeed, one of the hallmarks of effective organizations in the 1990s has been the growth and development of team-work and training through teams for organizational effectiveness. Companies such as Toyota have changed the language of the organization to reflect their commitment to teams as the basis for their work. Others are investing heavily in coaching for team playing and in team development and team learning strategies so as to ensure that teams become the building blocks for development in the organization. IBM has developed a world-wide programme to support and enhance the work of teams throughout the organization. The days of the prima donna manager who acts from the premise 'it's my way or the highway' are ending. The new rule for organizational design and effectiveness is team work. Only self-managing work teams can bring the range of professional talent, experience and perspective needed to analyse and improve the core processes of the organization.

## Characteristics of high-performing teams

The last thirty years has seen a great deal of research on the characteristics of high-performing teams. The research is remarkably consistent and reflects much about what we know about effective group work (Zander 1982). One leading figure in the field of team development and team work is Mike Woodcock – a British consultant with extensive experience of team development across a range of organizations (Woodcock 1979). Woodcock suggests that high-performing teams have a number of key characteristics, which include:

### A shared sense of purpose and vision

Team members are equally aware and committed to the work of the team in terms of its mission and values. They have a common understanding of what is expected, both in terms of outcome and in terms of the values that will inform the processes used by the team to achieve these outcomes. The team is focused and energized by this common understanding.

### Open communication

There are no hidden politics in the team. There is a great deal of direct, open and honest talk. People say what they think and they do not worry about consequences (in terms of punishment, subsequent rivalries, etc.) because they know that their comments will be understood as reflecting their genuine care and concern about the tasks faced by the team. Moreover, members will not be challenging the integrity or dignity of their colleagues within the team. While the communication will be honest and direct, it will also be respectful and focused.

### Trust and mutuality

Effective teams demonstrate a great deal of mutual respect, trust and understanding between members. They show a high level of mutual understanding and shared assumptions, yet can also be very argumentative and challenging (indeed, they need to be challenging to be sustainable). What 'binds' the team is its sense of responsibility both for the process it is using and for the task and the trust the individual members have in each others' skills, judgement and knowledge.

### Useful creative conflict

Not all team meetings and discussions are 'friendly' and 'nice': some will be tough and demanding, many will be stretching the knowledge and skills of those involved and some will examine issues that are difficult to resolve. Within the TQM approach, the level of trust and mutual respect, coupled with the extent of the shared values and vision, means that these conflicts are powerful, valuable and valued. They are the conflicts that will make the difference between the team being 'sound' and it being 'exceptional'. By striving to achieve beyond the comfort zone of the team, the team is able to develop strategies, solutions and processes that take it (and consequently the school) to new levels of achievement. Further, having engaged in a useful conflict and having used this conflict to make real progress in its thinking, the team actively seeks to learn from this conflict in terms of how it can improve its own thinking and ways of working. Rather than being avoided, conflict is regarded as both an essential and satisfying aspect of the work of the team. Another key component here is the idea that constructive conflict results from the team having a diversity of skills, backgrounds and styles of working available to it. Effective teams balance a number of different styles of working within their boundaries so that they can take advantage of different ways of working and viewing problems, something we explore below.

### Appropriate working methods

The most frequent complaints we hear from teachers about schools concerns the poor communication, lack of consultation and the waste of time inherent in some staff meetings. The working method adopted is usually the same for all problems and usually involves a small number of people (usually the same people) talking 'at' a large number of others.

Effective teams have effective ways of working. These methods will vary according to the problem in hand and to the interests and skills of the people in the team. These working methods will be discussed openly as being as important as the outcome (because process drives outcome) and will be regarded as opportunities for the team to learn how to best manage its work. Team members will always have full and complete access to all information; will know who is doing what and by when their work is expected; will know what resources are available to them; will know when the team is expected to work with others and will have a sense of what other teams in the organization are doing and how their work may (or may not) have an impact on their own work.

Effective teams also keep good records of what they have agreed to, what they have agreed not to do and how they have been working. They are also highly efficient in the way in which they manage time.

This may sound elementary and basic, yet it is surprising how many schools do some or all of these things poorly.

*Appropriate leadership*

Teams will generally have a chairperson responsible for the routines of meetings – ensuring that they take place, acting as a facilitator, making sure that issues are followed up and dealt with. But leadership in effective teams is largely determined by the situation (Schön 1984). Rather than being based on status in the organizational hierarchy, or upon length of service, it is based on the ability to lead the team through the issue or concerns or activity that is at the forefront of their work at that moment in time. For some teams, this leadership role will be exercised by one or two people for the duration of the life of the team. In others, leadership will be more varied because of the varied nature of their work. The key point here is that the team is not dominated by its leader – the leadership role is more facilitative, coaching oriented and developmental than instructional or controlling.

*Regular review and reflection*

As part of their process, effective teams will stop working on a task from time to time and review the quality of their ways of working. That is, they will undertake a process review aimed at how they work and what they could do to improve their ways of working. Never content to fall into a rhythm of familiar working method, the team asks 'What else could we do to make the way we work as a team more effective?'

Effective teams ask this question on a regular basis, not only when they are experiencing some difficulty in working or when the work of the team is completed. They review their own effectiveness systematically and periodically, and in their own terms.

### Enabling and encouraging individual development

To be effective, the team relies upon the knowledge and competencies of each of its members. If the team is to develop over time, then it has to encourage the individuals in the team to attend to their own needs for development. Another way of looking at this feature of effective teamwork is to say that the individual is never totally submerged in the work of the team – their own work and individual development remains important: without it, the team will experience atrophy. The implication is that the team has to start to develop an ability to help individuals recognize their needs for development and facilitate the professional and personal development needed. The team may need financial resources to assist in this work.

### Sound links with other teams

No team is an island within an organization. For the school as a whole to be achieving excellence and leadership in its chosen strategy, all teams in the school need to have a level of connectedness appropriate to the task in hand. Effective teams link themselves to other teams, share ideas and concerns, exchange ways of working that they have found to be effective and create cross-functional links whenever appropriate.

Teams within the organization do not spend their time fighting each other – this a destructive use of energy and is generally unproductive. Rather, they spend their time looking for 'win–win' advantages for teams through effective working relationships.

Our experience of facilitating teams within schools and other organizations suggests two other team requirements in addition to those outlined above. First, there is the key element of fun and comradeship. Teams that work well and are high achieving, are usually ones to which people look forward to, have fun while working and share highs and lows in a way that develops comradeship and affinity among team members. This comradeship binds the team but does not inhibit confrontation, useful conflict or challenge. What this espirit de corps does do is to ensure that the trust and mutuality component is high.

The second element we have observed in highly effective teams is the celebration of success and failure. The team itself rewards the work of its members by acknowledging their attempts to achieve, whether or not the attempt is successful. Using simple recognition devices (parties, stickers, small gifts, amusing honorary titles within the team, lapel pins and badges, etc.) the team recognizes effort and seeks to learn from both success and failure in an active way. Some have questioned the celebration of failure. Peters (1989) suggests that a team who does not fail from time to time is not trying – it is always playing safe. Occasional small failures should be celebrated for three reasons: (i) they represent the team's genuine and well-intentioned attempt to do something constructive; (ii) they provide an opportunity for significant learning (all problems are treasures from which we can improve); and (iii) the fact that the team supports its members who try (even though they failed) will encourage others to try.

## Valuing diversity within a team

Following the work of Carl Jung (1923), there has been a great deal of interest in the variety of styles within which people work. The interest extends to understanding team dynamics and quality in terms of the variety of styles needed for a team to be truly effective. The core question in this work is 'What is it about the style of working used by a person that can enhance the work of the team?' A related question is 'What kind of personal styles do we need to recruit to a team in order that the team will be effective?'

These questions have been explored, in their early work, by Barnard (1938); Brown (1960) and others. Belbin (1981) identified different team roles – such as the shaper, worker, resource investigator, challenger – and their value to the success of team work, and these are frequently measured using a variety of personal profile instruments, some of which are based on Jungian archetypes of personality (as measured by the Myer's Briggs Type Indicator) or some sociological features of the organization of effective teams.

### Key work team behaviours

Mergerison and McCann (1985) have extended the essentially sociological work of Belbin by examining the roles actually played in highly effective teams. They identified nine critical functional roles – essential tasks that need to be undertaken if the group is to be effective and efficient in completing its assignment. These nine roles (or types of work) were:

1 *Advising*. Gathering information and disseminating it to others. Ensuring that the necessary information is gathered from all possible sources and presented in a form useful for decison-making.

2 *Innovating*. Going beyond the state of the art and creating a new way of thinking or working that will change or advance the activity for which the team is responsible.

3 *Promoting*. Many good ideas and innovations are lost because they are not 'sold' well to others (many of whom developed the ideas that are now being 'improved'). An effective team has among its members some-one who is able to take innovative ideas and present them to others in a way that is both compelling and non-threatening.

4 *Developing*. Many innovators are poor at detailed work – they need others to fill in the blanks and develop the detailed specifications and procedures that will make their ideas work. In addition, many inno-vations can be achieved by several different routes, with the developer within the team outlining the specifications for alternatives and advis-ing on the best and most efficient way of turning an idea into action.

5 *Organizing*. Plans are one thing, action is another. Once the innovation becomes a fully worked specification, someone needs to organize its actual implementation.

6 *Producing*. Someone needs to do the work associated with the idea and the development work that has taken place. This person or group also needs to sustain this work over time.

7 *Inspecting*. So that the quality of the work is maintained and so that the opportunity for quality improvement can be built into the work of the team, someone needs to spend time looking at the 'output' of the team so as to ensure consistency, quality and adaptability to changing circumstances.

8 *Maintaining*. So that all of the diverse functions in the team can be effec-tive, and so that the work of the team can be maintained, the team needs a person with a commitment to both team and activity maintenance.

9 *Linker*. This is the co-ordinator and manager of all of this work – the leadership and facilitation role within the team.

These behaviours can be combined, with some playing two or three of the parts outlined here at different stages in the development of a task. What is critical, is that these tasks are performed effectively in a self-managed team. Weak teams or teams that fail often do not have individuals able to perform these roles or, if they do, these individuals cannot perform these roles effectively. One difference between the Belbin frame and that out-lined here is precisely that a person can perform more than one of the behaviours required in the work of the team.

Individuals within teams bring their psychological work styles to the work of the team. Some are more naturally lateral thinkers or more creative than others, who find advising and summarizing the work of others to be more satisfying (the adviser–explorer dimension). Others prefer to work on the organizing–controlling aspects of the work of the team –

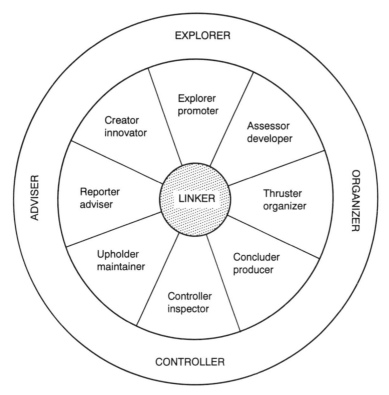

*Fig. 8.1*   The team management wheel (from Mergerison and McCann 1985).

detailed planning, inspecting, implementing, etc. When we add these dimensions to our understanding of team roles, it becomes possible to construct a model of the effective team that fully reflects the needed roles and personal styles of team members. Figure 8.1 shows the model developed by Mergerison and McCann (1985).

The eight double-barrelled types in the middle of this wheel refer to the role styles that individuals bring to the team, while the outer ring refers primarily to the psychological orientation the person brings to the work of the team. The wheel represents the behaviour styles needed within a team for it to be highly effective. It also represents the balance of skills that are needed within a team if it is to be high-performing. In selecting team members or in looking at team development needs, the idea is that the team should be able to handle these roles and styles from among its membership. These roles do not have to be available to the team in equal proportions.

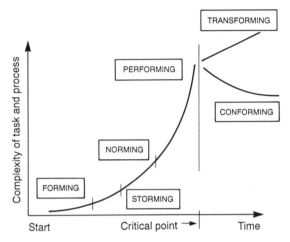

*Fig. 8.2*   Stages of team development (from Truckman and Jensen 1977).

## Stages of development of effective teams

Teams, once formed, are unlikely to be effective from day one: they need time to mature and develop. Even when many of the team members know each other well from other activities and settings, a new team with a new task is likely to take time to settle into its work.

Most authorities on group and team development recognize that there are several stages to the growth and development of teams. Most typically, there are seen to be five stages of team development (Fig. 8.2).

The idea of this framework is to identify the stages of development that teams pass through on the road to high performance, using as the staging points those moments at which the team is most vulnerable to failure.

The first stage is referred to as forming. At this stage the focus is upon defining goals and procedures that will enable the team to function effectively in a way that maximizes the talents, skills and interests of all members. This stage is usually a difficult one. Members of the team tend to: (i) keep feelings to themselves until they know more about others in the team, the situation of the team within the school as a whole and the real nature of the task in hand; (ii) act more secure than they actually feel; (iii) behave with a degree of insecurity about both the nature of the task and their own roles within the team; and (iv) hide animosity to others while focusing upon personal gain.

The politeness and symmetry of early team meetings soon gives way to storming. At this stage, conflicts emerge over roles, tasks and behaviours. Strong feelings begin to be expressed about the task, the way the team is working and the roles individuals are playing in the team. It is a time of considerable vulnerability in the team. The most important feature of this stage is to work through the issues, not to avoid them: through engaging directly in the understanding of the issues and the nature of the conflicts that are emerging, the team can become stronger.

As the team works through these issues it begins to accept its methods and its understanding of its own work as its norms – it is in the norming stage of its development. The key characteristic of this stage is acceptance – of roles, tasks, ways of working and diversity within the team. During this stage, a sense of shared responsibility and cohesiveness emerges.

Once norming is achieved, the team starts performing. Because understanding of roles and responsibilities is now high, the team becomes both effective and efficient in understanding how it can best meet the challenges set for it. It engages the skills and talents of individuals working through the team so as to respond to its purposes.

Once it becomes effective, there is a fifth stage where the team is again vulnerable. Its vulnerability arises from the choice between settling into a safe route (conforming) and continuing to perform as it has always done or choosing to re-examine all of its work in the light of the need for constant improvement (transforming). Many teams in education have settled for the safe option of conforming. Over time, performance levels stabilize into acceptable but not optimum levels – growth and energy decline as performance becomes comfortable. The alternative is to find ways of challenging and renewing the work of the team so that it can continually perform at increasingly high levels and transform its work from being acceptable to being outstanding.

## Maturity and self-management

As teams mature and become high-performing, they are entrusted with increasing responsibility. In some organizations, team maturity is seen as an index for the degree of self-management they are permitted. Table 8.1, based on the work of Hellriegel *et al.* (1992) suggests nine levels of autonomy for a team. As teams mature and gain respect within the school, they will pass from a low to a higher level.

In many schools, the level of team autonomy does not change over time. Once again, the model appears to be that the development of the team within the school is 'stuck' and is held at a certain point by history and circumstance. This is a choice schools are making, although often it is an unconscious one. By thinking differently about the way in which the school operates in terms of its team quality and in terms of the autonomy given to teams within the school, significant performance gains can be made. In many organizations, the growth of team work and the enhancement of team autonomy has lead to very significant performance gains over time.

*Table 8.1*    Levels of team autonomy

| Decision type | Level |
|---|---|
| Team can directly influence its Hoshin goals | 9 |
| Team can directly influence its process goals | 8 |
| Team can add additional tasks and goals to its work | 7 |
| Team decides when it will work and its timetable for completion | 6 |
| Team decides how it will work | 5 |
| Team determines who will work on the team and when new members will be recruited | 4 |
| Team makes its own decisions about leadership | 3 |
| Team members individually decide how they will perform their own jobs | 2 |
| Team members have almost no influence on decisions about how the team will function | 1 |

## The danger of group-think

One characteristic of teams within a school system is that they are very similar, both within a region and between one region and another. While there are small (and sometimes significant) differences between one team and another, one is more often struck by their similarities than their dissimilarities. One way of conceptualizing the cultural similarities of teams within schools is to look at the cohesiveness of schooling as a process.

To some extent, teaching and schooling have become stereotypical. Through a process of collective rationalization and self-censorship of deviations from what might be termed 'normative' schooling, the task of teaching and the nature of schooling is seen to be grossly similar from one organization to another. While there are differences – and some are significant – between teaching and schooling from one school to another, the similarities are greater than the differences in many cases. There is therefore an illusion of unanimity among educators about the task of teaching and the nature of schooling. We refer to this as an illusion precisely because there are examples of schools that have adopted radically different teaching and organizational strategies with powerful effects, but most schools adopt very similar strategies and tactics, exemplifying this unanimity.

One further feature of schooling needs to be mentioned here. There are, in each community and in many schools, self-appointed guardians of the traditions of the school. These can be teachers, parents or community members. They have high regard for the school and its past achievements and believe that the future will best be managed by reference to the past. They serve to protect the school from adverse information that might shatter or challenge the illusion of unanimity about the effectiveness of the school and its ways of working.

These features of schooling – collective rationalization, stereotype views, self-censorship, illusion of unanimity and self-appointed guardians – can become characteristics of group-think within and between schools about what schools can be and become. This is not inevitable, but it is a danger. The most likely danger arises within a team that sees little alternative to doing things as they have always been done. Indeed, group-think begins within a school: when all teams begin to see maintaining their ways of working as more important than finding new and more effective ways of working, or when these teams rationalize their proposals in terms of being 'no worse than anyone else'.

Some danger signs of group-think can be identified. We list five here:

1 *Incomplete surveys of alternatives.* The team within the school does not look at different ways of working or at ways of working adopted in different settings (i.e. health, industry) when considering a problem or a task. It simply looks for examples that reinforce the current ways of working within the school. This usually shows itself in a lack of contingency planning within a school.
2 *Incomplete surveys of goals.* When faced with a task or challenge, the team takes the line of 'least resistance' and seeks to minimize the value of the problem or task in terms of developing the school through the adoption of a wide range of goals.
3 *Failure to examine risks.* Group-think arises in two ways here. First, the team does not consider fully the risks inherent in maintaining current ways of working. Second, the team can fail to examine fully the risks inherent in its proposals for change.
4 *Poor information search.* This is strongly linked to the three features just mentioned. Group-think can occur when the team restricts its search for information. For example, when faced with a major challenge about student behavioural problems, does the team ask questions of counterparts in other occupations (e.g. social work, hospitals, child welfare) and other countries, or does it rely on its local network? Given the increasing ease of global communication, the potential for change and development of effective schooling through a more global search for knowledge is growing.
5 *Selective bias in processing information.* The achievement of outrageous goals by a team requires a great deal of hard work and commitment. In addition, risk-taking and uncertainty will need to be tolerated. Group-think teams may seek to avoid these challenges by looking for the 'quick-fix',

'least-resistance' response and will bias their reading of the available information accordingly.

If teams display these characteristics then there is a danger that the team is engaging in group-think and is not making the best use of available information or the talents of its members – the team is under-performing.

High-performing organizations are collections of high-performing teams. Whether it is Boeing's teams working on the design and construction of the Boeing 777, Ford's teams working on the design and development of its 2000-series cars and trucks or a school team working on reducing the time taken to achieve certain literacy standards in elementary (primary) schools – teams are the key vehicles for meeting challenging and demanding goals and sustaining their performance over time. Teams are the building blocks of organizations.

As TQM becomes more widely implemented, the success of self-managing teams in achieving outstanding performance becomes more evident. There is a growing realization that effective organizational development will come through increasing the sense of autonomy felt by workers in managing their own activities in terms of the Hoshin goals of the organization. If they are to respond to the challenges outlined in the early part of this book, schools need to look at their design in terms of teamwork. Only through increasing the autonomy of the individual school and the teams within that school can we unleash the power of the professionals working in these in organizations. The answers to the challenging questions for education rest not in the minds of ministers and their advisers but with teachers and their students. By empowering them to create success through their own self-managing work teams schools might substantially exceed the current levels of success.

# 9

# Daily management tools for effective TQM

> In God we trust – all others must use data!
> Anon

Some people have seen TQM as essentially about measurement: through measuring outputs we can ensure quality. This in part explains the growing interest in performance indicators in education and the assumption that these indicators speak to both quality and value for money. As we have shown, however, TQM is not concerned just with the outcomes of schooling, but with the whole nature of schooling as a process and experience for all staff, students and stakeholders. TQM is a comprehensive approach to the management of well-being and effectiveness in organizations, so that the organization can achieve sustainable steep-slope quality improvement.

While the whole strategy is what makes the difference to performance, some aspects of TQM do concern 'hard' data and information, but these are often misunderstood. The critical issue is: how can we collect good information so that we can make good decisions? The focus and emphasis is upon making decisions, not measurement.

In many schools, decisions are made on the basis of one or more of the following: (i) 'it seemed to work last time, let's assume it will again . . .'; (ii) 'I have heard that this worked well somewhere else . . .'; (iii) 'we could try this . . .'; (iv) 'I have heard a rumour that this is what we are expected to do . . .'; or (v) 'I think we should do this, don't ask me what the full consequences will be, but this is my best guess . . .'. Decisions are rarely made on the basis of a full and systematic evaluation of the options, and it is even rarer that changes are made on the basis of systematic and skilled data-based evaluation.

It is no different in industry. Many companies make decisions on the basis of inference, innuendo, imaginative leaps of faith and rumour. Decision scientists, who specialize in information systems and their development, frequently lament the failure of organizations to make well-informed and rational decisions, seeming to prefer instead to make decisions that are poorly informed and quasi-rational (Meyer and Boone 1989). Some of the major marketing and product development disasters of our time – the Ford Edsel, the IBM PC/jnr, Coca Cola's launch of the New Coke in 1985 and Bell's launch of the viewphone in 1972 – are multi-million dollar examples of the consequences of poor thinking and infor-mation collection. In all of these cases, and in the case of many other 'poor' decisions in industry, the critical decisions were made by those furthest from the customer and with the least understanding of the practical impli-cations of what they were deciding.

The tools of TQM are designed to help teams within an organization think more critically about the problems they face and the practices in which they daily engage. They are thinking-clarification tools. They are in-tended to aid the task of daily management by: (i) systematically examin-ing what is happening in the organization; (ii) standardizing 'best' practice within the work of the team; (iii) pointing out the possibilities for contin-uous improvement by facilitating the systematic scrutiny of practice within a team; and (iv) recording progress towards the achievement of measur-able goals. The classic tools of TQM are thinking tools. Where measure-ment is used, it is as an aid to understanding and decision-making, not as an end in itself.

In this chapter we outline an approach to systematic thinking and measurement that is intended to aid the task of daily management in TQM. There is not the space in a book of this kind to outline all of the measure-ment skills and thinking tools that may be required by an effective team seeking to fully implement TQM. We introduce key skills and point to relevant sources of valuable information and ideas about other skills that an effective team will need. What should be clear from this chapter is that schools need to invest in the development of thinking and analytical skills (including measurement) for all of their stakeholders if they are to make the best use of the imaginations and skills of those wishing to support the implementation of TQM, the achievement of goals and the fulfilment of the strategic vision of the school.

### Six reasons to invest in thinking and measuring

There are essentially six functions that a team needs to perform for which it needs clear and lateral thinking and some form of systematic approach to the collection and use of information.

1 *Collect basic information*. Before tackling a problem, a team needs good basic information about the extent, dynamics and nature of the problem. For example, if a school wants to tackle truancy an effective team needs information about truancy within the school over time (preferably over many years), by age, by time of day, by gender, by ability and by predictability. It may also need to examine the truants' own explanation for their behaviour. Rather than assuming that it knows all of these things, an effective team would collect the relevant information and develop insights on the basis of actual rather than assumed data.

2 *Convert ideas and information into measures*. Many good ideas are implemented with a 'let's wait and see what happens' approach – often good data about the idea, is not collected in a way that helps modify the idea, and the evaluation is often more subjective than it needs to be. If ideas are converted into measurable goals and the measures are taken frequently, then progress towards achieving the goal (and hence making the idea a reality) can be systematic. A team seeking to improve discipline in school could look directly at the impact of specific strategies if they devised ways of measuring these impacts – by doing so, they could secure wide-based support for effective ideas.

3 *Analysing processes*. When a team has the task of securing process improvements, it will often need to examine and understand the process, and to do this in a more objective way than has been the case hitherto. Using process mapping and other tools, the team can get inside its processes and better understand them.

4 *Designing improved processes*. Understanding a process is the first step to improving it. New thinking and analytical tools, such as the systems archetypes of Senge (1990) and the 'thinking hats' of de Bono (1987), can be used to seek improvements to processes and achieve steep-slope quality improvement.

5 *Establish standards*. For a team to implement change successfully, it needs to establish targets for both its work and the staging points for achieving major gains in its performance (this by date $x$, then this by date $y$ . . .).

6 *Manage performance*. Having achieved an acceptable level of performance against its established standards, the team needs to record how this is achieved (describe its effective process) and sustained. A failure to achieve this function may lead the work of the team to be temporary rather than permanent.

The discerning reader will notice that these six functions are circular. As soon as function six is reached, it is time to collect data and begin the process all over again. This is why these six functions are critical to successful TQM implementation: they are steps in the search for continuous improvement.

Table 9.1 Thinking and measuring tools and their uses in TQM

| Tool | Collect information | Convert to measures | Analyse process | Improve process | Set standards | Manage performance |
|---|---|---|---|---|---|---|
| Archetypes of systems (Senge) | ✓ | | | | | |
| Affinity diagram (Walton) | ✓ | | | | | |
| Arrow diagram (Mizuno) | ✓ | | ✓ | ✓ | | ✓ |
| Benchmarking (Camp) | | ✓ | ✓ | | ✓ | ✓ |
| Brainstorming (de Bono) | ✓ | | ✓ | ✓ | | |
| Cause–effect diagram (Walton) | ✓ | ✓ | ✓ | ✓ | | |
| Charts and graphs (Walton) | ✓ | | ✓ | | | |
| Check sheets (Walton) | ✓ | | ✓ | | | |
| Control charts (Oakland) | ✓ | | ✓ | | ✓ | ✓ |
| Cost–Benefit analysis (Oakland) | ✓ | | ✓ | | ✓ | ✓ |
| Five whys (Murgatroyd/Morgan) | ✓ | | ✓ | | | |
| Force field analysis | ✓ | | ✓ | ✓ | | |
| Histograms (Walton/Oakland) | ✓ | ✓ | ✓ | ✓ | ✓ | ✓ |
| House of quality (Murgatroyd/Morgan) | ✓ | ✓ | ✓ | ✓ | ✓ | ✓ |
| Mental mapping (Senge) | ✓ | ✓ | | ✓ | | |
| Pareto charts (Walton) | ✓ | ✓ | ✓ | ✓ | | ✓ |
| Process decision programme charts (PDPC) (Mizuno) | ✓ | | | | | |
| Process mapping (Murgatroyd/Morgan) | ✓ | ✓ | ✓ | ✓ | ✓ | ✓ |
| Run charts (Walton) | ✓ | ✓ | ✓ | | ✓ | ✓ |
| Sampling (Oakland) | ✓ | ✓ | | | ✓ | ✓ |
| Scatter diagram (Walton) | ✓ | | ✓ | ✓ | | |
| Six thinking hats (de Bono) | | | ✓ | ✓ | | |
| Six action shoes (de Bono) | | | | ✓ | | |
| Systematic diagram (Mizuno) | ✓ | ✓ | ✓ | ✓ | ✓ | ✓ |
| Three MUs (Murgatroyd/Morgan) | ✓ | | ✓ | ✓ | | |

## Tools for thinking and measuring by teams

Teams need skills to collect basic information; convert ideas, information and plans into measures; analyse processes; design process improvements; establish standards and manage performance. What are the tools and skills that the team can develop to implement these requirements? One key criterion to be applied in answering this question is that the tools selected by the team should aid the development of the team, while at the same time contributing to the achievement of team goals.

Given these six functions within a team for the use and development of thinking and measuring skills, what are the tools and skills that the team can develop? Table 9.1 is intended to indicate the kinds of tools a team can access. The list is comprehensive, but not exhaustive.

A variety of texts describe in detail exactly how these tools work, with examples provided from industry applications. Those working in schools will need to look carefully at these texts and examine the ways in which they can be helpful in developing the work of their team and in achieving the Hoshin goals set for them within the school. Especially valuable are those by Walton (1986), Oakland (1986, 1989), de Bono (1987, 1991), Mizuno (1988), Camp (1989) and Senge (1990).

In this chapter we provide a brief overview of each of the tools outlined here and suggest their applicability to the work of TQM and the school. The tools can become very complex and elaborate. There are no quick ways to adopt them and begin to use them on a wide scale: it takes time. More critically, the use of the tools has to become embodied in the culture of the organization and is part of the organization's way of communicating, both within and between teams. One key criterion for selecting a tool should be that its use aids the development of the team, while at the same time contributes to the achievement of the teams goals. That is, the tool must have process value as well as outcome value.

When used well and effectively, the thinking and measurement tools we outline here can make a significant and substantive contribution to the work of teams. In particular, they can:

1 Focus energy on appropriate and validated concerns.
2 Engender a spirit of systematic and continuous inquiry within a team – an essential prerequisite to continuous improvement efforts.
3 Provide a systematic basis for effective dialogue.
4 Support change and the achievement of Hoshin goals.
5 Minimize the personality basis for debate and argument in teams and maximize the data-based quality of the arguments.

When they have these consequences, these tools are powerful and effective.

The following sections describe and illustrate the relevance of all of the tools included in Table 9.1. Our aim in doing this is to provide an outline sufficient for readers to determine which tools may be of value and how best to begin the process of using them. The descriptions are not comprehensive, but basic. Readers should refer to the sources cited for more detailed accounts of the tools and their utility.

### Archetypes of systems

Systems thinking was developed as a means by which the complexity of processes within society could be simplified. The aim of systems theory is to develop an understanding of the properties and dynamics of naturally occurring events, which aids our ability to understand these events and affect them (von Bertalanffy, 1968). Systems theory has been used in the study of family systems, in organizations, social trends and problems and in the study of technological problems.

A key assumption of systems theory is that naturally occurring systems have implicit systemic features that, once understood, can enable us to better manage these systems. Senge (1990) suggests that there are ten implicit systems features, one or more of which will be present in a system. These ten are:

1 *Balancing processes with delay.* A teacher or group within a school acting towards a goal, adjusts their behaviour in response to delayed feedback. If they are not fully aware of their use of this mechanism, they will take more corrective action than is called for by the situation or (rarely) give up because they cannot see real progress being made.

   For example, in response to perceived discipline problems with a particular year group, the staff of a school agree to get really tough with and dramatically increase their rates of detention and suspension for this group. This had the effect of creating many parental challenges to the authority of the teachers and to the regime of the school. In the long-term, this response is too severe given the actual nature of the problem these teachers faced – it created more problems than it was trying to solve.

2 *Limits to growth.* A process feeds on itself and produces rapid (exponential) growth or expansion. The growth then slows down (much to the surprise and dismay of those concerned) and goes into reverse. It then becomes a case of 'the more we change, the more we stay the same'.

   For example, a school suddenly finds a very successful way of marketing itself. Student numbers grow annually by a significant figure – above 10 per cent. As it does so, the school finds it more and more difficult to sustain its ways of working and to give students the individualized attention on which its reputation (and marketing strategy) were based. As parents become more aware of these difficulties, numbers suddenly decline and then begin to 'free fall'.

3 *Shifting the burden.* A problem is 'fixed' by a short-term solution with positive and quick results. While many recognize that this solution is

short-term and that a longer term solution must be found, the veracity of the short-term 'fix' is such that their willingness to engage in the work needed for the long-term solution atrophies. The quick fix becomes permanent and the long-term fix is avoided.

For example, a school finds that more and more of its students are spending an extra year taking final year (Grade 12 or sixth form) courses. They do this to give them better grades for the increasingly difficult college and university entrance requirements. Rather than looking at re-designing the way in which the last two years of schooling are designed and managed, the school finds ways of making it easier to stay on for an extra year.

4 *Shifting the burden to the intervenor.* When an organization uses a consultant to solve problems, it will often shift the problem burden to this person. In doing so, the organization can 'disable' itself – render itself incapable of solving the problem without the help of this person. When this occurs, it is known as 'shifting the burden to the intervenor'.

For example, a school in South Wales asked one of the authors of this book to help solve problems in the design and delivery of pastoral care services in the school. For four years after the initial intervention the school sought this person's help each time there were problems in its pastoral care and counselling work.

5 *Eroding goals.* This is similar to shifting the burden, except that the focus here is upon goals rather than problem-solving. In this system, as the quick fix appears effective, then goals are revised downwards so as to minimize the effort involved in securing the more challenging goals. This is a serious system 'defect' of organizations pursuing Hoshin goals – it is much easier (and 'safer') to accept a less demanding, easier-to-attain goal than to enter into the challenge and discomfort of outrageous goals.

For example, a school set itself the goal of reducing the time taken to secure reading abilities at the age 8 level so that all students aged 6 or 7 could read at this level without exception. Significant success was achieved with this programme, except for a cluster of students who found reading difficult. Rather than work with these students in a customized programme, the school revised its goal to be 'for all those committed to reading, this school will ensure that they are able to read a year ahead of their age group . . .' – by making their guarantee of performance conditional, they eroded the original goal in favour of something safer.

6 *Escalation.* For one person to 'win' in an organization they feel that another person has to 'loose'. If the other 'wins' then there is a need for the person who has lost to be seen to win a greater advantage through aggressively pursuing their own goals. Often each side will see their defensive behaviour as a natural response to the 'aggressive' behaviour of the other – one Leeds United soccer player used to say 'I always get

my retaliation in first'. These situations can escalate quickly and often become major conflicts.

For example, a school was very split over the Principal's plan to integrate computers into all teaching at all levels of the school by 1995. Advocates of this position were demanding more and more of the scarce resources of the school. To fight back, those who opposed this development asked for more and more non-computing resources and professional development time. The battle escalated over a three-year period to a point at which available and scarce resources were being dissipated at an increasingly faster rate each year.

7 *Success to the successful.* When two activities compete for scarce resources and one wins, the winner increases the chances of securing subsequent resources, leaving the one who 'lost' struggling for recognition and resources. As time passes, more comes to the successful than to the loser of the first pass at resource allocations.

For example, two Principals propose new curriculum delivery plans, which require capital expenditure, to the same School Board. The Board funds one and not the other. As each year passes, the initially funded school secures more and more resources, always at the expense of the school that failed to secure the cash the first time round. The staff of this 'under-resourced' school become increasingly demoralized, while the staff of the 'resourced' school engage in ever more demanding work.

8 *Tragedy of the commons.* A school has had a history of being well resourced and has allocated these resources on the basis of the declared individual needs of teachers. However, resources are becoming more scarce, so the teachers intensify their efforts to secure resources as a statement of their own determination not to be affected by the reductions in budgets and resources. Doing this speeds up the problems in the school, meaning that the resources become allocated and used much more quickly now than ever before. A crisis develops, making it difficult for the leadership within the school to secure changes in the process of resource allocation. By not insisting on systematic resource constraints or moving to re-allocation of resources as the basis for resource allocation once the problems became evident, the leadership of the school has lost its ability to manage the allocation of resources effectively.

9 *Fixes that fail.* A quick fix that deals with a problem in the here and now has unforeseen long-term consequences, which may require even more use of the fix. A common example is that of individuals who borrow money to pay off their credit card debts, thereby ensuring that they will have to pay out more interest later. For a school, fixing a discipline problem that could have been fixed through a programme of social skills training, by suspension, could lead to the increasing use of suspension for 'offences' that otherwise might not have led to this punishment.

10 *Growth and under-investment.* A school is very successful and really needs to invest in new equipment, staff and buildings if it is to sustain its growth over time. However, the longer it delays making these decisions, the less likely it is that the growth will continue. So as to justify this under investment, goals and aspirations within the school are lowered.

How do we use these archetypes? First, they can be used to analyse the past history of a process – which one of these archetypes best describes what has happened to a particular process within the school? For example, looking at the school's response to truancy. Was this response a fix that failed? Did they first 'shift the burden' and then later 'shift the burden to the intervenor'? Second, the archetypes can be used as a way of checking proposals for change – are you proposing an escalation or to balance a process with delay? Finally, they are valuable ways of looking critically at the underlying processes of the school as part of any major review. We have presented these archetypes briefly, and with examples to illuminate their nature. One or more of these systems archetypes is likely to be at work at the school in a way that affects the performance of the organization. By examining the problems faced by a team at work in the school in terms of these archetypes – a way of making mental maps of problems explicit – the underlying structure of the problem being tackled can be examined. Senge (1990) presents some diagrams that represent these archetypes and, from experience, the more familiar team members are with these archetypes the quicker they can be recognized and the work of the team altered by this recognition.

### Affinity diagram

This is a visual way of representing connections between ideas. Developed by Kawakita Jiro (which is why it is sometimes referred to as a KJ diagram), the tool is powerful in representing clusters of ideas and their connectivities. The procedure for using the affinity diagram is simple:

1 The team decides on its focus. In our example here, we have chosen cycle time.
2 The team then collects narrative data. In our example, this would be about the ways in which time is poorly used in the school and the ways in which additional time would be used if it became available.
3 The narrative data is then transferred onto cards. Each card represents a key idea – for example, waiting for people to arrive is a key idea.
4 The cards are then sorted into groups or clusters of similar (like-minded) ideas.
5 The cards are then labelled with the key idea or implicit idea that binds all of the cards in the cluster. For example, all of the cards involving waiting could be clustered under the heading 'idle time'.

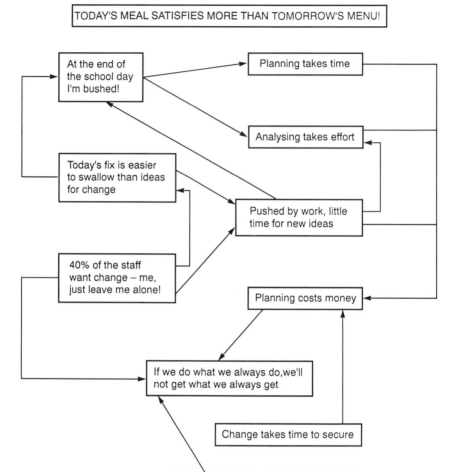

*Fig. 9.1* Affinity diagram – resistance to change.

6 Arrows are then drawn, which show the links between one cluster of ideas and another.

7 The team then presents its ideas to others and tests its understanding of problems.

The affinity diagram is most useful when the team: (i) is uncertain about the facts and the problem is hard to understand in all of its implications; (ii) there is a need to set-up thoughts systematically before entering into a more detailed and objective analysis; (iii) thoughts about the problem in hand are varied and need to be examined in depth; (iv) pre-existing ideas and assumptions make it difficult to achieve Hoshin goals – there is or has been group-think; (v) there is little unity in the team and the team needs to focus its energies to make progress; and (vi) the leadership of the school needs to listen to staff explain what a problem is and how it might be tackled.

Figure 9.1 is a simple affinity diagram developed by a group of school administrators looking at resistance to change within their school. The diagram they developed had a total of 56 cards – we show here only a fraction of their ideas. They said that the process really helped their understanding of this problem and helped to clarify the way in which some of their attempts to solve this problem had failed and how they had unwittingly fallen into some of the system archetype problems identified earlier in this chapter.

## Arrow diagram

The arrow diagram is a way of showing a process visually. It is used extensively in project management and computer systems development as a way of showing the stages and steps in a process. It is especially useful in: (i) fine-tuning a process so that all involved with it understand; (ii) systematically recording a standardized procedure; (iii) changing a procedure and showing the full effects of the change; (iv) highlighting key areas in the process where delays or problems can occur. Arrow diagrams are increasingly used in many descriptions of process flows (they are also known as flow diagrams): the more complex the process, the more valuable the diagram.

Figure 9.2 shows the process a student should use when appealing a grade at a school in British Columbia. The process is taken from the student handbook and is written for students to use.

Imagine an arrow diagram for the most complex processes in the school, for example, timetabling decisions, examination arrangements and budget processes. Constructing them often highlights problems. In addition, their construction provides a basis for training others and for standardizing good practice.

## Benchmarking

Setting benchmarks for performance is a critical process in successful TQM implementation. There are essentially two kinds of benchmarks: (i) those that reflect what the school is currently capable of – we can call these service guarantees; and (ii) those that state what the school is aiming at. Benchmarks can cover such things as response time for queries and concerns from parents; time between student enrolment in a course and mastering key skills; the time taken by a teacher to receive, grade, comment on and return a work assignment from a student; the skill levels to be

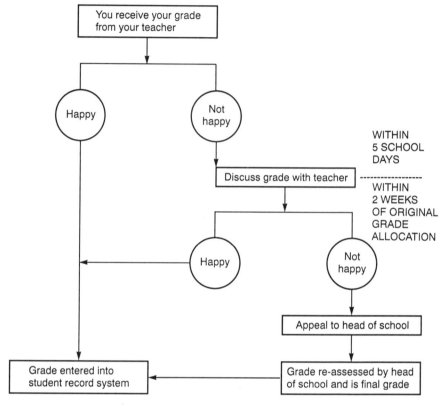

*Fig. 9.2*  Arrow diagram – grade appeals.

attained by students during a course (expressed in terms of time). Benchmarks are most useful when: (i) there is a specific and recognized gap between the performance of the school and the expectations of primary stakeholders; (ii) the team associated with a task wishes to set performance targets; and (iii) the team is seeking to re-think a process and wishes to work backwards from what the process will achieve (benchmark) to how this work will be completed.

Benchmarking can be achieved in many different ways (Camp, 1989). The following, however, are the basic steps:

1 Establish precisely what the problem is (use affinity diagrams and other tools). Express this problem in terms of just what the customer expectations are for the process you are trying to improve.
2 Looking at other schools and other organizations who experience similar problems (including businesses, hospitals, other social agencies), establish what the most outstanding organization does with this problem

and express this in terms of a benchmark. For example, if a local school guarantees to its students that all assignments handed in by 2 p.m. will be returned fully graded, commented upon and completed by noon the next day, treat this as the benchmark goal to aim at.

3 Process map (see pp. 114–19) your own processes so that you can see how you can achieve this benchmark performance on a continuous, sustainable basis. Summarize current performance as the existing benchmark and then show the improved performance goal which you are aiming to achieve.

What makes benchmarking important to an organization is the fact that the benchmarks are available to customers for the process concerned. For example, the fastest growing optical services are those that guarantee eyewear ophthalmic prescriptions made-up in one hour or you don't pay. The service guarantee is critical in ensuring that lenscrafters and eyemasters sustain this level of performance and look constantly at new ways of making-up eyewear prescriptions in less time so as to minimize financial risk to them. Beta Shoes of Canada guarantees to have a shoe available for you, in your size (even if it has to be specially made), within 24 hours of you placing your order. The New Orleans Sheraton International Hotel guarantees room service delivery of your menu selection for breakfast, lunch or dinner within 20 minutes or you don't pay. These achievements – and they are achievements – come from systematic attempts at benchmarking performance and then establishing systematic ways of ensuring that this performance level is maintained and constantly improved. Schools can engage in these processes too.

Examples of school benchmarks from a Sixth Form College in Britain are: all homework handed in by noon will be returned, fully marked, by 4 p.m. on the next full school day; the time taken between application in the first year of the programme and receipt of the final timetable for studies will be two working days; students will have access to a personal computer for 2 hours a day within one day of booking the services; all students will be able to complete university application procedures (including a careers interview, an on-line course search and a talk with a student currently studying in the programme selected) within ten days of initiating the procedures, and there are a number of others. The key to them is that they indicate a service commitment, or guarantee, which is measurable by the school and the customer.

### Brainstorming

Many teachers are familiar with brainstorming and with its use in classroom activities. It is therefore surprising how infrequently it is used as a method for problem-solving among the staff of a school or for developing ideas for improvement during staff meetings.

Brainstorming is valuable for: (i) getting at the basic ideas for solving a problem that the school faces; (ii) mapping the key elements of a customer's expectations for a process; (iii) looking creatively at a new process or a new idea; and (iv) beginning to work on the task of achieving outrageous goals. The danger of brainstorming is that it often is used to develop 'quick fixes' to complex problems, and can therefore become a starting point for a fix that fails.

The procedure for brainstorming is simple:

1 Getting to understand:
   (a) write a short statement of the problem on a blackboard or on a flip-chart – the statement needs to be one that everyone involved understands in the same way;
   (b) choose one person to facilitate the process and to be neutral to the issues;
   (c) ask everyone involved to suggest ideas or solutions or aspects of the problem (one or other of these three) by shouting out their suggestion. Record these on the board/flip-chart as succinctly as possible. The idea is to get as many ideas as possible on the board. Encourage humour, craziness and off-the-wall thinking, as these ideas sometimes contain the seeds of radical ways of tackling problems.
2 Getting manageable:
   (a) review the list with everyone concerned to make sure that all of the ideas are understood;
   (b) during the process of review, remove any duplicate items – do so with the agreement of the parties concerned.
3 'Dotmocracy':
   (a) having got the list succinct and devoid of duplication, spend 5–6 minutes removing clearly outrageous or unworkable proposals, suggestions that are irrelevant to the problem in hand or ideas that are inappropriate for this group to work with;
   (b) give each person 4–6 'stick-on' dots (available from all stationers) and ask them to place their dots against the ideas/suggestions that they think should provide the focus for subsequent discussion;
   (c) count the dots to establish which issues have the most support for exploration in the team.
4 Getting in deep: having used dotmocracy as a basis for building an agenda, call a second or subsequent meeting to explore the issues identified.

This process works well if it is kept short, is facilitated in a way that does not favour one group or one position over another and is involving, lively and fun. Brainstorming is a powerful way of moving from *status quo* thinking on an issue.

## Cause–effect diagram

This is also called a 'fishbone diagram' because it frequently resembles the skeleton of a fish, with the problem statement represented by the head of the fish. It is also known as an Ishikawa diagram (it was invented by Kaoru Ishikawa). The idea is that, by looking at some basic questions, the causes of a problem can be better understood before action is taken to resolve it. These diagrams are essential if the school wishes to avoid falling into the archetypes of fixes that fail or shifting the burden.

Cause–effect diagrams are most effective when: (i) the school is seeking to diagnose a particular problem with more than one cause; (ii) the school wishes to change processes and needs to understand these processes better before doing so; and (iii) when a team within the school is seeking to understand the links between its work and that of others.

There are a number of steps in the completion of a basic cause–effect diagram:

1 Identify the problem being examined in a short sentence and treat this as the head of the fish in the fishbone.
2 Identify the four basic parameters of the problem's cause that need to be examined by the team. The most frequently used 'causes' in our use of this tool in schools are: policies, procedures, people and equipment. Other, more relevant, headings can be substituted. However, having more than 4–6 headings tends to confuse the problem rather than clarify it.
3 Under each heading, look at the probable causes. Do this by brain-storming or using other techniques outlined here (the five WHYs (see pp. 174–6) are especially useful).
4 Having completed the basic diagram, discuss the basic underlying cause(s) – make sure that you are not looking at symptoms – and circle the cause, so that it becomes the topic to focus the team's energy on.

Figure 9.3 is a cause–effect diagram developed by the secretarial team in a very large school in Britain. The problem was that the school sent out student acceptance letters late – so late, in fact, that many parents had assumed that their son or daughter had not been accepted into the school. The diagram reflects the views of the support staff at the school about the problem: they have circled 'priorities not set clearly' because, in the view of this team, this is the process they need to focus their energies on. Look too at the variety of issues that this particular incident reveals.

## Charts and graphs

One of the most impressive aspects of organizations that have dedicated themselves to TQM is the appearance throughout the organization of appro-priate and relevant charts and graphs. These show how the team is doing against some benchmarked performance on a day-by-day or week-by-week

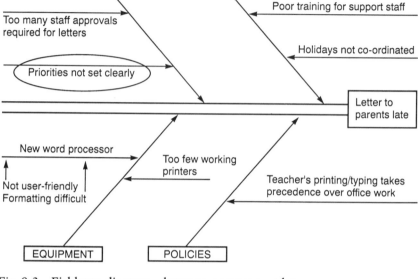

*Fig. 9.3*   Fishbone diagram – letter to parents sent late.

basis. Some of the most powerful initial steps in TQM have been achieved by simply showing people what their performance looks like.

For example, in one school, which aims to get to zero discipline problems in terms of students being sent to the school office by 1994, a chart is updated daily showing the number of discipline cases referred to the Principal today in comparison with the same day last year and the benchmark agreed for the year as a whole. This chart is then shown outside each teacher's room, showing the number of referrals by that teacher. These are powerful ways of showing all in the school just what the target is and how they are doing.

Figure 9.4 shows another school demonstrating its performance on a key area. The school was challenged by the US National Basketball Association (NBA), if it achieved perfect attendance (as defined by the School Board) for a full semester, it would be entitled to send all of its students to a special show put on just for the schools in the district on the day of the NBA All Stars Game presented by the All Stars and few surprise visitors. To achieve this would involve a 46 per cent improvement in attendance over the 13 weeks of the semester – a massive goal. As you can see, the school was able to achieve this. What is more, this level of attendance has been maintained in the year since the game.

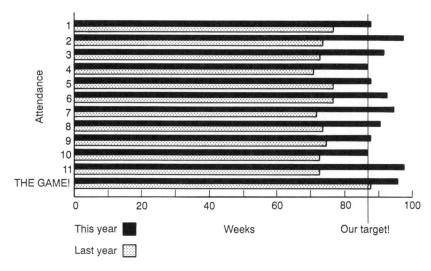

*Fig. 9.4* DuPont School attendance – let's get to the All Star game!

There are essentially four kinds of charts and graphs a school can use: (i) bar chart – such as the one used here or some other form of bar chart; (ii) line chart – in which data are presented as a line rather than as a bar or a series of bars; (iii) pie chart – in which proportions are shown as slices of a pie; (iv) pictorial graph – in which volumes are represented pictorially.

The most powerful use of such graphs is when those most affected by the process being measured or recorded complete the graph or chart themselves.

### Check sheets or logs of specific activities

These are among the most simple recording devices for events. Each time an event occurs, a check mark is made on an appropriate recording sheet. At the end of an agreed time period, a count is made to see how many times the event has occurred.

For example, the school office at a school in Northern Alberta keeps a record of parent complaints by week of the school year. The school is especially concerned to look at four areas of complaint: (i) lack of information; (ii) concern about a decision; (iii) not understanding information provided; and (iv) lack of personal contact. They record the incidents of parental concerns against this list each time they occur, as shown in Fig. 9.5.

The check sheet requires little effort and is simple to use and can be a 'quick and dirty' source of basic information about what is actually happening in an organization.

| Issue | Week 1 | Week 2 | Week 3 | Week 4 | Week 5 | Total |
|---|---|---|---|---|---|---|
| Lack of information | ///// | ////// | ///// ////// | //// / //////// | //////// //// / | 49 |
| Not under-standing | / /// | /// | //// | //// / | /// | 18 |
| Lack of contact | / ///// | //// / | //// | /// | /// | 20 |
| Concern over decisions | //// | / | /// | // | //// | 14 |
| TOTALS | 19 | 14 | 22 | 22 | 24 | |

Fig. 9.5 Check sheet – parental complaints.


## Control charts

These are difficult tools to use, at least for those without a statistical background. Once mastered, however, they are extremely valuable in looking at the underlying features of a process or system.

The primary use of the control chart is to determine whether something is or is not in control. It involves calculating the acceptable range of behaviour within a system – the upper and lower limits – and then looking at those behaviours that fall in and out of these ranges. Let us illustrate this in terms of discipline problems in a school.

Over the past fifteen years, a school has had thirty trainee teachers. The school is interested to know how well they handle discipline issues. A simple measure is the number of reported incidents of discipline problems occurring in the classrooms of these teachers and which have earned detentions, suspensions or some other punishments.

A bar chart showing the incidence of discipline reports could be constructed for each teacher and a mean could be calculated. Deviations from the mean could then be examined. But if we look at the upper and lower limits for the 'system' of trainee teacher discipline, we could construct a more useful chart (Fig. 9.6).

There is a technical calculation for the upper and lower limits (Oakland 1986), using the following process: (i) calculate the mean of the variable you are considering – in this case, the number of discipline referrals; (ii)

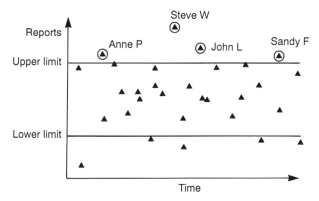

*Fig. 9.6*  Process control chart – trainee teachers and discipline. The circles show the out of range (problematic) trainees.

calculate the average proportion of discipline problems by dividing the total number of problems by the number of observations multiplied by the total number of problems minus one:

$$\bar{p} = \frac{\Sigma x}{n \times (\Sigma x - 1)}$$

(iii) to get the upper and lower limits we use the formula:

$$\bar{x} = \pm 3 \sqrt{x} \; (1 - \bar{p})$$

The point is that judgements about trainee teachers would be different if other, less objective, methods were used. Control charts are used to: (i) encourage the making of decisions on the basis of best available data; (ii) help understand how performance and the nature of a process within a school are linked; (iii) provide a determination as to whether or not a process is in or out of control. Statistical process control, which gives rise to control charts, is a major tool in TQM and cannot be ignored by a school wishing to show leadership in the adoption of quality principles and practices. (Oakland (1986) provides one of the most accessible texts on this subject, but see also Walton (1986).)

### Cost–benefit analysis

On many occasions in our work with Local Education Authorities in England and Wales, and School Boards in North America, we have been amazed at how major investment decisions are made without reference to any systematic analytic study of the cost–benefits of the investment. This applies not just to capital investments – buildings, equipment, computer hardware – but also to investment in curriculum planning, development and implementation.

Cost–benefit analysis does exactly what its title implies: provides a systematic basis for looking at the benefits to be derived – the added value – from a decision to spend or not to spend money, time and people's energy on an activity. It can be used to: (i) chose between several possible investment choices; (ii) determine the worth of an improvement; or (iii) identify the benefits (even non-obvious benefits) of a proposed solution to a problem.

There are several ways of calculating a cost–benefit analysis (Fogarty *et al.* 1989) and examples of their application in education can be found in Blaug (1968) and Gear (1975). Perhaps the most useful approaches to this tool, and the easiest to understand, are those provided by Garvin (1988) or Oakland (1989).

In our example, a school faces the decision to buy or not to buy a dedicated computer facility, which will aid the teaching of modern languages. The facility costs Canadian $200,000 (£100,000). During the last two years, the number of students choosing to pursue modern languages as an option has been growing steadily by around 20 per cent per annum. Some recent studies suggest that this number could double, as the Government is giving a push to language studies (especially French and Japanese). If the number of students increases significantly then there will be substantial additional costs. Using Computer Managed Learning (CML) and self-pacing, the same results can be achieved at a lower cost – at least that is the claim from the language staff. The Board completes the cost–benefit decision tree analysis (which is just one method it uses) to help think through its options. The decision tree is given in Fig. 9.7. The tree shows various decision options calculated by looking at costs × probability. The end calculation is reached by:

To buy = ($360k × 0.4) + ($400k × 0.2) + ($300k × 0.4) = $344,000

Not to buy = ($1.4m × 0.4) + ($200k × 0.2) + ($100k × 0.4) = $640,000

Probabilities were the best guesses the board could make about the likelihood of growth (0.4), stability (0.2) or decline (0.4) and the costs of each scenario are calculated on the basis of best costs available data.

To do a more detailed cost–benefit analysis, the Board would have to look at all of the related costs of both 'buy' and 'don't buy' decisions, but the decision tree above strongly suggests that they ought to look at the proposition. This is a basic use of cost–benefit analysis.

### The five WHYs

This is an old systematic thinking technique, with no one being very clear as to where it originated. The method is simple: when someone outlines a problem, the task is to get beneath the obvious diagnosis of why the problem occurred (the first why) into a more analytic (some say structural)

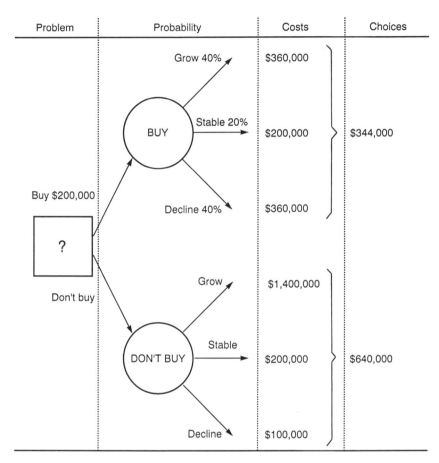

| Problem | Probability | Costs | Choices |
|---|---|---|---|

*Fig. 9.7* Decision tree framework for buy/don't buy decision. The grow, stable and decline rates are the same.

understanding of the problem. By asking WHY five times, this deeper understanding of the nature of the problem usually follows.

The following is an example from a five WHYs completed by a team looking at why parents did not attend the twice yearly parents meetings held to discuss student progress:

Problem: A large number of parents do not attend parents meetings (approximately 60 per cent do not do so).

1 WHY? They have traditionally not done so.
2 WHY? They do not see a relationship between their attendance and changes in the performance of their son or daughter.

3 WHY? Because we use the evening more as a report-on-progress session than as a contracting-for-change session. We do not help them see a connection between their work and the performance of their sons/daughters.
4 WHY? Because we have not trained our staff to develop change and performance contracts with parents and students. What is more, staff have not explored the implications of this.
5 WHY? Because systematically improving performance of students with the full involvement of parents is not a priority in this school at this time.

By using the five WHYs, this team has a better understanding of the problem. It is not simply a technical matter, but a matter of some significant educational importance. Notice that if the team had stopped after the first why (the most typical point for such an analysis to stop) it would have concluded that the problem was to be expected. By going beyond the first why, it now realizes that the issue is one that goes to the heart of the performance improvement strategy of the school.

The five WHYs is used frequently as an adjunct to other techniques described here, but can often be used to help any staff member or student think a little more deeply about a problem they have. It is one of the tools that can help avoid fixes that fail.

**Force field analysis**

When a change is proposed or when a process is in trouble, it is often useful to look systematically at the forces driving the change or supporting the process and those opposing the change or restraining the process.

Conducting a force field analysis involves the following steps:

Step 1   Define the current problem (possible with a cause–effect diagram and/or the five WHYs).
Step 2   Identify the drivers and restrainers for this problem and record them in the form of a balance sheet, with driving forces on the left and restraining forces on the right. Brainstorming or the Six Thinking Hats tool (de Bono 1987) can be used as a basis for doing this part of the task.
Step 3   Have team members evaluate the most important tensions in the balance sheet so that these can become the focus for planning and action.

This sounds simple, yet it can often lead to valuable insights about how an issue is being understood among a staff and can, because it is very visual, open up the possibility of hitherto hidden synergies.

A small school of 150 students and 9 teachers in a small, rural community is considering using distance education as a method for increasing option choices and ensuring that the students at this school have the

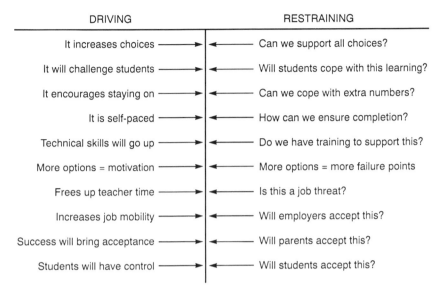

| DRIVING | RESTRAINING |
|---------|-------------|
| It increases choices ⟶ | ⟵ Can we support all choices? |
| It will challenge students ⟶ | ⟵ Will students cope with this learning? |
| It encourages staying on ⟶ | ⟵ Can we cope with extra numbers? |
| It is self-paced ⟶ | ⟵ How can we ensure completion? |
| Technical skills will go up ⟶ | ⟵ Do we have training to support this? |
| More options = motivation ⟶ | ⟵ More options = more failure points |
| Frees up teacher time ⟶ | ⟵ Is this a job threat? |
| Increases job mobility ⟶ | ⟵ Will employers accept this? |
| Success will bring acceptance ⟶ | ⟵ Will parents accept this? |
| Students will have control ⟶ | ⟵ Will students accept this? |

*Fig. 9.8*   Force field analysis – distance education in school.

same access to education as students in urban schools. The nearest urban school is a good distance away. Figure 9.8 shows a force field analysis completed by the staff of the school during a one-day staff inservice event or retreat.

This development activity helped the staff understand the issues and enabled the leadership team in the school to identify key issues to work on. The most important issue – at least in the view of the staff team – was between self-pacing and ensuring completion, and it was this that this team chose to focus on.

### Histograms

Histograms are bar graphs that can be used to display the frequency of distribution of continuous data. The simplest are those that involve a single variable (e.g. discipline referrals, absenteeism). Most effective histograms show the average (as a mean, mode or median) over a period of time for some behaviour or activity.

Histograms can be used in a variety of ways in a school. They are most useful as indicators of how the team is performing against some kind of benchmark. Figure 9.9 is for the zero discipline target set by Dupont School.

### House of quality

This has been fully described and explained elsewhere in this text (see Chapter 6). We will here just mention three additional points: (i) an

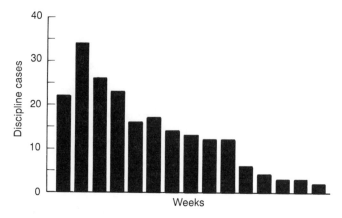

*Fig. 9.9*   Histogram – achieving zero discipline problems.

effective use of the House of Quality process is one that involves stakeholders designing their own matrix of WHATs and HOWs – doing this brings the voice of the 'customer' into the heart of the work of the school; (ii) a House of Quality in which the WHATs have been developed by the customers and the HOWs by the staff becomes a useful framework for an independent evaluation of the performance of the school – the independent evaluators examine the WHATs versus HOWs matrix as analytically and objectively as possible; and (iii) the House of Quality is a visual way of communicating to others just what the school is about and how it goes about its business.

### Sharing mental maps in teams

It is frequently assumed that team members share a common set of understandings (mental maps) about a problem. For example, that all teachers would recognize the value of everyone in the school focusing on language skills across the curriculum, whether they are teaching chemistry, history, language, arts or music. Yet when debate is engaged about proposals or ideas related to some topic, very different perspectives and understandings emerge. In our example here, some teachers think focusing on language means checking spelling, while others look at it in terms of encouraging expression or developing précis skills. By encouraging people to examine and explain their mental maps, we can increase shared understanding and promote a more common process for the work of a team.

Senge (1990), reviewing the work of cognitive action theorists, suggests that our mental models not only help shape our understanding of the organization of which we are a part, but determine the actions we take within them. This is a view supported by several others (Argyris 1982;

Gardner 1985). It stands to reason, therefore, that effective teams engage in a significant degree of sharing of mental models, and that they do so not to ensure total agreement but to ensure enhanced understanding of the position taken by each other. David Kreutzer, of Gould–Kreutzer Associates, has developed an effective process for a team to share mental maps. Using magnetic hexagons on which ideas can be written and erased, the ideas behind a particular proposal, construct, process are examined by a team. Here are the steps in using the hexagons:

Step 1  Brainstorm (see pp. 167–8) the key ideas or principles that lie behind a process, decision, construct or proposal. Each new idea is placed on a hexagon and put up on a magnetic board.

Step 2  Having ensured that all the key ideas are out on the board (this can often take 30–40 hexagons), the group is then asked to identify the core ideas – the three or four key ideas that 'drive' the construct, process or proposal. What are its essential ingredients? These ideas are then placed in the centre of the board (preferably by being re-written on different coloured hexagons).

Step 3  Once the key ideas are on the board, the team is asked to work at the board to fit the hexagons together so that they build a conceptual map of the idea and show the connections between one element and another. They can add hexagons, duplicate them, move them around, re-write them and so on. As they work on the task, they are asked to share understandings and relevant information or concerns.

Step 4  Make sure that all connections are shown. If one cluster of ideas around one 'driver' construct hexagon should be connected to another cluster, show this connection with an arrow, thus showing the affinity between one idea-set and another.

Step 5  Record the final mental map on paper, with the hexagons drawn in.

If hexagons are unavailable, then Post-it® notes can be substituted, although the hexagons have a more powerful visual impact.

The process just described brings ideas and mental models out into the open where they can be shared and understood. This is an effective method for capturing ideas, showing the relationships between ideas and enhancing shared understanding within a team. But there are many more uses of the hexagons once the basic steps just outlined have been completed. For example, different colours can be used for different kinds of inputs into the process – doing this might highlight the number of opinions (red) versus facts (grey) or opportunities (yellow). It may also point to the need to increase the amount of information (grey) or elaborations (orange) needed. Another creative use of the hexagons is called 'throwing ideas to the wind' – making sure step 5 has been completed, take all of the hexagons off the board and start again to construct a different mental model by

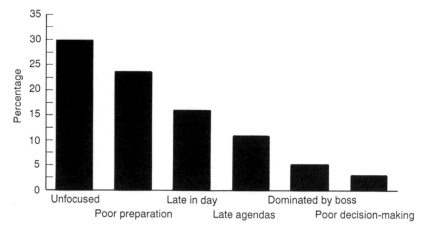

*Fig. 9.10*   School staff meetings in our system – why they are not as useful as they could be.

throwing the hexagons at random on the board. Look at the pattern of ideas that emerges and try to work to complete that pattern – what does this pattern suggest in terms of new ways of thinking and seeing?

Hexagon processes are, from personal experience, practical and effective ways of developing mental maps and models within a team. Using hexagons can significantly improve the clarity with which a team approaches a problem or task and can significantly aid team building.

### Pareto charts

Pareto, an eighteenth-century mathematician, suggested that 80 per cent of a problem is due to 20 per cent of its total set of causes. If we don't remember this, a lot of time can be spent focusing on a range of causes that will make little difference to the problem in hand. By using a Pareto chart – a special kind of histogram – we can look at a problem and identify primary causes and seek to effect the causes that matter most.

The easiest way to understand this tool is to look at an example. School staff meetings are often thought to be badly managed, wasteful of time and energy and not a good way to get things done. In one school system we asked 400 teachers to indicate on a card the single most important problem they had with staff meetings. We counted the cards in terms of the primary items identified and showed a graph of this count, with the most frequent to the left and then the next most frequent and so on. The result is given in Fig. 9.10. Such a chart can help an individual school or a system look at what to focus on to make a difference to the problem at hand. In this case, getting the meetings more focused and the people attending them better prepared would remove some 54 per cent of frustration with the problem. Changing the time of staff meetings to first thing in the morning rather than at the end of the afternoon may also make a difference.

This simple device is very valuable in sorting out the wood from the trees, yet it is rarely used by school teams in their attempts to solve problems.

### Process decision programme charts (PDPCs)

Even the best laid plans of mice and men go awry. When problems arise, solutions are not always apparent, although a well prepared plan has built-in contingencies. PDPC charts are simply another form of flow-diagram showing how to respond with anticipated contingencies, by which we mean pre-planning for all the 'if this . . . then we will . . .' events that could occur in the implementation of a process or activity.

The primary uses of PDPCs concern: (i) planning for new curriculum introduction; (ii) establishing the best and most effective use of available technology within a school; (iii) timetable planning; and (iv) staff planning. A full description of the process used to construct these charts is provided in Mizuno (1988).

### Process mapping

We have already described the basic steps in this process in Chapter 6 (see pp. 114–19). We will just stress two points here. First, the critical use of process mapping is to work from the outside (who is the customer and what do they expect from this process) in (how do we meet and then exceed the expectations of the customer), not the other way around. The aim is to make the processes we use more 'value added' for the customers for that process. The second point is that, although process mapping involves a great deal of work, it is critical that the processes used in the school are understood and examined critically all of the time. As school comprises sequences of routines, significant improvement in the process of schooling will come from a re-examination of these routines. Process mapping is a very useful tool for this task.

### Run charts

In the behavioural treatment of children with learning disabilities, the first step is to benchmark the occurrence of the problem then, during a period of treatment, to measure the occurrences of the problem; this measurement should be continued after treatment has ended (Lerner 1971). The behavioural charts used to examine the occurrence of the behaviour that the therapist is seeking to reduce or eliminate are run charts – they show the way in which a behaviour runs over time.

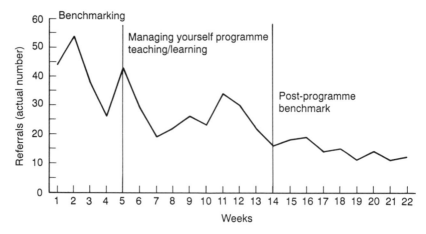

*Fig. 9.11*   DuPont School – discipline referrals to the office.

In constructing such charts, (e.g. Fig. 9.11, which concerns discipline problems in school), the key question is one of definition. If a team is seeking to make a difference to the process in a school, they will want to look carefully at the best and easiest way of measuring the behaviour of the process. For example, discipline problems at a school could be examined in a variety of different ways. In the school above, they have chosen to measure these simply in terms of the number of students in the school who are referred to the Principal for discipline reasons by the teacher. The reason this measure was chosen over any other is that the underlying aim of the staff is to develop self-discipline among the students in class. They want to encourage the idea that discipline is everyone's problem, not just the job of the Principal. To develop this idea, the team has launched a programme called 'Managing Yourself' for both teachers and students to help develop an awareness of self-management for discipline control. Thus the measure they chose to affect their actions reflected this strategic goal.

Run charts are everywhere in committed TQM schools – in classrooms, corridors, student note books, teachers' lesson plans and in staff rooms. By showing the behaviour of the system that is under scrutiny, and demonstrating the target for change simply to as many people as possible, all parties are encouraged to contribute to improvement.

## Sampling

To look at the effectiveness and quality of a process it is not necessary to look at all occurrences of process. If we want to know how well students in a particular year group are at a particular skill, we do not need to test and examine all of them. Sampling is a statistical process for determining how many incidences of a process should be examined so as to obtain valid information for a systematic evaluation.

There are many sampling methods – random sampling, stratified sampling and stratified random sampling – and the choice of these should be made on the basis of sound judgement of the validity of the sample and the reliability of the data that results from sampling.

For a TQM school, sampling parents or students on a regular basis about their satisfaction with the work of the school using a standard instrument could be a valuable indicator of customer satisfaction. Sampling also ensures that the same people are not asked time and time again to complete questionnaires, participate in interviews or attend focus groups. At the same time, sampling provides valuable and relevant data to help a team look at what is happening in the school.

## Scatter diagram

These are simple diagrams showing the relationship between two variables. They are used to examine what happens to one variable ($x$) when another ($y$) changes.

For example, one school sees as a key strategic goal the development of positive self-concepts in its students. It is using a systematic measure of self-concept, which examines the number of positive self-statements someone makes in response to a questionnaire. The assumption is that the number of positive statements would increase with age if the school is achieving its objective. By sampling the students (see above) frequently, the school is able to examine its achievements systematically.

How it does this is to collect 75 questionnaires, each month which show the length of time the student has been at the school (in years) and the number of positive self-statements. These data are then plotted on a graph (Fig. 9.12) and the graph is used to discern patterns of relationship.

Once again, one key variable that the school is trying to affect by its strategic interventions, such charts, would be displayed in a variety of key locations in the school.

## Six thinking hats and six action shoes

Edward de Bono has developed a world-wide reputation for teaching creative and lateral thinking. He has introduced many devices to help teams think through issues more creatively and powerfully, so that their decision-making is better informed, they have taken into account more of the options and have avoided group-think. Perhaps his most important contribution has been the CoRT programme (de Bono 1973), which seeks to develop systematic thinking skills within an organization.

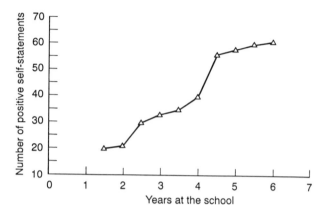

*Fig. 9.12*  Our positive self programme.

His most popular contributions to organizational development, however, are his books *Six thinking hats* (1987) and *Six action shoes* (1991), which propose basic ways of working and thinking about problems and their solutions. They are also powerful as ways of effective team work.

*Six thinking hats* suggests that a team faced with an issue, opportunity or a problem can make systematic use of different thinking modes (hats) in looking at a problem. De Bono suggests that different hats can be used (either metaphorically or in fact) at different stages of a meeting to represent these different styles and that, if used systematically, can be successful at getting to the heart of a problem.

---

*Six thinking hats – different hats for different styles*
*('Watch my Hat!')*

White hat: Facts
Red hat: Feelings
Black hat: Negative judgement
Yellow hat: Constructive suggestions
Green hat: Brainstorming
Blue hat: Conductor of the thinking orchestra

---

Having thought systematically about a problem or an opportunity, a team then has to make some decisions about what action it can take. De Bono's *Six action shoes* suggests that a team can adopt six action styles and that, before deciding on an appropriate action, a team should look carefully about what the actions would look like for different action styles.

*Six action shoes – different shoes for different actions*
*('Read my feet!')*

Navy formal shoes: Routine behaviours
Grey sneakers: collecting information and thinking
Brown brogues: Pragmatism – doing what can be done
Orange gumboots: Action to reduce danger
Pink slippers: Sympathy, compassion and help
Purple riding boots: Playing the status role

To master the ideas implied here it is necessary to look at the books. Certified training is also available in the use of these methods from the International Centre for Creative Thinking. Our reason for including them in this chapter is that they are useful devices for encouraging and enabling teams to become more self-managing over time. Further, they are effective in getting to the heart of problems and deciding what action can be taken. We have used them extensively with school staffs to show how staff meetings can be managed differently and how problems can be looked at as opportunities for adult learning.

### Systematic diagrams

What is a school trying to do and how do the objectives of the individuals within the school link back to the overall objectives of the school? If teachers are asked this question they often answer 'I don't know!'. A systematic diagram is a device that permits an organization to look at the way in which objectives and tasks are interconnected. The basic structure of such a diagram is given in Fig. 9.13. Every objective of a teacher can be linked back (right to left) and every objective of the school should be linked across (left to right) the work of others. Showing this diagrammatically will often clarify how objectives are to be met and measured. It also tends to indicate gaps between the rhetoric of a school and its actual plans for making its objectives a reality. Further details of the methods that can be used will be found in Mizuno (1988).

### The three MUs

This tool gets its name from the Japanese words for waste, strain and gap or discrepancy (muda, muri and mura). It involves a team looking at a problem or process or opportunity and asking three basic questions:

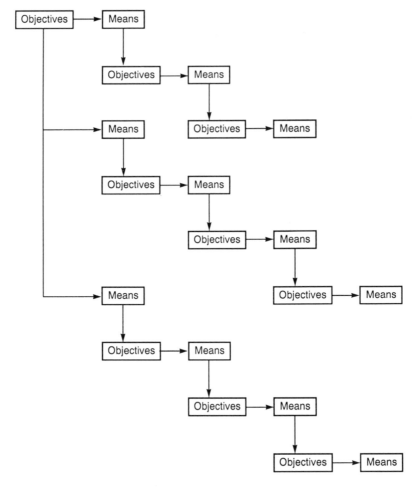

*Fig. 9.13* Basic structure for a systematic diagram.

1 What is wasteful in the way we work (or could work) this process?
2 What are the strains we experience in making this process work – the pressures and difficult demands?
3 What is the difference between what we say we are going to do and what we actually do?

Rather than just asking these questions in general, it is helpful to ask the questions about one or more of the following: our use of people, our methods of working, our use of time, our use of the school's building, our

*Table 9.2*    Three MU chart

|  | Waste | Strain | Gap |
|---|---|---|---|
| Use of people | | | |
| Methods of working | | | |
| Use of time | | | |
| Use of the building | | | |
| Use of new technology | | | |
| Other . . . | | | |

use of our new technology. A simple chart can be constructed to help a team use this tool (Table 9.2).

### Computer tools for team working

There is a variety of tools available to teams that make use of computers. For example, the House of Quality is available as a computer-based system. Other valuable tools include idea generators, creative problem-solving tools, strategy development tool and model builders – a summary of such tools is provided by Proctor (1991).

### Tooling the team for high performance

There are many more valuable tools, although this listing and brief description provides a list of the most commonly used tools in the practice of TQM through teams.

Two points need to be made clearly in ending this chapter. First, the more systematic teams become in using these tools the more likely it is that they will do good work. All high-performance teams aim to enhance the quality of teamwork by systematically encouraging and enabling learning. Second, tools, of themselves, do not solve problems, people do. Tools aim to help a team develop competencies that will both improve the quality of its thinking and decision-making and equip it to make better use of the available data about an issue or a problem. In the end, however, a team bites bullets and makes choices. The problem in educational organizations, in many cases, is that not enough time has been given to quality thinking and effective data analysis before the bullet has been bitten. The result is often that the bullets explode while still in the mouth. Becoming systematic takes time, but can produce outstanding results in terms of sustainable, steep-slope quality improvements.

# CHAPTER
# 10

# Implementing TQM in the school: Challenge and opportunity

TQM is not another applications programme; it is not just another 'bolt on' and 'belt up' programme that we can add to existing practices. It is a wholly reconceived approach to the total management of educational institutions. It is an approach whose time has come because of the significant changes now taking place in the external environment, as we saw in Chapter 1. The school must now achieve higher standards of performance for its students – more value must be added for its stakeholders. This can only be accomplished by visionary leaders in the school enabling their staff and their customers to define the possibilities for schooling anew and assisting them to achieve what is possible. Implementing TQM is essentially about improving all customer–supplier processes, with the consequence of enhanced performance as evidenced by hard and fast measures. The key message of this book is that quality – higher standards of achievement across the board – can only come about from a concerted, integrated and dynamic effort.

Implementing TQM is not easy and the process of achieving the Hoshin goals and securing steep-slope quality improvement is long and often arduous: there are no short cuts for the developments of teams, for training team members in the thinking skills and systematic tools required for effective TQM implementation.

There are no ready-made programmes for TQM. While we have suggested some step-by-step processes, we do so on the assumption that, from the experience of a range of schools applying TQM, ideas and sets of proven TQM applications will emerge over the next few years, which other schools can put to immediate use. However, we stress that TQM implementation is, by its nature, arduous and painstaking.

The history of total quality management implementation in business and industry is a complex one. The failure rate for implementation is high – some say as high as 70 per cent (Clemmer 1990), although this figure is often inflated because it includes those who fail because they took one look at the commitment TQM implies and decided that it was not for them. Some educational organizations that have moved down the TQM road have found that it takes time to secure the basics (longer than was thought) and even more time to secure some gains but, once the initial phases have been passed through, the gains begin to be consistent and of growing importance to the well-being of the organization.

In this chapter we will examine the problems associated with creating a total quality management programme in a school and show how these can be overcome by thinking through the implementation strategy carefully and by looking at the sources of strength within the school that will aid implementation. The substance of this chapter is derived from practical experience and from a series of discussions with TQM consultants and practitioners conducted between 1989 and 1992.

## Why TQM sometimes fails

When failures are investigated, two major sets of reasons emerge. The first can be referred to as 'initiating' or 'start-up' problems. The second set of problems are concerned with the 'post-launch' issues that TQM stimulates. Before looking at these two classes of issues in depth, three general points need to be made.

There is a word used in some organizations to describe the reaction of staff to a new set of ideas coming from the 'top' of the organization. The word is BOHICA – it is an acronym for 'bend over, here it comes again!'. When used by staff, it suggests that if they just wait long enough, this new programme will pass over and they can get on with their business. Teachers sometimes say 'this is old wine in new bottles', 'what we have here is the latest firewater panacea' or 'these gimmicks, like TQM, come and go but teaching always remains the same' and they conclude that if they do what they always do they will get what they always get. If TQM is positioned as just another programme and is seen as an adjunct rather than a centrepiece in terms of the work of the school, then staff are likely to BOHICA-it. Without exception, effective TQM implementers have seen TQM as a way of integrating all of the work of their organization and focusing that work upon a set of core ideas. TQM has not been another programme, it has been the central platform for all of the work of the organization.

A second general point is that TQM implementation is often seen as a way of securing financial and service gains. Indeed, TQM will lead to significant efficiencies in the long-term: rarely will it do so instantly or quickly. Because many organizations have waited until their financial position or market circumstances drives them to TQM, they often do not have time to wait for the outcomes and so adopt a second strategy, called downsizing or layoff. TQM thus sometimes becomes thought of as part of this downsizing (also known as 'rightsizing') strategy – as another way of cutting out waste and inefficiency. This pairing of ideas can be detrimental to the adoption of TQM in any organization. While a school may have to lose staff in the short-term, the aim of TQM is to reposition the school for survival and rejuvenation in the long-term. Linking cost-cutting and TQM can be fatal to the TQM initiative.

The third general point we wish to make here is that TQM works as well as the investments made in the development of skills and competencies permit. One way of looking at TQM in schools is to suggest that it provides a focus and an agenda for the adult learning work that needs to take place within the organization. To be implemented effectively, TQM requires that all staff master a range of tools valuable to the task of continuous improvement, that they work in teams to learn more about the nature of current processes and to develop the opportunities to improve them. If staff are not enabled to make use of the opportunities for improvement, they are unlikely to secure sustainable steep-slope quality improvement, no matter how empowered they might be.

## Some general inhibitors to TQM implementation and success

Having made these general points, now let us examine the most common problems in the adoption of TQM within schools.

### Problems with start-up of TQM

Experience of applying TQM to date suggests that there are four common problems in the start-up of TQM initiatives. These are: (i) lack of visible enactment by the senior staff of the school; (ii) poor plan for the deployment of TQM in the school; (iii) lack of an adequate database on which to develop TQM initiatives; and (iv) lack of appropriate skills within the organization to secure TQM advantage. We will look at each of these in turn.

#### Lack of viable commitment by leaders

When a Principal/Headteacher seeks to initiate change the critical question for staff concerns his or her level of commitment to the process. Commitment is measured in terms of visible and tangible things, not in terms of rhetoric. Staff will look to the behaviour and actions of the Principal and the top team rather than the words spoken. If they do not see in the behaviour of the top team a genuine and sustained commitment to quality, then it is unlikely to be produced from below. The behaviour that will be examined critically will include: (i) how quality is demonstrated in the way staff matters (recognition, rewards, promotion, workload allocations, etc.) are treated within the school; (ii) the extent to which data drive decisions in the organization; (iii) the extent to which the skills required for TQM and the tools of TQM are demonstrated by the top team; and (iv) the way in which recognition and rewards are distributed in the organization. If no substantial behavioural change is noticed, then TQM will be seen as a rhetorical programme, not an action-oriented programme. Where TQM is lived daily by the top team and all of their actions can be seen as TQM-centred, then TQM will become well established in the organization.

*Poor plan for TQM deployment*

When TQM developments begin in an organization there is often a focus on quickly forming teams and getting the teams to start to work. A number of problems then arise. These include: (i) just what should these teams focus on? (ii) do all teams need to do the same thing, or can teams work in their own way towards their quality goals? And (iii) do all the teams need to develop the same skills or can skill development be a team responsibility? These questions, and many others like them, can delay effective implementation or stall it to a point where the team no longer functions. The view of many TQM developers is that teams should form when teams are ready to form and that they should work on real problems that, if only they were dealt with, would make a substantial difference to the way in which the school works as a centre for learning and achievement. Thus it is likely that effective team work begins with cross-functional teams working on specifics, rather than departmental or 'line' teams working on improving their everyday work. Further, there is the question of whether involvement with TQM should be mandatory or voluntary – should we 'let it grow' or 'make it grow'? The answer to this question will vary from school to school, but in almost every case of successful TQM implementation it is some combination of requirement to act and volunteering how to act that leads to success.

A further element here is the weakness of focus for many implementations. School TQM initiation teams (usually the top team) seem always to want to launch TQM as a way of dealing with a specific set of issues, rather than as a way of dealing with the strategic future of the school in its entirety. TQM is a whole-school, whole-staff, whole-issue strategy, which can be especially helpful in dealing initially with some long-standing problems. If presented solely in terms of the long-standing problems, then TQM will be seen as the solution box for these problems and not as a general way of working.

### Lack of good data on which to build TQM initiatives

Many organizations are shocked at how little they actually know about their operations in measurable terms. While many collect a great deal of information, when they seek to use it to actually change the operation or affect behaviour within it, they find the data to be lacking or weak in some or several respects. For example, schools collect attendance data but experience suggests that these data are kept for one purpose (generalized record keeping) rather than for changing behaviour. Data should be designed as the primary mechanism for showing how a process operates and what the outcomes of the process are. Schools need to undertake a data audit of the available data and to look at what these data could be used for in terms of managing systematic change and quality improvements. In many cases they will be surprised at the paucity of the data available. Before launching TQM it may be worth identifying six key issues that the school faces in terms of strategic positioning, and then asking a task team to look at what data it would need to have available so as to examine the process associated with these issues and the outcomes of these processes. Such a team should ask the question 'What feedback data do we need to provide to our colleagues concerned with these questions and what is the simplest way of securing and sharing these data?' Such a team could also benefit from thinking through the use of the tools presented in Chapter 9 as ways of understanding these data.

One consequence of not having good data at the launch of a TQM initiative is that the first step for TQM will be to collect it. This develops an association between TQM and measurement and encourages the notion that TQM is about measurement. It is not. TQM is about continuous improvement and the search for quality, measurement and record keeping aid the achievement of these objectives.

### Lack of appropriate skills

TQM leaders in school systems are not 'seats of their pants' managers. They are strategically focused leaders who use data to make decisions and seek to empower their staff. They have strong people skills, a strong ability to communicate vision, optimism and purposiveness. They have a high level of tolerance for ambiguity, patience and integrity. They are respected both for what they themselves have achieved but, more importantly, for what they have enabled their staff to achieve. They are insightful about people and can demonstrate their trust in others through delegation. They do not panic easily, take a long-term view of issues and are not driven by expediency or opportunism. These are the leadership skills required for effective TQM implementation.

But the organization also needs to develop other skills. First, there needs to be a skill-set within the school that enables the staff to go beyond the 'quick fix' mentality and look at the medium- to long-term. We refer to this skill set as 'sightedness', referring to short-sightedness (adopting quick fixes that often fail) and long-sightedness (doing what is necessary now to aid the long-term achievement of goals). Staff within and outside the top team need to be long-sighted. Second, the school needs to develop critical thinking and analysis skills for the organization, notably some of the thinking skills described in the previous chapter (e.g. archetypes, brainstorming, five WHYs, force field analysis, mental mapping and six thinking hats/action shoes). Training all staff in some or all of these skills is a useful first step. Third, some of the staff need to develop competencies in databased skills (e.g. benchmarking, charts and graphs, control charts and the House of Quality) and process mapping. If a cross-section of staff is able to look systematically at how to collect and use information and all are capable of critical thinking and evaluation, then there is a potential for teams to be effective. Finally, all staff need to develop the skill of working in teams.

All the comments made here concern positioning the school so that it is both ready and able to benefit fully from TQM. Simply declaring the school to be a TQM school and willing it to happen will not lead to any sustainable steep-slope quality improvement.

### Post-launch problems of TQM

A variety of problems can be discerned post-launch. The most common are: (i) team mania – too many teams and not enough support; (ii) measurement mania – too many measurements leading nowhere; (iii) over-zealous selling of outcomes and very little initial achievements; (iv) fixing problems without looking at processes; and (v) losing momentum. Let us look at each of these problems in turn.

#### Problems of team formulation and purpose

In one school with a staff of 54, a total of 22 teams dealing with both departmental issues and cross-functional issues were formed in the first semester of the first year of a TQM development by the Principal. By the end of the second semester of this same year only three of these teams were functioning fully – two of them were cross-functional and one was a departmental team in mathematics, which had set itself a goal of increasing all students' comfort with and enjoyment of mathematical work. The Principal had created teams artificially and these teams were unsure of what they had to do, how they might work and what outcomes their work was supposed to lead to. Poor preparation and over-zealous use of teams had 'teamed' the school to 'death' (according to one teacher). Teams are only useful as focal points for the development of competencies, the promotion of shared understanding and the achievement of particular goals. Teams for the sake of teams are likely to be counterproductive.

### Problems of paucity of process and performance data

Measuring activities, processes or outcomes; benchmarking processes and process mapping processes all require effort. Doing them for the sake of doing them leads nowhere. Teams working on real problems, which make use of appropriate tools to first understand these problems and then act on them, measuring the consequences of their actions, are powerful. TQM launched as a strategy for measurement and accountability will lead to a great many charts, tables, models and indicators, but may not change the processes of the school or the outcomes of these processes. Measures should be used sparingly, in a focused way, with the intention that they enable understanding and facilitate the systematic examination of the consequences of change. In many organizations with which we have worked we find ourselves not only reducing the number of measures taken, but changing the ones that remain so that they are more focused on the issues and more useful to the teams working on these issues. In other organizations with little or no history of measurement, we focus on creating an efficient and focused set of simple measures of key strategic processes (not all processes, just those that have most impact on the achievement of strategy), which can aid teams seeking to improve these processes. As one team member in an internationally recognized telephone company pointed out 'the more time we spend measuring processes, the less time we have to improve them!' The idea is that measurement should serve the task of improvement.

### Problems of scope of TQM strategy

Launching TQM as 'the answer to our prayers, dilemmas and uncertainties' and as a means for solving all problems will always lead to failure. TQM requires a great deal of effort and an openness and ability to rethink problems and issues. As more and more investment is made in understanding processes and issues within the school, achievements become smaller and problems become understood in their complexity. Solutions seem to move further away rather than nearer to hand, especially when logical problem-solving and databased analysis are used to drive understanding. The fact that the solutions are likely to lead, in the medium- to long-term, to substantial gains, sometimes does not offset the feeling that a great deal of work is being invested with very little initial returns.

Part of the problem here is that the staff of a school have been encouraged to think of their organization as having an annual existence. Problems are defined, examined and tackled in the context of a single school year. Almost no other public sector organization works with this assumption so endemically enshrined. In a typical TQM process, a year might be taken in understanding a problem, six months spent in bench-marking the processes associated with the problem and then a further year spent in making changes to the processes associated with the problem. There are no quick fixes, yet TQM is sometimes presented to staff in schools as if it could make a substantive difference right now. Such a 'selling' of TQM will lead to disaffection, as few critical processes in a school can be changed that quickly.

*Fixing problems without fixing processes*

One school Principal suggested that he could halve the discipline problem in the school by simply suspending or expelling more students more often. He then asked 'would this be a TQM solution?' Here is a potential problem-fix that does not necessarily lead to a process change in the work of the school. As the problems re-appear, the school simply suspends or expels those that do not conform. The questions we asked of this Principal were: (i) How did these students get into the school in the first place? (ii) What is it about these students or their experience of schooling that is causing them to react in the way that they are? (iii) What strategies are being tried in the school to develop responses to the concerns which arise in (ii)? and (iv) What would doubling the suspension rate and quadrupling the expulsion rate do for the achievement of the school's long-term strategic objectives and vision? Once these questions begin to be examined (using the six thinking hats), we realized that the 'quick fix' solutions – suspension and expulsion – would actually make the school's overall problem worse: it would be a fix that failed.

This story is not uncommon. Because of the renewed focus on 'time-on-task' and pragmatic work in schools, the staff seek a quick 'resolution' to a problem so that they can re-engage in the 'real' work of the school. They focus on outcome-oriented solutions – how can we modify process outcome to get better results – rather than process-focused solutions. Doing this can damage sustainability and can also lead to the assumption that the underlying process cannot be the problem.

Most major successes in TQM have come from passing the outcome barrier and re-thinking the process – working smarter, not harder. While keeping an eye on outcomes is an important part of understanding process (Schaffer and Thomson 1992), process improvement will lead to sustainable outcome change.

*Losing momentum*

TQM produces some results in terms of team quality, some small gains in understanding and occasionally some outcome gains in the first period of its introduction. But initially there is a lot of work – work that one teacher described to us as 'worry work'. People are asked to develop new ways of working – teams, tools and different focal points for their work. It is unsettling. Where is all this leading? If this question cannot be answered clearly and convincingly, then the initiative is likely to fail. People will make significant investments of time and effort in an activity only if they know what it is likely to lead to. If they do not know where the work is heading, momentum will be lost and gains will be low.

Putting these pieces together suggests that an effective launch and follow-through for any school-based TQM initiative is essential. A failure to secure both these elements – launch and follow-through – could lead not just to TQM being a failure but to a crisis of leadership within the school.

## Effective development of TQM in the school

There is no one way to engage a school in TQM work. What is suggested here are the key elements for TQM engagement in an organization seeking to adopt TQM as the centrepiece of its strategy for achieving its vision. The pieces are presented sequentially, but schools may need to undertake these tasks in different sequences (or, more likely, with overlapping or parallel sequences). What is important is that all elements outlined here are present.

### Phase 1: Top team TQM commitment

All successful TQM implementations require major and substantive top team commitment. That is, the persons holding positions of responsibility in the school and to whom others look to for guidance and leadership should all buy into the TQM strategy and act accordingly. The slightest digression or perception that lip-service is being given to TQM will lead to rejection. It is critical that the top team understand what it is they are getting into, recognize the work it will create and commit to achieving their vision through TQM. There are three stages to this process.

*Stage 1: Induction and training a school's senior staff in TQM*

This book provides a comprehensive account of TQM and its potential for the school and all top team members need to understand all of the key ideas contained here. This should take the form of reading, discussion and site visits to schools, hospitals, businesses and other organizations that have adopted TQM. The top team should particularly understand the leadership role they will be expected to play and the implications TQM has for thinking differently about processes and the roles of customers in the achievement of the vision and mission of the school.

### Stage 2: Apply TQM to the school

The top team, having understood the key ideas of TQM and having seen them in action in some location, then need to connect these ideas to the experience they have of their school. It is not as if TQM is a standard programme available which, if they could only adopt correctly, would make all the difference in the world to their school. TQM has to be customized and refined for their school by them as a group. This will take a great deal of open discussion within the team. The team should discuss: (i) what does this all mean for the way we work as a team? (ii) what does this mean for the way we work with staff, students and stakeholders? (iii) what is it that TQM will need to bring to us over the next 3–5 years for it to be successful? (iv) how does TQM need to be launched and what is the most likely reaction of our staff colleagues? (v) what are the barriers to effective TQM implementation in our school and how can we systematically over-come these? and (vi) what will be the gains and positive outcomes for all of our staff?

### Stage 3: Commitment

If the first two stages are passed through and the team still wishes to proceed (if there are doubts, keep working until the doubts are either removed or are so serious that it becomes self-evident that TQM will not work for the team), individuals need to develop a self-contract about their role in the launch and follow-through and share these contracts in the top team. The team also needs to define what behaviours they need to engage in collectively to demonstrate their commitment to all staff. In particular, this discussion should focus on decision-making, the use of data and rewards and recognition for staff – from experience, these are key areas.

### Phase 2: Designating and training the implementers

Before launching TQM to all staff, the top team needs to identify some key implementers who will be critical to both the successful launch and to the follow-through that the launch requires. These individuals need to be recognized as positive supporters and their skills need to be strengthened. Further, they should be asked to attend a session in which the key ideas of TQM are developed in relation to the vision statement of the school. Of particular importance is a discussion of the idea that, to achieve high performance and to enhance learning, the management of the school needs to be based around teams not individual champions.

Implementers are crucial in that they provide peer leadership for TQM, can support TQM initiatives because they have appropriate team or tool skills and can provide direction to a team in terms of what TQM can lead to for the school. They should be selected for their ability to work in teams, their openness to new ideas and their ability to demonstrate skills data use and critical thinking. These people should be potential team facilitators, peer-group educators and cross-functional team leaders. They need not have formal status in the organization, but must have the requisite skills.

### Phase 3: Positive launch

With the support of the top team and its implementers, the school needs to find a way of successfully launching a TQM strategy that engages and inspires staff and other stakeholders without: (i) making promises for TQM that can never be achieved; and (ii) without creating a 'here comes the next panacea' syndrome.

The most successful launches we have seen in schools begin with a great deal of honesty rather than hype. The top team outline what is likely to happen to the school under a given set of assumptions over a 4–5 year period and explore with the staff the idea that 'if they do what they always do' they will have problems sustaining their work. This then leads to questions about how the school can sustain its work towards the achievement of a vision while at the same time securing process gains and improved achievements. TQM is thus launched as a naturally occurring strategy in response to real issues, rather than as the 'latest' management technique from North America and Japan.

Most schools do not call their TQM programmes 'Total Quality Management' programmes. They chose a name that fits the strategy and circumstances of their school. For example, one school in New Mexico calls their programme 'Quality First' while another calls it the 'Q-Program'. In industry, TQM initiatives go by many names – 'People First', 'Customer Service', 'Quality Program'. What something is called is not as important as what it does. The name, however, does need to reflect the actual strategy of the school.

### Phase 4: Getting TQM going

Essentially, the school faces two choices: (i) it can encourage teams and individuals to initiate activity on an as-soon-as-a-team-is-ready basis and support their efforts to do so – this is the strategy pursued by Shell (Canada) with significant results; or (ii) it can require departments and teams to start to work on the specific areas of their operation that require a TQM focus – this is the strategy pursued by many TQM initiators with varying results. The first strategy is voluntary and the second is mandatory.

The benefit of the voluntary strategy is that everyone involved begins by being committed to the task in hand and looks to the top team for help in achieving their objectives. The downside is that the tasks chosen are often short-term, cross-functional tasks, which have some impact but rarely change the basic processes of the organization. Further, the volunteers are likely to be those who would volunteer for any development and would make such a development work because of their commitment. In the setting of the school, given the nature of the tasks associated with schooling and the nature of the problems faced in schools, this strategy is hardly the most attractive.

The disadvantages of the mandatory strategy are many and varied. First, not all staff will like being required to undertake new work. Second, the teams that operate will do so with very varying degrees of success. Third, the skill levels of teams will vary significantly. Finally, some teams will 'go through the motions' but are unlikely to produce results. On the positive side, if all staff are being asked to look at process some key issues may get tackled. Second, if 75 per cent of the staff become involved and become committed this is a significant gain. Before choosing the mandatory option senior managers should therefore make a judgement on the level of involvement likely to ensue. Third, at some point senior managers in the school should make it explicit that TQM is the approach to organizational development and management they wish to use and that pursuing this approach is not optional.

What tends to get the mandatory strategy off the ground is work associated with Hoshin goals linked to a strong sense of vision (see Chapters 4–7). Once this work is completed, then more buy-in follows. Teams start to form naturally and others do not want to be left behind.

A common question at this stage of the process is 'What do we do with those who do not want to get involved?' First, it needs to be recognized that, whatever the strategy, not all will be involved to the degree that a top team would like. Second, the key task is to focus support, energy and attention on implementers (the behaviours we wish to reward and encourage) rather than defectors and detractors. Third, at some point it is necessary to make clear to staff that the programme is not optional – it is the basis on which the future of the school will be based: engagement within a time scale is a requirement of the position. This may sound like a tough stand, but the strategy and success of the school is what is really in question here.

## Phase 5: Invest and recognize

As the work of TQM begins to unfold in the organization, the role of the top team becomes 2-fold: (i) invest in the continuous improvement of skills and understanding among all staff; and (ii) recognize and reward success.

Most schools have professional development activities. In a TQM school focused on vision and success, these days become opportunities to enhance skills and focus energies within the organization. Rather than encouraging staff to leave the school, the school needs to use these days as opportunities to connect the schools to skills and ideas available in the community and to see school-based professional development as the key to success.

Not all of the available time should be spent talking and working as a staff within the school. One or more days should be set aside for teams to visit other locations – other TQM schools, colleges, businesses, hospitals, dental clinics, non-profit agencies, retailing organizations, distributors and others – to try and learn just what issues they are tackling from a TQM perspective, what skills they find make the difference to continuous improvement work and how the team work in these organizations adds value to their work. Connecting staff to TQM developments elsewhere brings new perspectives to the school, can open opportunities for the school to use resources available locally and can lead to long-term invest-ments by others in the TQM work of the school.

Investing in the development of staff is no reason to exclude other stakeholders. It is not uncommon for a TQM workshop designed primarily for teaching and administrative staff in a school also to have parents, teacher aides and some students as participants.

To make these investments in staff development, the school should have a staff development programme developed by teams and the top team working in collaboration. This plan should focus on what it is that the staff needs in terms of skills and ideas that would aid the school achieve its vision over a 3–5 year period.

As TQM activities and ideas unfold in the school, there is a need for these to be fully recognized by the top team. Recognition, in the form of descriptions of success, small presentations, granting of extra leave, recog-nition at a full staff meeting or student assembly, gifts and prizes – what-ever it takes to show that the ideas and work of teams are fully appreciated.

The more subtle recognition that is required is for the top team to demonstrate their commitment to TQM in their daily actions – to behave as a team, using the tools, in making decisions that are clearly seen as TQM decisions. In doing so, they may wish to call on the skills and expertise of others on the staff to facilitate discussion, to demonstrate the application of a tool or skill or to assist in the understanding of issues requiring their attention. This subtle work is a recognition that the top team is not immune from the work it is asking others to do and that it is visibly engag-ing in the real work of TQM.

### Phase 6: Re-focus and re-invigorate

After a period of time, the whole staff needs to review where these TQM investments and efforts have taken them and what needs to be done to sustain the work and to maintain alignment and commitment. Teams need to be re-invigorated and challenged to continue to work on tasks that are clearly beneficial to the achievement of the Hoshin goals and the school's overall strategy.

The systematic review of development should not be undertaken only by top team members. The work is best done as a self-evaluation by all teams in the school, co-ordinated by the top team and key implementers. Re-focusing and re-invigorating are tasks for the top team.

These six steps place emphasis on leadership, modelling, coaching, educating, guiding and shaping – key roles for the top team and implementers.

There are problems and pitfalls in the implementation of TQM. Effective implementation requires close attention to the six phases noted here. Not all schools who embark on the road to TQM will be successful: it is a tough road with many opportunities for failure and success. The key to success is commitment, communication and the development of a culture dedicated to making vision a reality through actively pursuing a focused strategy dedicated to meeting and exceeding customer needs.

# Postscript

This book contains many ideas, insights, tools, resources and case examples. You may, however, still be wondering whether you and your school should be making a positive commitment to the implementation of the TQM model set out in this book. To answer this question we suggest you respond to the following questions by rating yourself on a five-point scale (1, minimum; 5, maximum):

1  *Leadership.* To what extent are you and your senior management colleagues currently creating and building-in 'quality values' in the way the school is run?
2  *Information and analysis.* To what extent are you and your senior management colleagues collecting data and information on a systematic basis and analysing them for quality improvement and planning?
3  *Strategic quality planning.* To what extent have you and your senior management colleagues integrated your stakeholders' quality requirements into your strategic plans?
4  *Human resource utilization.* To what extent have you and your senior management colleagues created the structures and opportunities to realize the full potential of all members of staff for quality?
5  *Quality control of what the school does.* To what extent have you and your senior management colleagues implemented systems for ensuring quality control of all that the school teaches and provides, and also integrated this quality control with continuous quality improvement?

6 *Quality results.* To what extent can you and your senior management colleagues demonstrate improvements in quality excellence by evidence that includes quantitative measures?

7 *Customer satisfaction.* To what extent do you and your senior management colleagues implement effective systems to determine customer requirements and demonstrate the success you are achieving in meeting them?

These seven questions address all the main components of a school-wide TQM policy. We suggest that if the score you gave yourself is less than 30, then you should lose no time in making a positive commitment to the TQM model we have set out in the book. Also that even if you have rated yourself 30 or more, you could still find that what we have presented could increase your score to a maximum and, more importantly still, to a maximum in the eyes of your customers.

# References

Aga, A. (1991) 'Client services in the engineering area and its management at a college of further education' (unpublished thesis). Wales: Polytechnic of Wales.

Argyris, C. (1982) *Reasoning, Learning and Action – Individual and Organizational*. San Fransisco: Jossey-Bass.

Armstrong, L. (1991) 'The customer as honoured guest' *Business Week*, December/January bonus issue, p. 104.

Atkinson, P. (1991) *Creating Cultural Change – The Key to Successful Total Quality Management*. London: IFS Ltd.

Barker, J.A. (1990) *The Power of Vision*. Minnesota: Charthouse International (video).

Barnard, C. (1938) *The Functions of the Executive*. London: Routledge.

Barth, R.S. (1991) 'Restructuring schools – some questions for teachers and principals' *Phi Delta Kappan*, October, pp. 123–8.

Belbin, M. (1981) *Management Teams*. London: Heinemann.

Bennis, W. and Nanus, B. (1985) *Leaders – The Strategies for Taking Charge*. New York: Harper and Row.

Berg, L. (1968) *Risinghill – Death of a Comprehensive*. Harmondsworth: Penguin.

Berry, T.H. (1991) *Managing the Total Quality Transformation*. New York: McGraw Hill.

Blaug, M. (ed.) (1968) *Economics of Education, Volume 1*. Harmondsworth: Penguin.

Bowles, S. and Gintis, H. (1976) *Schooling in Capitalist America – Educational Reform and the Contradictions of Economic Life*. London: Routledge.

Brown, W. (1960) *Explorations in Management*. London: Heinemann.

*Business Week* (USA) (1991/92) December/January, pp. 21–3.

Camp, R.C. (1989) *Benchmarking – The Search for Industry Best Practices that Lead to Superior Performance.* Milwaukee: Quality Press.

Clemmer, J. (1990) *Firing on All Cylinders – The Service/Quality System for High Powered Corporate Performance.* Toronto: Macmillan of Canada.

Coleman, P. and La Roque, L. (1990) *Struggling to Be 'Good Enough' – Administrative Practices and School District Ethos.* London: Falmer Press.

Collins, J.C. and Porras, J.T. (1991) 'Organizational vision and visioning organizations' *California Management Review,* Fall, pp. 30–52.

Davies, J. (1972, 1973) 'Management by objectives in local education authorities and educational institutions (Parts I and II)' *British Educational Administration Bulletin,* 1(1) Summer 1972 and 2(1) Autumn 1973.

Davies, J. (1975) 'A discussion of the use of PPBS and MBO in educational planning and administration' in L. Dobson, T. Gear and A. Westoby (eds) *Management in Education – Some Techniques and Systems.* London: Ward-Lock/Open University Press.

Day, G.S. (1990) *Market Driven Strategy – Processes for Creating Value.* New York: Free Press.

de Bono, E. (1973) *CoRT Thinking Programme.* Oxford: Pergamon Press.

de Bono, E. (1987) *Six Thinking Hats.* Toronto: Key Porter Books.

de Bono, E. (1991) *Six Action Shoes.* New York: Harper Business Books.

de Pree, M. (1989) *Leadership is an Art.* New York: Dell.

Donaldson, G. (1989) *The Corporate Restructuring Cycle.* Harvard Business School (mimeo).

Drucker, P. (1954) *The Practice of Management.* New York: Harper and Row.

Dyer, J.W. (1991) 'A school and its customers' (unpublished thesis). Wales: Polytechnic of Wales.

Fogarty, D.W., Hoffmann, T.R. and Stonebraker, P.W. (1989) *Production and Operations Management.* Cincinatti: South Western Publishing/APICS.

Gardner, H. (1985) *The Mind's New Science.* New York: Basic Books.

Garvin, D. (1988) *Managing for Quality.* New York: Free Press.

Gear, T. (1975) 'Application of decision trees to educational planning' in L. Dobson, T. Gear, and A. Westoby (eds) *Management in Education – Some Techniques and Systems.* London: Ward Lock/Open University Press.

Ghemawat, P. (1991) *Commitment – The Dynamic of Strategy.* New York: Free Press.

Glasser, W. (1990) 'The quality school' *Phi Delta Kappan,* February, pp. 425–36.

Green, S. (1988) 'Strategy, structure and cultural symbolism' *Long Range Planning,* 21(4), pp. 121–9.

Hall, V., Mackay, H. and Morgan, C. (1986) *Headteachers at Work.* Milton Keynes: Open University Press.

Handy, C. (1989) *The Age of Unreason.* London: Business Books.

Hellriegel, D., Slocum, J.W. and Woodman, R.W. (1992) *Organizational Behaviour* (6th edn). St Paul: West.

Humble, J.W. (1968) *Management by Objectives.* London: Industrial, Educational and Research Foundation.

ISO 9000 (1987) 'A positive contribution to better business (1992)' BS5750/150, 9000/EN, 29000: 1987. Booklet produced by Department of Trade and Industry's Managing into the 90s Programme within the Enterprise Initiative.

Johnson, P. (1989) *History of The Modern World, from 1917–1980*. London: Weidenfeld and Nicolson.

Jung, C. (1929) *Psychological Types*. London: Routledge and Kegan Paul.

Juran, J. (1979) *Quality Control Handbook* (3rd edn). New York: McGraw Hill.

King, R. (1989) *Hoshin Planning – The Developmental Approach*. Mehuen, MA: Goal/QPC.

Kotler, P. and Fox, K.A. (1985) *Strategic Marketing of Educational Institutions*. New Jersey: Prentice Hall.

Lapointe, A.E., Mead, N. and Phillips, G. (1988) *A World of Differences – An International Assessment of Mathematics and Science*. London: Educational Testing Services.

Lerner, J.W. (1971) *Children with Learning Disabilities*. New York: Houghton-Mifflin.

Liswood, L. (1990) *Serving Them Right: Innovation and Powerful Customer Retention Strategies*. New York: Harper and Row.

Marland, M. and Rogers, R. (1991) *Marketing the School*. London: Heinemann.

McGaw, B., Banks, D. and Piper, K. (1991) *Effective Schools – Schools That Make a Difference*. Hawthorne: Australian Council for Educational Research (mimeo).

Mergerison, C.J. and McCann, D.J. (1985) *How to Lead a Winning Team*. Bradford: MCB Press.

Meyer, N.D. and Boone, M.E. (1989) *The Information Edge*. Homewood, Ill: Dow-Jones Irvin.

Mills, A.R. and Murgatroyd, S. (1991) *Organizational Rules – A Framework for Understanding Organizational Action*. Milton Keynes: Open University Press.

Mitchell, B. and Cunningham, L.L. (eds) (1990) *Educational Leadership and Changing Contexts of Families, Communities and Schools*. Chicago: University of Chicago Press.

Mizuno, S. (1988) *Management for Quality Improvement – The 7 New Quality Tools*. New York: Productivity Press.

Morgan, C. and Morris, G. (1989) 'What the teachers say' in C. Riches and C. Morgan (eds) *Human Resource Management in Education*. Milton Keynes, Open University Press.

Moss-Kanter, E. (1991) 'Transcending business boundaries – 12,000 world managers view change' *Harvard Business Review*, 69(3), pp. 151–64.

Murgatroyd, S. (1984) 'Relationships, change and the school' *School Organization*, 4(2), pp. 171–8.

Murgatroyd, S. (1988) 'Combatting truancy – a counselling approach' in K. Reid (ed.) *Combatting School Absenteeism*. London: Hodder and Stoughton.

Murgatroyd, S. (1989) 'KAIZEN – school wide quality improvement' *School Organization*, 9(2), pp. 241–60.

Murgatroyd, S. (1991) 'Strategy, structure and quality service – developing school wide quality improvement' *School Organization*, 11(1), pp. 7–19.

Murphy, J. (1992) 'School effectiveness and school structuring – A comparative analysis of two lines of school improvement'. Paper presented at the International Congress for School Effectiveness and Improvement, Victoria, British Columbia, Canada, February.

Myer, M.W. and Zucker, L.G. (1989) *Permanently Failing Organizations*. Beverly Hills, CA: Sage.

Oakland, J. (1986) *Statistical Process Control*. London: Heinemann.

Oakland, J. (1989) *Total Quality Management*. London: Butterworth.

Ott, J.S. (1989) *The Organizational Culture Perspective*. Pacific Grove, CA: Brooks-Cole.

Palazzoli, M.S., Anolli, L., diBlasio, P., Giossi, L., Pisano, I., Ricci, C., Sacchi, M. and Ugazio, V. (1981) *The Hidden Games of Organizations*. New York: Pantheon.

Palazzoli, M.S., Boscolo, L., Cecchin, G. and Prata, G. (1978) *Paradox and Counter Paradox*. New York: Jason Aronson.

Paul, R.H. (1991) *Open Learning and the Nature of Management*. London: Kogan-Page.

Peters, T. (1989) *Thriving on Choas*. New York: Knopf.

Polak, F. (1973) *The Image of the Future*. Amsterdam: Elsevier.

Porter, M.E. (1980) *Competitive Strategy – Techniques for Analyzing Industries and Competitors*. New York: Free Press.

Porter, M.E. (1985) *Competitive Advantage – Creating and Sustaining Superior Performance*. New York: Free Press.

Porter, M.E. (1990) *The Competitive Advantage of Nations*. New York: Free Press.

Proctor, P.A. (1991) 'The importance of creativity in the management field' *British Journal of Management*, 2, pp. 223–30.

Reynolds, D.R., Jones, D., St Leger, S. and Murgatroyd, S. (1980) 'School factors and truancy' in L. Hersov, and I. Berg (eds) *Out of School*. London: John Wiley & Sons.

Reynolds, D.R., Sullivan, M. with Murgatroyd, S. (1987) *The Comprehensive Experiment*. London: Falmer Press.

Reynolds, D.R. and Murgatroyd, S. (1977) 'The sociology of schooling and the absent pupil' in H.C.M. Carroll (ed.) *Absenteeism in South Wales*. Swansea: Faculty of Education.

Roach, S. (1991) 'Services under siege – the restructuring imperative' *Harvard Business Review*, 65, pp. 8–9.

Rutter, M., Maughan, M., Mortimore, P. and Ouston, J. (1979) *Fifteen Thousand Hours*. London: Open Books.

Samuels, G. (1991) 'The Q-word in action' *Education* (UK), 22 November, p. 412.

Schaffer, R. (1991) 'Demand better results and get them' *Harvard Business Review*, 69(2), March-April, pp. 142–9.

Schaffer, R.H. and Thomson, H.A. (1992) 'Successful change programs begin with results' *Harvard Business Review*, 70(1), pp. 80–9.

Schein, E. (1984) 'Coming to a new awareness of organizational culture' *Sloan Management Review*, 25, pp. 3–16.

Schön, D. (1984) 'Leadership as reflection in action' in T.J. Sergiovanni, and J.E. Corbally (eds) *Leadership and Organizational Culture – New Perspectives on Administrative Theory and Practice*. Urbana, Ill: University of Illinois Press.

Schonberger, R. (1989) *Building a Chain of Customers*. New York: Free Press.

Senge, P. (1990) *The Fifth Discipline – The Art and Practice of the Learning Organization*. New York: Doubelday.

Sergiovanni, T.J. (1990) *Value Added Leadership – How to Get Extraordinary Performance In Schools*. New York: Harcourt, Brace-Jovanovich.

Skinner, W. (1981) 'Big hat, no cattle – managing human resources' *Harvard Business Review*, 59(5), pp. 106–14.

Spady, W.G. and Marshall, D. (1991) 'Beyond traditional outcome based education' *Educational Leadership*, May, pp. 23–6.

Stein, H. (1986) 'Unconscious factors in organizational decision making – a case study from medicine' *Organizational Development Journal*, 4(2), pp. 21–4.

Truckman, B.W. and Jensen, M.A.C. (1977) 'Stages of small group development revisited' *Groups and Organizational Studies*, 2, pp. 419–42.

von Bertalanffy, L. (1968) *General Systems Theory*. Harmondsworth: Penguin.

Walton, M. (1986) *The Deming Management Method*. New York: Putnam.

Whiteley, R.C. (1991) *The Customer Driven Company – Moving from Talk to Action*. New York: Addison Wesley.

Woodcock, M. (1979) *Team Development Manual*. London: Gower Press.

Zander, A. (1982) *Making Groups Effective*. New York: Jossey Bass.

Zeithaml, V.A., Parasuraman, A. and Berry, L. (1990) *Delivering Quality Service – Balancing Customer Perceptions and Expectations*. New York: Free Press.

# Index

HAVERING COLLEGE OF F & H E

174110